Seeds of Time

THE BACKGROUND
OF SOUTHERN THINKING

By Henry Savage, Jr.

Henry Holt and Company, New York

Preface

Voices of the ages, even from the most remote past, reverberate and echo. Filtered and amplified, they speak through us today. And ever and always, those voices reflect the environments whence they came. We speak today in the light of times and conditions perhaps long gone.

If one is to hear with empathy those who speak today, one should have a measure of familiarity with the events, circumstances, and conditions from which emanated those voices of the ages.

To that end, this volume is an attempt to show why, with singular solidarity, the South thinks and acts as it does by a relation of the aspects of the region's history that gave rise to those thoughts and acts. Back of the mid-twentieth century mind of the South lies a long history—a history that is frequently glorious and inspiring, in aspects romantic and glamorous; often blatantly crude, with overtones of appalling ignorance and blind bigotry, of periods of idolatry to false gods; but one which throughout is, in the main, tragic beyond words. Until recently it was a tale of lost opportunities and withdrawal from the mainstream of Western civilization. It involves the stories of many leaders of superb stature but also of many who were talented demagogues, as disgusting and false as any the nation has produced.

It is from all these that we hear the voices of the ages speaking in the South today.

"If you can look into the seeds of time,
And say which grain will grow and which will not
Speak then to me, who neither beg nor fear
Your favours nor your hate."
                                —Macbeth

Table

of

Contents

1. The South Becomes Part of the World   3
2. The South Becomes Part of the World of Man   7
3. The South Becomes Part of the White Man's World   12
4. The South Becomes Part of a New Nation   31
5. The South Becomes a Kingdom: 1   49
6. The South Becomes a Kingdom: 2   69
7. The South Becomes a Kingdom: 3   85
8. The South Becomes a Kingdom: 4   101
9. The South Becomes a Kingdom: 5   109
10. The South Becomes a Nation   118
11. The South Becomes a Conquered Province: 1   137
12. The South Becomes a Conquered Province: 2   153
13. The South Becomes a Conquered Province: 3   169
14. The South Becomes a Conquered Province: 4   176
15. The South Becomes a Conquered Province: 5   187

16. The South Becomes a State of Mind   194

17. The South Becomes the New South: 1   201

18. The South Becomes the New South: 2   227

19. The South Embraces Change: 1   242

20. The South Embraces Change: 2   259

21. A Postscript for the Day   275

SEEDS OF TIME

The South Becomes Part of the World

T HE HAND WHICH WROTE the turbulent history of the South started writing it long ago—long before living creatures moved out from the sea to dwell on the land. And yet that Hand was even then writing into the minds of those who now claim the region as their home, a measure of the thoughts and views they entertain today.

Through all of time, down to a mere yesterday, the story of the South is written in the stones underlying and outcropping from its diverse soils. It would require volumes to tell what men who know the language have read there; we have space for but paragraphs of their story.

For millions of millennia, half of all the time since finite earth time separated itself from eternal celestial time, the creating Hand wrote on an unpaged manuscript, and there was still no North America and no South. No lands resembling them were yet emergent from the boiling oceans.

At last there came a time, perhaps a thousand million years later, after a variety of life had come to occupy the earth's warm seas, that a lofty range of mountains rose from those seas, mountains which were to form the eastern margin of the United States. Remaining to us today from this earliest of the permanent land areas of the earth is the Southern Piedmont. Eons would have to succeed eons until from this beginning, the surrounding areas would be built up through successive convulsions and long, slow alterations to resemble the land we recognize today as the South.

Before that time would come, at intervals of hundreds of millions of years, other towering mountain ranges, mostly parallel to and westward from that which once strode, lofty and gaunt, along the red hill country of the South; each in turn, under the violent action of the elements in a violent young world, would give the great bulk of their substance to form the Southern coastal plain and the wide land area extending westwardly toward the Mississippi.

Meanwhile, time after time, today's land areas to the west, the Mississippi valley and Texas, rose irregularly from the shallow seas which covered them, only to be submerged again by the warping of the aging surface of the earth. Many of the submergings extended for vast periods of time—time enough for the lime-bearing remains of tiny sea organisms to build layers of limestone, thousands of feet thick in places, on the floor of those temporary seas.

All these momentous changes in the face of the South, the rising and leveling of mountain ranges, the inundations of the seas, the elevation of the plains, took place incredibly slowly, so slowly that along the margins of those seas long gone, swamps, verdant with ferns and primitive trees, lasted long enough to build from the remains of those plants the rich coal beds of the Southern highlands and Alabama and the oil fields of Mississippi, Louisiana, and Texas, these to be tapped in our day by drilling through ten thousand feet, and more, of the debris of later ages. Again, events which came to pass when our ancestors were still fishes were already playing a major role in the lives of those Southerners living today in our changing South.

Before those coal and oil deposits could be created to become a latent rich heritage for us today, the seeds of life, the protozoa of the sea, would have to evolve through countless mutations into algae which could move out of the sea as lichen and primitive ferns, eventually to specialize into mosses and ferns much like those with which we are familiar today, and on into primitive trees bearing recognizable relationships to the palms and pines which are now the floral hallmark of the South. In the intervening hundreds of millions of years since Nature tucked away black gold into the folds of the earth, plants of the types entombed there gave rise to a vast variety of specialized forms adapted to all sorts of conditions—and the South's richest commercial resource, its forests, stretched across the length and breadth of the region.

Meanwhile, from those same seeds of life in the sea, through parallel processes, came the creatures of the earth. After evolving countless ages in the sea, the first creatures to take up residence on the young earth were the scorpions and spiders. In terms of the long reaches of geological time, they were soon joined there by insects, much like those that plague us today. All the while, the family tree of man and of other higher forms of life was gestating through fishes to lungfishes, through amphibians (branching off to give rise to reptiles and birds), through primitive egg-laying mammals, to the higher mammals, and thence to primates and man. During that long process, there were periods during which reptiles ruled the face of the earth and the emergent mammals were but incidental—except for their inherent potential.

At last there came a day, but a moment ago on the geological timetable, when man raised himself on two legs, manipulated material objects with his hands, and gave thought to his problems of existence in a viciously competitive world. But even that was long, long ago and no man had ever set foot in America or the South. And for those regions, the most significant geological event of all had yet to occur. The world grew cold.

It was perhaps a million years ago that rising new mountain ranges and changing ocean currents brought layers of ice, thousands of feet thick, creeping down from the north eventually to cover most of the continent, bringing with them much of the soil which had been accumulating all across present-day Canada. In the ages which followed, this great ice cap repeatedly melted back, only to build up and creep down again across the Great Lakes to the Ohio River. Each time a melting age came to pass and the ice cap receded, much of the resulting water found its way to the sea through the Mississippi valley, bringing with it vast quantities of the rich earth born far to the north, filling the remains of the great inland sea, and pushing back the Gulf of Mexico—creating, in those formerly inundated areas, vast expanses of relatively flat alluvial lands, areas which, with those long before built along the eastern coast, would eventually, in millennia to come, prove themselves ideal for plantation crops.

At last, some twenty thousand years ago, the latest glacial encroachment slowly receded northward and the land we know today as the South appeared, much as it did long later when the intrepid De Soto toiled through its forests and across its mountains and swamps to its great river, where his followers would give his body to its waters. It was already a land of rich red hills, of vast alluvial plains, of incredibly rich river swamps and deltas. It was already a land of tall pines, sweet gums and cypresses, of magnolia and jessamine. Even then its forests and prairies teemed with turkey and wild pigeons, with bison and elk, and, above all, with the exquisitely graceful Virginia deer, a creature destined to play the part of empire builder far in the future, after strange new creatures had crossed the sea and laid claim to this land that had lain so long unclaimed.

The differences were minor and few. The Mississippi was yet to shrink to a wraith of its former expanse as the glacier-fed waters of the Great Lakes found other outlets to the sea. Wild horses, camels, great elephants, giant ground sloths, and fearsome saber-toothed tigers still roamed its hills and plains. But essentially, it was the same land De Soto gave his life to see.

And still nowhere had its soil felt a human footfall.

The South

Becomes

Part of the World of Man

2

For a long, long time, the red man held the stage. His act is finished and he is gone. But he left us much to remember him by. All across the land, he left monuments more enduring than stone; verbal monuments, commemorative of his part in the piece. His name is on waters from the Potomac and Ohio to the Arkansas. Some of these names fairly flow with the streams they designate, lazily on the Suwannee, the Yazoo, the Coosa, and Tallapoosa; or blithesome and sparkling on the Hiwassee and Tennessee; or roaring on the Watauga and the Catawba. All have a touch of the exotic and romantic, from the Rappahannock and Roanoke, Pee Dee, Santee, Edisto, Savannah, and Altamaha in the east, through the tongue twisters of the Gulf plains, the Ocmulgee, the Chattahoochee, the Apalachicola, and Tombigbee, to the Mississippi and Arkansas of the west. Our mountains are his towering monuments; the Appalachians and the Ozarks (*aux arcs* for the men with bows who lived there). Even our states he named; Alabama and Mississippi, Tennessee, Arkansas and Texas, Kentucky and Oklahoma. Our wide waters bear his names from the Chesapeake Bay, Currituck and

Pamlico Sounds to the Gulf of Mexico. Long after his day, his place names keep recurring in our history; at Hatteras and Chickamauga, Kennesaw Mountain, Appomattox and Tuskeegee. Even our market places commemorate him; Tulsa, Chattanooga, Natchez, Biloxi and Mobile, Pensacola, Tallahassee, and Savannah.

It was at least fifteen thousand and perhaps even twenty-five thousand years ago that the Indian began to play his part in America. Being a minority red man in the yellow man's domain, he was, perhaps, driven eastward to Alaska from northeast Asia along a land bridge or island chain which rose from the north Pacific in that day, when so much of the earth's water was held fast in the continental ice caps. From there, he pushed south along the coast from which the warm Pacific currents had begun to drive back the ice cap. At length there came a day when the posterity of those first settlers entered our stage, when a band of red nomads stood in awe and gazed eastward across the still greatly swollen Mississippi. Remains of those early nomads, who sustained themselves by gathering the fruits and roots of the forest and by hunting its creatures, place them there at least ten thousand years ago.

As with other Stone Age men, insulated from civilization, their progress toward civilization through the centuries which followed was painfully slow. But gradually, they abandoned the caves which had sheltered them and devised huts of various types; of hides, or bark, sticks, grass and clay, or palmetto leaves, thereby rendering any fruitful spot a possible home. The primitive spear was augmented by darts, bows and arrows, and spear-throwing devices. Pottery making was discovered. But the most significant step of all came when the red man turned to farming and began providing himself regularly with his staple necessities, corn, tobacco, beans, squash, and melons. This development brought in its wake the more or less permanent Indian villages which, for at least a thousand years, were spread across the whole breadth of the South. What with villages to be administered and fields to be protected, a measure of orderly government became necessary. Commonly, it was spread beyond the towns to embrace whole tribes and even, sometimes, extensive federations.

This was the stage of the red man's development when sails appeared from the east—sails which presaged a tortured future and ultimate doom. At first mystifying, then terrifying, word of those sails and the manner of those who commanded them must have spread from the Timucuan towns of Florida, through the Apalachee of west Florida, up through the far-flung towns of the Muskogee federation in Georgia and Alabama, to Choctaw and Chickasaw relatives on the Mississippi, and on to the Hasinai and Akokisa beyond the Sabine River in Texas. From the Coosabo, the Siouan and Tuscarora of Carolina and the Powhatan of Virginia, the threat of later sails along those shores must have drifted westward through their inland kinsmen; the Santee, the Wateree, the Catawba and the Waxhaw, on to the great Cherokee federation in their resplendent domain in the mountains of Carolina and Tennessee, and on to the numerous back country allies of the Powhatan. As the sixteenth century accumulated years, it was these far-flung peoples, with others too numerous to name, who held a loose tenancy over the land we call the South. How tenuous was their hold upon it, in spite of their hundreds of tribes and thousands of villages, can best be told by reference to their numbers. Although there is reason to believe that ravages of the white man's diseases, particularly measles and smallpox, added to their constant intertribal warfare had reduced their numbers from earlier times, authorities agree that at the time of the first white settlements, there were, in the whole region from the Potomac to the Rio Grande, no more than 200,000 Indians—fewer than the population of any one of a dozen Southern cities of today.

In spite of the fewness of his people and even though he was so quickly driven from the scene, the Indian left us a variety of heritages of lasting historical significance.

As will be seen later, through trade ties and alliances, Indians were destined to play a major role in securing for British America all of the South lying west and south of the Carolinas and Georgia. Through the campaigns, as a fellow fighter with the colonials in that bit of empire building and often as their wily enemy, he taught them his method of warfare. In years to come, on this heritage would hang the difference between success and failure; when Francis Marion, the partisan leaders at Kings Mountain, and many others so tellingly demonstrated the superiority of Indian methods in wilderness warfare. A famous, but less tangible, facet of that heritage was the Indian war whoop which came from white men's throats as they charged up the steep sides of Kings Mountain—to echo down through the years to be heard again across the bloody fields of Tennessee and Virginia in the spine-chilling Rebel yell.

Destiny was again in the making, when the Indian from his patch supplied his white neighbor with seed for new ground. From those seeds grew the early tobacco plantations of Virginia and the corn to furnish the human and animal brawn of the slave-based cotton kingdom of later years.

Mention of the plantation system calls to mind another way in which the Indian unwittingly played an important, if indirect, part in the evolution of the slave-based plantation system. Very soon after Columbus discovered the Indies, the Spanish began to colonize them. To build their towns and operate their newly established sugar plantations, they enslaved the natives. Even by Spanish accounts, those free spirits, unsuited to slave labor, were so brutally treated that they died like flies. To replace them, almost every expedition to the mainland soon had as one of its objectives the capture of continental Indians. By 1515, conditions were already so bad among enslaved Indians that a movement to free them was started by a priest, Bartolomé de las Casas, who had come to Cuba with Columbus on his second voyage. His proposal met with such violent opposition from planters that, on at least one occasion, he was forced to seek sanctuary in a convent. Undaunted, he continued his struggle until he was widely known as "the Apostle of the Indies." Faced with little progress and consumed with zeal for liberty for the Indians, he finally proposed the acquisition of Negroes from the Portuguese in Africa as substitutes for the Indian slaves, a proposal which was accepted, but one which he lived to regret. Thus, by the time De Soto made his three-year march of exploration, conquest, and conversion across the primeval South, he was attended by Negro slaves as burden bearers. From this center of infection in the Spanish Indies through British Barbados to the Carolina settlements, and through each spot on the mainland where the Spaniards took up residence from St. Augustine on, the infection was to spread on Southern soil to meet another focal point at Jamestown, where, in 1620, a Dutch ship of war in need of supplies acquired them in exchange for "twenty Negars."

Although the Indian himself has passed from our scene, figuratively and in fact, his blood still flows in Southern veins. A recent study reports that forty percent of Southern Negroes have Indian blood, as do unnumbered whites.

Leaving behind a romantic aura, the Indian has made his exit from our stage. But the part he played was a major part, even an essential part, upon which hangs the drama of the South.

The South

Becomes

Part of the White Man's World

3

A s THE FIFTEENTH CENTURY drew to a close, the world was
witnessing one of the most aggressive national expan-
sions in all history. Stimulated by the successful conclusion of their
centuries of struggle to drive the Moors from their last foothold on
Spanish soil and fed by the dual stimulus of a fanatical missionary
zeal and a desperate need for wealth and resources which their poor
homeland lacked, the men of Castile, in a mere half-century, armed
with cross and sword, had gained footholds here and there over half
the world; they had plundered and subdued the civilizations of Mexico and Peru and had established a plantation society throughout the
West Indies. More than that, by virtue of decree of the Pope, reinforced by numerous voyages of exploration and discovery, both along
the coast and into the interior, Spain held technical title to most of
both North and South America. But the bold and ruthless expeditions
sent into and across the South of today had found little of value by
Spanish standards. The De Vaca, De Soto and Pardo expeditions
found only rich land, extensive forests, and barbaric natives—none of
which offered quick returns in material riches or converted souls.

With the exception of D'Ayllon's abortive attempt to establish a colony on the swampy shore of Carolina, Spain's glorious half-century passed without actual possession of an acre of Southern soil.

But the cards were being dealt and the game was being played back across the sea, amid the royal intrigues of old Europe's rival capitals. A rising France and an upstart England were both jealously eying Spain's treasure fleet, whose route from Mexico and Central America ran along with the Gulf Stream up the east coast of Florida. The temptation it offered prompted French settlement attempts, first in Carolina and then in Florida. As a protective countermeasure, Spain promptly proceeded to exterminate the French trespassers in Florida and reinforce its title to the mainland by establishing St. Augustine and a series of mission forts along the coast to Carolina.

The same incentive which prompted French efforts to colonize Florida, to offset the overweening power of Spain, was a powerful factor in the plans of Queen Elizabeth and Sir Walter Raleigh to plant a colony on the southern coast of the American mainland. The lost settlers of Roanoke Island were pawns in the game.

Reason to the contrary, notwithstanding, the bountiful and sunny South proved incredibly inhospitable to European settlement. For almost a half-century, vegetating St. Augustine, which was little more than a military post, remained the only permanent foothold of the white man north of Mexico. No other section was to prove so difficult to seize. We read of at least a dozen valiant, but tragic and futile, settlement attempts and several little known "lost colonies" as the Spanish and French tried to take hold of the Gulf coast, and the English and Spanish vied with each other for possession of the South Atlantic seaboard. It remained for private enterprise, emanating from rising mercantile England and operating through a business organization remarkably similar to a modern corporation, to ring up the next and most significant success in that seventeenth-century struggle for empire.

Back of that day in May, 1607, when the *Susan Constant*, the *Goodspeed*, and the *Discovery*, the largest of a hundred and the smallest of twenty-five tons, dropped anchor in Chesapeake Bay after a voyage of more than four months, lay years of planning and promotion. They were years of organization, stock selling, and well-directed but grossly optimistic propaganda; before the London Company could recruit and equip the initial contingent of one hundred and twenty prospective settlers and provision those tiny, history-making craft. Nevertheless, for these Jamestown settlers, the Southern shore was no more hospitable than it had been to those who had tried before and to many who later tried to establish themselves along it. After a year and a half, but thirty or forty of those first settlers remained alive. Although, meanwhile, their number had been augmented by one hundred and forty new settlers; in May, 1610, when the remnants of a fleet that set out with six hundred additional settlers arrived in Jamestown, "out of the ruins of the place tottered sixty wretches, more like ghosts than human beings, to tell their sorrowful story." To keep those remnants from abandoning the settlement, their leaders resorted to hanging, and even burning at the stake, captured deserters. After nine years of struggle and the investment of fortunes, there remained but three hundred and fifty survivors of the fifteen hundred who had been led to this paradise on earth by the glowing propaganda of the ill-fated company. And those hardships were to continue for years; through storms, famine, and Indian wars, one of which, in 1622, took three hundred and forty-seven lives, a third of the population of the colony.

But even in the face of these calamities there was significant progress. Those who survived their trial by ordeal began to develop productive plantations, from which, within a decade, they were exporting tobacco to London. In 1619, they secured an amendment to their charter which would prove of great historical significance. Shares in the company were issued to each settler, these shares carrying with them a suffrage right in the selection of the local governing assembly. From this beginning would grow the Virginia House of Burgesses, the prototype of all subsequent American legislative bodies. But between the arrival of those three little ships and a happier day when a respected House of Burgesses would be serving as a model for representative government, lay those early years, and many more, of incredible suffering.

Eventually, born of the travail of those years of struggle, there emerged the colonial Virginia of our mind's eye. But even that picture is of a much later Virginia, and it is a picture which has been so embellished with glamour that the true scene has become badly distorted.

Meanwhile, in this distant outpost of Britain, there would come to pass developments of great future import. From the colony's inception, its labor force, the bottom rung of its society, was largely composed of bond servants. Back in England, some of them had been so reduced by fate that selling themselves for a period of slavery, usually three to seven years, seemed a fair price for escape from their unhappy lot. Many others chose such servitude when the gallows was the other alternative, in that day when the gallows was the penalty for a hundred or more offenses now considered minor misdemeanors. Regardless of their low estate, these people came to America with traditional English pride of race, which through centuries has been exhibited throughout the world wherever the British have come in contact with colored races. In Shakespeare's *Othello*, there is ample evidence of the existence of that prejudice back in England in the previous century. Even during the years when the Virginia colony was womenless, both bond servants and their masters, the numerous small landowners, resisted the temptation to embrace blatantly willing native women customarily offered as temporary wives to visitors to their towns. The famous exception, John Rolfe, when he proposed to violate traditional taboo by wedding Pocahontas, was strongly advised against the step by Governor Thomas Dale. "Pocahontas," he warned, "is of a different and despised color;—of a hated race, not one of whom has ever looked above the meanest of the Colonists."

It was into this early colonial society, where the traditional British pride of race was meeting its first application in the field, its earliest confrontation with realities, and the conviction of white supremacy was emerging as a resultant, that the previously mentioned Dutch man-of-war bartered "twenty Negars" to augment the colony's labor supply—a labor supply which was chronically deficient, with a wilderness yet to be brought under the plow and a labor supply subject to erosion, as bond servants completed their terms of servitude or deserted their masters.

The presence of those Negroes, and the few who arrived from time to time in the decades that followed, served further to crystallize the colonial Englishman's assumption of racial superiority into a forceful, if yet unwritten, law that he and his posterity might retain the pride of race which was their heritage. By 1630, this conviction had already assumed the force of law. In that year, a Jamestown bond servant was publicly flogged before an assembly of Negroes and others for "defiling himself" by indulging in intimate relations with a Negro woman.

For some time after the arrival of the first Negroes in Virginia, there was no clear distinction between their servitude status and that of the white bondsmen who long comprised most of the population of the colony. English law at the time countenanced slavery only for heathens. But soon the Bishop of London ruled that conversion to Christianity did not prevent Negro servants from being retained in bondage. Colonial enactments providing that the children of Negro women should inherit their mothers' servitude, and prohibiting cohabitation of whites and Negroes, and others regulating relations between master and slave, completed the legal framework of the "Slave Code," which, in most respects, would be followed in the other colonies both northern and southern. But even with the institution formalized and sanctioned by law, its growth was relatively slow until the eighteenth century.

A hundred years, four generations, after the first settlers arrived at Jamestown, there were in all Virginia less than 100,000 people, spread thinly across the whole tidewater region up to the fall line where Richmond, Petersburg, and Washington now stand, and southwardly to North Carolina. Of that number perhaps 10,000 were Negro slaves, the use of whom had only recently become popular as the supply of bond servants dwindled. Estimates made in 1670 had counted but 2,000 slaves. Now the slaves were rapidly replacing the bondsmen and ex-bondsmen who, through the years, had furnished the farm help of the tobacco planter; a change accelerated by the reluctance of erstwhile bondsmen to labor at the same tasks performed by blacks. Through the years, most of those who had settled in Virginia had come there through selling their services for a period of years in return for the cost of their ocean passage. The vast majority of the oldest families of Virginia and much of the rest of the South had come to the colony under such arrangements. Commonly, when their years of bond service had run, they stayed on with the planter as wage laborers. But as Negroes began to arrive in numbers, more and more of these poor, humble, and usually illiterate people trekked off to the west where they took up their head rights in wilderness hinterland. Here they built their shacks, usually of squared logs, and began subsistence farming with a patch of tobacco as a cash crop. Necessity, born of their isolation and their moneyless society, soon called up from among them artisans of ability. The more industrious and the more fortunate began expanding their patches into fields and their shacks into houses and were soon thinking of themselves as planters or, at least, were looking forward to that estate for their children.

Even at that late date, Virginia was all but totally rural. Jamestown, only a few years before, had been abandoned in favor of Williamsburg where the first few buildings of the colony's only town, had just been completed. Here and there across the older areas some of the more successful planters had built durable and pleasing residences and had begun to pattern their social life on that of the English squire, with whom but a tiny handful could claim any blood connection. However, the simple cabin of squared logs was still the home of most Virginians. Those necessities of life which could not be improvised were still acquired mostly by barter, with tobacco as the medium of exchange. Waterways and Indian paths continued to be the only arteries of communication between those widespread but mutually isolated Virginians.

Already on the older plantations, nearly a century of tobacco culture had exhausted all available suitable soil, and many planters were acquiring fresh lands to the west. To provide the manpower necessary to carve these new plantations from the wilderness, the demand for slave labor mounted, a demand which was met during that period with Negroes from the West Indies.

That was Virginia a hundred years after the *Susan Constant*, the *Goodspeed*, and the *Discovery* dropped anchor off the marsh-girt peninsula at Jamestown.

Meanwhile, four hundred miles to the south, another focus of influence had come into being. Under the aegis of the earliest written constitution, a document liberal by seventeenth-century standards but aristocratic in the extreme by twentieth-century standards, and under the sponsorship of a group of speculative noblemen, who not only owned the territory but were heavily involved in the African slave trade, ships and colonists for Carolina had set out in August, 1669, to plant a colony on that shore which had repulsed so many earlier attempts at settlement. After a voyage plagued by misfortune, storm, and shipwreck, the settlers finally disembarked on the Ashley River where they built their first huts and planted their first crops, including cotton. Here they successfully sustained themselves in the face of attack by neighboring Indians and a Spanish force from St. Augustine. Ten years later, they moved their settlement to the peninsula at the confluence of the Ashley and Cooper Rivers and named it Charles Town.

Before proceeding with the fortunes of their city and the colony it was to dominate for so long, it is appropriate to point out some other significant features of the colony's Fundamental Constitution, which, incidentally, had been drafted by the famous philosopher, John Locke. Agreeable to its obvious intent to create in Carolina a landed aristocracy, replete with orders of nobility, all to be supported by agriculture, and agreeable with the involvement of the proprietors in the African slave trade, Negro slaves entering the colony entitled their masters to the same head rights or land allotments as any other ordinary settler—a considerable inducement to the acquisition of slaves. Another provision of great future significance was that granting the colonists the right to select representatives to the governing council, from which quickly grew the colony's powerful representative assembly.

Another historically significant aspect of infant Charleston was its dominance, during early years, by those who had come there from the island of Barbados, England's rich little colony off the northern coast of South America, where a prosperous plantation society, based on Negro slavery, had long been well established. Supplementary, but equally important historically, was the delivery, by a New England sea captain, of a bag of rice from Madagascar to permit his Charleston host to experiment with rice culture in the region. As a result of those coincidences, within a very few years rice, produced by Negro slave labor on fields arduously wrested by them from the neighboring swamps, was as dominant a staple in Carolina as tobacco was in Virginia.

The Lords Proprietors of Carolina had carefully planned for an agricultural aristocracy in their domain, but environment, more authoritative than they, ordered otherwise. For the first half-century, settlement was confined to tidal rivers of the coast. Nowhere did it extend as much as fifty miles inland, for lands suitable for rice culture lay mostly on tidewater streams. But beyond that lay other reasons for the colony's restriction. As a frontier settlement constantly exposed to attack by the Spanish, who still regarded the Carolinians as trespassers, and by numerous Indian tribes to the south and west, who were being persistently goaded by the Spanish and the French along the Gulf to make war, it would have been folly for Carolinians to spread their settlements into the hinterland as had been done in Virginia. Thus, the capital city on the sea turned to trade and, through trade, found prosperity. For the people of Charleston, trade offered a more than adequate substitute for agricultural production. For engaging in the Indian trade no other colony was so advantageously situated—with the way open around the southern end of the Appalachians all the way to the Mississippi. By sea, the city was conveniently located for trade with the Indies, both by merchant ships and through the not unwelcome pirates who, in those times, infested Southern waters. Attracted by its prosperity and a wider religious tolerance than prevailed anywhere else, settlers flocked to the town and Charleston quickly became not only the South's only city but also America's most cosmopolitan community, with substantial population influxes from many less tolerant lands.

When the Virginians marked the hundredth anniversary of their colony, there was little outward resemblance between the two foci of

Southern culture other than the fact that both were becoming more receptive to Negro slavery on a relatively large scale. But in a less obvious yet important respect, there was a marked similarity. From the beginning, South Carolina's precarious frontier position and, later, its active trade called for an effective and responsible local government as strongly as did the widespread plantation society of Virginia. In both colonies, citizens soon learned jealously to guard their governments. In doing this, they developed a long sustained and consuming interest in political institutions and in politics. In both colonies, especially among those of the upper classes, a feeling of political obligation developed, an obligation to accept public service as a primary duty. These were the beginnings of the South's tendency toward political institutions controlled in large measure by the privileged few.

From the earliest days of the Carolina settlement, the Spanish in Florida had constituted a constant threat to its safety but they had not proved a very effective deterrent to the Carolinians' Indian trade. However, in the closing years of the seventeenth century, from another quarter such a threat did make itself felt, as French traders appeared on the Mississippi, inciting and alienating the natives in that region. By 1702, the Le Moyne brothers, Iberville and Bienville, had planted colonies at Mobile and Biloxi and were laying plans for the strategically important settlement of New Orleans.

To counter these French moves, the Spaniards made a third, and this time successful, attempt to locate a settlement at Pensacola.

West of French Louisiana lay Spanish Mexico from which, eventually, Texas would be carved. Although for a century Mexico City had been a thriving colonial capital, replete with schools, hospitals, and cathedrals, the region that was to become Texas, except for a few forts, missions, and trading posts, remained Indian territory. But the natives were being converted and absorbed as citizens, a method of conquest at which the Spaniards had proved themselves most adept.

In remaining colonial years, the two-thirds century leading up to the Revolution, changes which occurred in the South were mostly ones of degree, continuations of developments already under way in its first hundred years after the settlement at Jamestown. The only significant exceptions were the philanthropic settlement of Georgia and the establishment of New Orleans and its satellite, slave-based plantation society.

During the middle years of the American colonial period, England was being swept by a religious revival and a newly awakened, but powerful, wave of social consciousness. These waves swept into high places. Many high-placed Englishmen were seized with a desire to improve the lot of their less fortunate brethren. One of the products of the movement was an organization under the aegis of James Oglethorpe, military hero and an able member of Parliament while still in his twenties. Oglethorpe's group was especially moved by the sad lot of thousands of unfortunates who were languishing in debtors' prisons. They proposed that these people be released for settlement in America in the disputed region south of Carolina, claimed by both England and Spain. Upswelling benevolence provided funds for the undertaking. The imperial interests in the Spanish rivalry supplied the colonial charter and territorial grant. In 1733, these dreams of Utopia and dreams of empire met on the banks of the Savannah, as Georgia was launched on a high moral plane—a refuge for the poor, where alcohol, slavery, and large landholdings were forbidden.

It took but two decades to convince Georgia's promoters that their high moralistic society could not persist in the face of the realities of a frontier settlement in raw, violent, expansive eighteenth-century America. Its unique moral curbs were abandoned, and Georgia quickly began to assume the economic and social aspects of its neighbors to the north and east. Oglethorpe's dream of a just and orderly society, free of both oppressive wealth and men in bondage, had failed, but it fully played its imperial role and secured Georgia for the English. That a man of his stature, highly regarded by his peers, could devote so much of himself and his fortune to alleviate the sufferings of his less fortunate fellow Britons and also serve as deputy-governor of the Royal African Company, England's principal slave trading organization, illustrates the prevailing British attitude of the day—benevolence for the white man only.

A considerable measure of the royal interest in the establishment of Georgia stemmed from the recent success of Bienville in realizing for France his long-sought hope of establishing a city near the mouth of the Mississippi which might effectually control that salient key to the vast French domain, extending from Canada and the Great Lakes to the Gulf of Mexico. In 1718, he had established New Orleans. Within a few years it had superseded Biloxi as the capital of Louisiana and had grown so fast that it was rivaling Charleston. Many who came to New Orleans were sufficiently affluent to bring with them groups of Negro slaves. Many others in the boom town soon acquired them. By 1723, there were so many slaves in the colony that a "Code Noir," governing the institution, had already been enacted. Although this slave code was somewhat softer than its counterpart of the English colonies, it reflected a similar assumption of white superiority. The other two great American colonial powers, Spain and Portugal, owing perhaps to their long association and gradual fusion with the Moors, did not display anything like the solicitude for racial integrity that the French and English did, and in their colonies racial mixing with both natives and blacks was commonplace.

The compelling motive back of Bienville's establishment of New Orleans was to checkmate the far-ranging Indian traders emanating from Charleston. Within a few years after the English launched their Carolina enterprise, those dauntless wilderness men were deep in French territory, alienating from the French and Spanish alike, the Indians settled in their back yards. For all their energy and ability, Bienville, Iberville, and their devoted lieutenant, Tonti, were no match for hundreds of daring, frequently crafty, unscrupulous, and immoral Carolina traders, as they spun their web of informal treaties and cemented them with trade in English goods superior in the eyes of the natives to those offered by the French and Spanish. While much of the power of the Carolina wilderness men can be attributed to their numbers, even more influential with the natives were the textiles, rum, axes, hoes, mirrors, guns, and ammunition which they received in exchange for the red man's principal commodities, deer skins and enslaved enemies (for sale in the West

Indies). Whether motivated by visions of empire or simply a desire to retain their trading area for themselves, Carolina traders soon cleared the way for the establishment of Georgia, by forcing the abandonment of Spanish outposts along its coast, while their fellow traders to the west were laying claim to all French America east of the Mississippi from the Ohio river to Spanish Florida. The names of traders such as Maurice Matthews, Thomas Welch, Thomas Nairne, and Price Hughes have been all but ignored by history. Nevertheless, their claims on behalf of Britain and the manipulation of the native tribes under their influence prevented the tight encirclement of English coastal colonies and laid the foundation for the acquisition of a subcontinent for English America. More than that, they provided the vanguard for the settlement of the back country, first to the mountains, and then over and around them to the Ohio and Mississippi. However, for the moment, that is ahead of our story.

Beginning with the early years of the eighteenth century, older Southern settlements were witnessing a changing scene, fraught with great and tragic significance. Until then, although Negro slavery was an established institution in all the colonies, in none of them was it of really great consequence. Even in South Carolina, because of its rice culture most dependent of all on Negro slaves, they probably comprised less than twenty percent of the population, not greatly exceeding in number the colony's Indian slaves. Elsewhere the proportions were much less. However, those slaves already present, wherever they occurred in a region devoted to growing extensive crops for sale and export, constituted in themselves an inexorable force to multiply their numbers. In Virginia, for example, landless whites and bondsmen as their terms expired, eschewing competition with Negroes on the tobacco plantations, knowing that it meant wages at subsistence level, tended more and more to migrate west and south in search of farms for themselves. Their leaving heightened the chronic labor shortage on the plantations. To meet that shortage called for the importation of yet more blacks. Farther inland, many an erstwhile bond servant, having acquired more land than he and his family could cultivate and aspiring to planter status, was realizing that to attain that status he must meet the planter's competition. So he, too, entered the market for slaves.

Along the Carolina rice coast, to a lesser degree, the same forces were at work. In addition, rice culture itself created a special condition calling for the employment of Negroes, who were largely immune to malaria. Experience had demonstrated that the white man's susceptibility to malaria precluded his use in the miasmic fields of that swamp grown crop. As rice production increased, the demand for slaves mounted. The rise in the slave population of South Carolina from less than 2,000 at the beginning of the century to more than 40,000 at mid-century reflects the accelerating change, a change which was already disturbing many of the section's leaders, as the slave populations of many areas far outran the white population. By 1765, slaves constituted more than two-thirds of the population of the rice coast.

Slave imports reached their height about 1734. In that year, 70,000 blacks were landed in the British colonies, mostly in Maryland and the colonies to the south of it, wherever plantation crops were grown. By then, the slave trade was entirely in the hands of merchant fleets of England and New England. As prices rose, with the mounting demand for slaves in the English colonies, many were acquired in the West Indies, but vast numbers were brought directly from West Africa; from Sierra Leone and the Grain Coast, from Gambia, the Ivory, Gold, and Slave Coasts, from the Cameroons, Gabon, and Angola. In return for cheap rum, gaudy textiles, and baubles, slavers received, from the native chiefs and professional slave catchers, their pathetic cargoes; always with the critical eye of a livestock dealer inspecting his purchases for disease, strength, age, and breed, for all these had great bearing on the price which the cargo would fetch when placed on the auction blocks back in the colonies. Most prized were the Senegalese, of Negroid and Arabian amalgam. Considered the most intelligent, they would bring top prices, to serve as house servants and drivers of their fellow slaves. Coromantees were always a problem for, although unusually honest, they were known to be fierce, haughty, and stubborn and likely to become mutinous under harsh treatment. Whydahs, Nagoes, and Pawpaws of the Slave Coast were always considered choice cargoes as the best prospective field hands because of their strong physiques and cheerful and submissive dispositions. But for the swamp labor of rice plantations, Mandingos, in spite of their thievish ways, were most sought after. Unless a better cargo was unobtainable, Eboes and Gaboons were eschewed, as generally weak, moody, and subject to suicide in slavery. Into the Southern melting pot, already at work blending a wide diversity of whites, were dumped all these black peoples, at least as diverse among themselves as the whites.

With those blacks as the mudsill of the structure, planters around the older coastal settlements were beginning to erect a society which, given sufficient of the essential ingredient of time, would flower into something resembling a real aristocracy. In tidewater Virginia and in and near Charleston as genuine an aristocracy as America has known had already flowered. At the same time, planters themselves were becoming fearful of what they were doing, of the risks they were running, of the price the future might have to pay for their advancement. By 1750, in South Carolina, they had already become so fearful of the black tide that they voted to tax themselves and their fellow citizens for funds to give free ocean passage to whites who would settle in the colony.

This inducement to immigration and the encouragement offered by other Southern colonies set in motion a stream of immigration through the Southern ports of entry and into the unsettled hill country to the west. In response to these inducements and attracted by the prevailing religious tolerance came waves of Germans from the Rhineland. Swiss refugees settled in groups all over the region, especially in South Carolina. Scotch Highlanders in numbers came to central North Carolina. Huguenots continued to join their earlier-arrived fellow Frenchmen along the James and the Santee. Fleeing economic austerity at home, Welshmen took up new homes along the Pee Dee.

But most numerous of all were the Scotch-Irish. Under overseas passage conditions described by Henry Laurens as worse than those on slave ships, they arrived in hordes at all the colonial ports from New York south. But wherever they landed, they generally tended to migrate to the same general region—the Southern back country. Those landing in the South, as they moved westwardly into the rich red hills of the Carolinas and Virginia and into the picturesque and fruitful valley of Virginia, commonly met the vanguard of contingents of what was to become one of the most significant and headlong migrations in American history. Back of it lay centuries of austere living and long years of acute suffering for a people endowed with pronounced and all but immutable attributes, which were to prove of telling significance in the story of the South.

About the time the English were struggling to keep their tenuous foothold at Jamestown, a long drawn out Irish revolt was finally being suppressed. Among the punitive measures meted out to the revolting Irish earls was the forfeiture of their extensive estates in Northern Ireland. To occupy the forfeited region and offset the Catholic power in Ireland, Scotch Lowlanders, mostly staunch Calvinists, were encouraged to migrate to the region. Even thrifty farming in rugged North Ireland did not obviate the necessity for other income. To survive, many turned to the home manufacturing of textiles. After a turn in the wheel of political fortune, they found themselves politically and economically oppressed. They were excluded from public office. Their Presbyterian marriages were not recognized. Tithes to the Anglican church were required of them. Finally, by 1700, they found themselves subject to heavy discriminatory trade restrictions. The resulting poverty and dissatisfaction set up a stream of migration to America. By 1730, more than 6,000 a year were leaving. Most of these, or their descendants, within a generation or two were finding homes in the American South.

If you would understand the South of today, note well the characteristics of these people, for the odds are that most contemporary Southerners number many of them among their ancestors; and to this day, their posterity have dominated a wide section of the South, the hill country from the Potomac to north Georgia and westward to the Mississippi, the mountain regions to the west and the valley regions west of the mountains. Once the coastal planters were unseated, it was from these people that much of the Southern leadership came. They were the stock of Patrick Henry, Andrew Jackson, James K.

Polk, John C. Calhoun, and Andrew Johnson, to mention but a few. Typically, they were tough and spare of physique. A background of centuries of austere living had eliminated the weaklings. In common with German religious refugees, many of whom trekked south along the same roads to settle widely in the valley of Virginia and western North Carolina and in lesser concentrations in many other sections, they had a fanatical devotion to their reformed church. In common with the Welsh, who were settling among them in numbers, they had the Celtic bent toward religious observances with a minimum of ritual and a maximum of emotionalism, even to liberal indulgences in the supernatural. Add their intense individualism to those religious characteristics and their social characteristics consistently follow. Independent, intractable, resentful of regulation and regimentation, they were ever ready to resist any authority seeking to curb their individualism. These characteristics plus their emotionalism gave them their propensity to violence. They were inordinate romantics, lovers of fine phrases and florid oratory and ever strongly partisan in causes which appealed to their emotions, be the causes positive or negative, programs or prejudices.

On the eve of the Revolution, these were the peoples who had staked out their land claims, built their cabins, and cleared their little fields across the whole back country, from the Potomac to Georgia, up to the resented "Proclamation Line," marking the boundary of the territory reserved for the Indians by royal proclamation in 1765. There they had lived for years, decades, and even generations, in rural isolation. In all the vast territory they had taken for their own, there was no town, scarcely even a village. There were no roads, no schools, no churches, no courts, no elections, even little or no government, during most of those years. In effect, they were all but walled off from the outside world. Even as the issues leading to the impending war were debated and the tensions between the coastal settlements and the mother country mounted, these back country people remained all but oblivious of the impending crisis. They drank no tea, read no newspapers, and seldom saw a document calling for a stamp; and they themselves had few or no representatives in the colonial governments which nominally governed them.

In 1750, in the valley of Virginia, they were observed living "like savages" with no clothes but deer skins and no food but deer and bear meat and johnnycakes.

Governor James Glen of South Carolina, reporting on a trip to the back country of that province in 1753, observed that, although the people had been long settled there, they had "never had any Minister or School Master among them although most of them had good crops and large herds of cattle, hogs and children, equally naked and fully as nasty." Fifteen years later, a missionary to the same people stated that they "Live in Logg Cabbins like Hogs—and their living and Behaviour as rude or more so than the Savages." Discord was rife. Among them, there was only one thing on which they agreed, "That of getting drunk."

It was about the time of the latter observations that the back country was beginning to feel the results of some outside concern for its welfare. Perhaps it was reports such as one from a missionary in Georgia in 1753, that the whites there were "as great Heathen as their Slaves," or contemporary estimates that not over twenty percent of the American colonists had any church or affiliation because of their rural isolation, that stirred the missionary zeal of younger sects in England. At any rate, first Baptist and later Methodist missionaries, from 1750 on, began to penetrate the back country in numbers. Thus began what came to be known as the Great Awakening, the first of many waves of evangelism and religious revival which were periodically to sweep over the South in years to come. Their success was immediate and overwhelming. To the long isolated and lonely, newly organized churches, providing the first social organizations they had known, quickly became the very heart of their social existence. The democratic governments of the new churches provided an outlet for their innate devotion to politics. But even more important was the religious appeal of the new sects, offering as they did, a maximum of emotional outlet and a minimum of prescribed ritual. To a people, so many of whom were naturally endowed with emotionalism and supernaturalism, the appeal was enormous.

As the war clouds of 1775 began to gather, although superficially there was little resemblance between the slave-holding plantation society of the tidewater South and that of the far more numerous rude interior, there were, nevertheless, highly significant resemblances —resemblances so important that they would eventually relegate their difference to relatively minor considerations. The most salient of those resemblances, the one from which, in the main, the others flowed, the one which was so deeply to color the South's predilections and largely determine its destiny, was the extreme ruralness of both. Although Virginia was the most populous of the colonies, and North Carolina had more people than New York, and South Carolina was even more thickly settled; Charleston, itself, in numbers but a small town, and far away New Orleans, vegetating under resented Spanish rule, were the only cities in the entire region between the Potomac and the Rio Grande. Here and there, widely separated, were but a handful of towns and most of them would be more accurately described as villages. Both in the coastal regions and the back country, this extreme ruralness placed all but insuperable obstacles in the way of establishing schools or any other institutions for social living. Isolation in both groups enhanced individualism to such a point that people became notoriously resentful of all but the minimum of law and order and consequently, extremely difficult to govern. On the positive side, that same untrammeled individualism was productive of a passionate devotion to liberty. Loneliness, born of isolation, combined with the lack of towns and inns generated the traditional hospitality of the region. Furthermore, as cities generate liberalism, the Southern ruralness made for extreme conservatism, both political and social. Together these qualities and bents comprise a substantial portion of the foundation upon which the social structure of the South was built. Finally, by physically precluding practical democracy, the isolation of the citizenry enabled the intelligent, educated, and able planter-merchant class to retain control of the machinery of government and the leadership of a nation for generations, and leadership of the section until relatively recent times.

From its widely diverse origins, from alien and conflicting cultures, from the descendants of traditionally warring peoples, came the white man's South. No other section of the country had origins which were more diverse; and yet, no other section of the country would become more nearly a unit or more cohesive in its thinking. Already, as the colonial period closed, the South was not just a product of English culture—neither was it French, Spanish, German, or Scotch. Already it was well on the way to becoming something quite different from any of these. It was frontier American, maturing along its seaside edge. And so it would be regarded for a while—until the mainstream of American development deflected from it, leaving it a great eddy. Then it came to be known as Southern.

Although a century and a half after Jamestown most of the present South was still in the red man's hands and the traditional South was not yet born, already present and carving out inexorably a destiny of glory and despair were the determining factors of the region: its soil and climate; its forests, coal, and oil; an agricultural economy based on cotton, tobacco, corn, and rice; its rural society, the plantation system, and the Negro slave; its political institutions, the domination of those institutions by the most privileged; and widespread illiteracy, soil exhaustion, and stark poverty of the majority. These are the heritage of the people of the South (already not English but American yet, because their way of life did not become nationally dominant, eventually known as Southern) be they English, Scotch, Irish, German, Spanish, French, Indian, or Negro; a heritage which welded them into a closely knit unit and moved them together as one down a tragic road to the brink of ruin. These are the components from which the traditional, glamorous South was built. Here, likewise, are the makings of what, long later, was to be known as the "nation's number one economic problem." They are also the elements from which, through sheer necessity, would eventually evolve the industrial South—which would inevitably become a drastically changing South.

But most of all, these are the forces which have molded the South's mind and shaped its attitudes; a mold of mind and attitude that make for painful adjustments in a changing South today.

The South   4

Becomes

Part of a New Nation

EVER AND ALWAYS, crisis has been all but endemic in the South. And that was especially true of the first century and a half after Jamestown. During those years, crises had followed or overlapped crises in such close succession that Southerners could know peace and quiet only through their dreams of a remote future—a future always separated from the present by new crises impending. Just as they had begun to draw easier breath, as the heavy clouds which had so long rolled in from the south and west—the domains of the Spanish, French, and Indians intermittently flashing death-dealing lightning—had lifted; new storms, charged with violence, rolled in simultaneously from east and west. From the west came the storm, first of protest, then of violence, from the crude and undisciplined masses who had almost in one moment grabbed for themselves the whole Carolina hinterland, from the coastal settlements to the mountains. From the coast rolled the even more ominous clouds, presaging already inevitable sociological conflict with the mother country across the sea.

Almost a century had passed since Virginia had had her first east-west conflict culminating in Bacon's Rebellion in 1676, when Nathaniel Bacon led hinterland farmers into a bloody war with the planter-dominated colonial government. In the years that followed, Virginia's plantation society spread widely over the colony all the way to the mountains, leaving only a few isolated and completely neglected areas as seedbeds for discontent. Not until well into the Revolutionary war period, when settlers poured over the mountains into the Kentucky and West Virginia portions of her wide domain, would Williamsburg again have to struggle with the back country problem. On the eve of the Revolution, the Georgia back country was still the land of the Creek and the Cherokee. However, in both the Carolinas, geography and the settlement pattern wrote a very different story.

Below Virginia, along the fall line, the sand hills sweep southwestwardly, with increasing width. Only a little more attractive to settlers than the soil poverty of those sand dunes of the interglacial Atlantic Ocean of ages past was the acid, sandy soil of the pine barrens which occupied much of the area between the sand hills and the coastal plantation country. Generally speaking, a wide insulating barrier lay between the long-settled low country and the attractive, fertile Piedmont country to the west. By 1765, the southward migrating hordes composed mostly of English erstwhile bondsmen, Scotch, Scotch-Irish, Irish, and German yeomanry of economically low estate, had so filled the back country that they already far outnumbered the white colonists of long-settled areas. And still they kept coming. Largely reflecting this land rush was the tripling of North Carlina's and the quadrupling of South Carolina's white population during the Revolutionary period, despite the fact that the area was, for several years, the scene of the most devastating fighting which occurred in the entire war.

Isolated from the seats of colonial government, this back country horde was, to say the least, sadly neglected. In North Carolina, gradually and grudgingly, it was given what amounted to little more than token representation in the colonial assembly. Such local administration as was provided for the back countrymen was commonly arbitrary and venal, and the reins were tightly held in the seaside capital.

In South Carolina, even as late as 1765, the very existence of numerous fellow colonists in the interior was all but ignored by the Charleston oligarchy. In response to bitter resentment felt by the North Carolina back countrymen for the lack of democracy and maladministration in their regions and the, at least, equal resentment of the South Carolina back countrymen for their neglect, the Carolina Regulator movement was born.

In both colonies, with but a minimum of organized leadership, the Regulators moved directly and militantly to force concessions to their grievances. Also, in both provinces, they promptly arrogated unto themselves the province of law enforcement in their raw and lawless region, their vigilante riders administering summary justice to horse and cattle thieves and outlaw bands which plagued the whole frontier. And while, in both provinces, armed conflict with the government ultimately climaxed the movement, those acts of violence were preceded by a series of bitter remonstrances addressed to the authorities, begging relief from their complaints.

In North Carolina, Regulators seized courts, drove out government officials, and organized a numerous, if motley, militia which threatened to march on the seat of government at New Bern. When relations between the east and the west had deteriorated to that point, Governor Tryon seized the initiative and marched out against the Regulators. On the Alamance River in the spring of 1771, Tryon's well-trained force of 1,500 faced a determined, more numerous, but poorly organized Regulator force. In the battle that followed, the Regulators were routed. Several of their leaders were captured and hanged. Before the movement reached this tragic climax, the years of Regulator agitation had already secured a considerable measure of the reforms they had sought. With their partial success in that field and disastrous failure on the field of battle, the movement collapsed.

At the same time in South Carolina, the Regulator movement was following a closely similar course. There the "Remonstrances" addressed to the Assembly were more colorful, cutting, and ironic. In response to a report that John Rutledge had called them a "pack of beggars," they urged the coastal aristocrats to look back but a little ways to their own origins and they would see that their own forebears were "even such as we are now." Their military brushes with colonial authorities were on a smaller scale than the Battle of Alamance, but when they began preparations for a march in force to Charleston, the Assembly met the threat with expediency, hurriedly granting their despised fellow citizens just enough, in the way of concessions, to stem their surging discontent. Armed revolt had barely been avoided. With its partial success, the movement died. But much of the bitterness and many of the animosities remained.

The events of the Regulator years are now of little import. The house burnings, the hangings, the skirmishes, even Alamance itself where thousands were involved, are in themselves of only passing interest today. But the spirit back of those events is of great significance. The fierce independence of Rutledge's "pack of beggars," their emotionalism in the face of injustice, their Celtic-German fanaticism which tended to sweep them to extremes, their readiness to resort to violence to obtain their objectives—all these remained, to become part of the living heritage of the millions now spread over the South who are the posterity of those tens of thousands who occupied the Carolina back country in Regulator days. And even to this day wherever frontier-like conditions persist (and they yet persist in hundreds of isolated, poverty-ridden areas all across the region), we still see the Regulator spirit manifesting itself in bursts of emotionalism, contempt of law, resentment of its restrictions, direct action, violence—all in the old Regulator tradition. The uncouth and informal Regulator type of violence joined the traditional formal military and dueling predilections of the coastal elite to create a regional propensity—a militant South, quick on the trigger—a people who find it hard to learn that few problems can be resolved through violence.

In the parlous years following the collapse of the Regulator movement, the spirit which evoked it continued to dominate the Southern hinterland. It was that freedom-loving, oppression-hating spirit which, according to eyewitness accounts, led the men of western North Carolina to anticipate, by more than a year, the action taken on behalf of all the colonies on July 4, 1776. And it was that same spirit that moved their colonial assembly to become the first to authorize its delegates to vote for independence in Philadelphia. As the War of Independence got under way, the bitterness and the animosities born of the Regulator struggles, which made patriots of so many of those against whom Tryon had marched in North Carolina, and Tories of so many of those to the south who were so openly despised by the Charleston aristocracy, resulted in Carolina becoming the scene of the war's most cruel and devastating struggle, as patriots and Tories sought to exterminate each other.

But those events take us ahead of our story.

Let us go back to the crisis which confronted the South in 1765, back to the awesome clouds which threatened from both east and west. Despite the potential violence it packed and despite the scars it was to leave across the land, the storm from the west was local and relatively insignificant in the face of that vastly wider storm front which was moving in from the east along the whole coast from Georgia to Maine.

Even as the English settlements were planted along the American seaboard, new and different conditions confronting them and their wide separation from the homeland had foreordained divergent destinies for the two centers of English culture. With the close of the French and Indian War, the threat of French encirclement was removed. New Orleans and the territory west of the Mississippi had passed into the palsied hands of Spain, whose imperial star was in rapid decline. The long standing fear of attack from the south was ended as the Floridas passed into British hands. For the first time since their forebears had landed on American soil, Americans could feel secure from alien attack. For the first time, they could feel that they themselves were the masters of their destiny. For the first time, they could afford to express the feeling of independence which had been evolving in their hearts from their earliest days.

After the middle of the eighteenth century, many colonial leaders could look back on three, four, or even five generations of American ancestry, and with each generation, the ties binding colonials to the mother country had loosened. They had long since thought of themselves as Americans. And their America was booming. Its population was increasing at a phenomenal rate. So, too, was its economy. Its expansion potential westward was all but unlimited. Wide and fertile areas to the west were there for the taking—taking, that is, from Indians and Spaniards whose lands the British colonists had pre-empted without scruple in the past.

Many of the more prescient on both sides of the Atlantic, who coolly considered these facts, even then realized the inevitability of an independent British America. In retrospect, that inevitability seems too obvious for any other outcome to have been possible. The only uncertainties that remained were when and under what circumstances the colonies and the mother country would come to a parting of the ways.

Viewed in this light of inevitability, the events leading up to the War of Independence and the details of the long struggle itself become largely superfluous to this account. A brief sketching of highlights will suffice.

After the Treaty of Paris, which formally concluded the war which had cost France her American empire, England enjoyed a position of unchallenged dominance in the Western world. In the Seven Years War, she had beaten the combined forces of France and Spain. But it had been a costly war and the government was pressed for funds. To make matters worse a postwar depression soon made tax revenues even more difficult to collect. And to hold her preeminence, it was essential that she maintain much of her wartime armed forces. Some of these were on the American mainland. To George III's new Prime Minister, George Grenville, it appeared reasonable to require American colonies to support those troops which were to be left there. To that end, the ministry secured the passage of quartering acts to provide for the physical needs of troops, and a variety of taxes to provide their pay. Grenville had already made himself unpopular, both with the powerful land speculators and the landless poor seeking cabin and patch sites on the frontier, by sponsoring the Proclamation Line of 1763, beyond which settlement was forbidden. Now his new taxes were roundly denounced and so energetically evaded that they produced more protests than revenue. With fatuous and contemptuous unconcern, Mr. Grenville persisted. The stamp tax followed.

By the time the Stamp Act was to go into effect, the colonies were determined to resist its enforcement. At ports north and south, arrival of the stamps was the signal for defiance, violent protests, and riots. Virginia, elder sister and most populous among the colonies, led the way in daring formal protest. Whipped to a frenzy of fury by the words of Patrick Henry, "the forest-born Demosthenes," the House of Burgesses formally declared that the British Parliament had no right to levy the Grenville taxes, but the majority refused to follow Henry all the way and adopt the nullification resolution he proposed. Their temerity enhanced by Virginia's action, eight other colonies promptly followed her lead. Fortified with this unity of resistance, the colonies dared to pool their strength, through the Stamp Act Congress, to speak for all Americans. Those pressures, underlined and given tangible reinforcement through a telling boycott of British goods, attained their objective in the repeal of the Stamp Act in 1766.

When news of the repeal reached America, there was high rejoicing—and a new cockiness—all through the colonies. In Charleston, a statue of William Pitt, who had had a major hand in the repeal, was ordered erected. In triumphant joy, little heed was given the ominous wording of the resolution which affected the repeal. Coupled with the repeal was a blunt assertion of the absolute right of Parliament to make any laws of "sufficient force and authority to bind the colonies and the people of America." On that sour note, the curtain rang down on the first phase of British-American conflict.

Between this act and the one to follow, there appeared, in Williamsburg, a remarkable pamphlet, *An Inquiry into the Rights of the British Colonies*. In this essay, Richard Bland, a leading figure in the Virginia House of Burgesses, went beyond the current issues of American rights. He delved into the inalienable rights of man and limitations of governments to the consent of the governed, ideas which, in years to follow, would glow in the minds of colonial leaders, until ultimately another Virginian would couch them in the graceful and ringing words of the Declaration of Independence.

More than two years were to pass before the curtain lifted on the second act of the drama, one which was to prove annoyingly repetitious of the first, even as tension mounted toward the climax. Neither Grenville, now superseded as prime minister, nor a majority of Parliament, where Grenville remained a potent force, had any real awareness of the growth of feeling of independence and nationalism in the colonies. To them, the colonists remained British subjects and as subject to the will of Parliament as any other Englishmen. With a blindness born of ignorance, spurred on by a contemptuous Grenville and a bullheaded king, Parliament, in 1767, proceeded to enact a whole new series of revenue measures calculated to require of the colonists substantial aid in meeting imperial expenses. The only concession to American feelings lay in the form of the new taxes, import duties rather than direct or internal levies such as the stamp act. The distinction was entirely lost on Americans. Actually, their reaction to the new duties was even more spontaneous and violent than it had been to the stamp tax. All the while their patience had been running lower and their nationalism running higher.

American response to the Townshend duties, as the new taxes were known, was a clamor of protest and, more tangibly, a crippling boycott of British imports. Sparked by Boston, most dependent on trade of American ports, nonimportation measures were adopted all down the coast. Placing principle above profit, merchants joined with other partisans of liberty in Charleston so effectively that, in 1770, trade with England had dropped to half its usual volume. This was strong medicine. Idle ships and sailors and the pinched pocketbooks of British merchants spoke to Parliament far more authoritatively than the distant colonials. Parliament heeded their behests and removed the Townshend duties—except those on tea which were retained more as a continuing assertion of authority than as a source of revenue. Back in America, the boiling cauldron quieted to a simmer which continued for two more years while Americans sipped smuggled Dutch tea and ignored dutied English leaves.

While no one was satisfied with the situation, neither was anyone very unhappy over it; that is, until the spring of 1773, when the British East India Company found itself in distress. Its warehouses were bulging with unsold tea. To the company's officials and the government the solution was obvious. Surplus tea could be dumped on the American market at prices below the price of smuggled Dutch leaves. A system of distribution through exclusive licensees in American ports was set up and tea ships sailed for America. To Americans this was the last straw. And they were determined to bear no part of even that straw. As the tea ships arrived, starting in Boston, there were salt water tea parties all along the coast to Charleston. When disorders in Boston continued and mounted with each new restricting measure, it was decided to teach Americans proper civil obedience by making an object lesson of that city. Its port was ordered closed. That stern action became the occasion for display of American unity, North and South. The day Boston's port was closed was observed in Virginia as a day of fasting and prayer. The suffering which the closing incurred brought generous response from the South. Charleston and Georgia promptly sent more than two hundred barrels of rice to beleagured New Englanders. South Carolina continued to send aid, ultimately exceeding the contributions of any other colony.

With the spring of 1775, in New England and to the westward, rioting changed to skirmishes, skirmishes to battles, and battles into campaigns as American colonial leadership, with reckless daring, challenged the world's greatest military power. Royal governors were expelled. Representative assemblies assumed control. The following year, the focus of armed conflict jumped all the way to the far South. In North Carolina, a superior Tory force was routed by Whig militia at Moores' Creek Bridge. In Charleston harbor a half-built, half-manned, half-armed palmetto log fort turned back a fifty-ship British armada, operating in conjunction with several thousand troops attacking by land. This signal victory of the Carolinians at Fort Moultrie was of momentous significance. Militarily, it discouraged the British from making any further attempt to subdue Southern colonies for another two and a half years, leaving them free to continue their accelerating growth and serve as an area of supply for the beleaguered east. Even more important was its demonstration of the patriot ardor of Carolina leadership.

A popular school of thought holds that all wars have their origins in economic interests. Either this theory is incorrect or South Carolina in the American Revolution must be an exception. The years of tension before the Revolution were, for South Carolina, its period of greatest progress and prosperity. England was the market for most of its enormous rice crop. Its indigo planters waxed rich on the bounty England paid for the production of that popular dyestuff. Conflict with England obviously spelled economic disaster. Christopher Gadsden, Henry Laurens, John Rutledge, and William Henry Drayton were loyal South Carolinians. But they were also cosmopolitan men of breadth, who could look beyond the narrow confines of their province. They and their forebears had long resided in America. When the rights they cherished as Americans were trampled upon in Boston, they were compelled to stand and be counted as rash rebels rather than as discreet and expedient Tories. To only a little less dramatic degree, the same compulsion brought the bulk of Virginia planter-aristocrats into the rebel camp, less dramatic only because tobacco planters were not enjoying a comparable prosperity at the time. All these men, gifted Carolina leaders and aristocratic titans of Virginia, in the overwhelming crisis which confronted them, were thinking of themselves first as Americans and only secondarily as Carolinians or Virginians.

On the day the British fleet was loosing its broadsides against the miserable log fort on Sullivan's Island, the continental thinking of Southern leaders was being dramatically displayed six hundred miles to the north in Philadelphia. That day, a slender, red-haired young genius from Virginia, Thomas Jefferson, rose before the worry-worn assembly of bewigged gentlemen of the Continental Congress and read the elegant flowing words of the Declaration of Independence, which he had prepared pursuant to the motion of his fellow Virginian, Richard Henry Lee. In the Declaration, Jefferson skillfully blended, with simplicity and dignity, the political philosophy of yet another Virginian, Richard Bland. Back of that day lay long months of wrestling with theories and realities—months during which the Virginia and South Carolina delegations, together with Benjamin Franklin and John Adams, dominated deliberations. There is little exaggeration in the statement that Southerners provided the bulk of the intellectual and moral force that provided the propulsion for launching the new nation.

It was during the debate on the Declaration of Independence that the first scintilla of a crack in the foundation of the new nation appeared—a crack which was to widen into a gaping chasm fourscore years in the future. Jefferson, along with most of the Virginia leadership, George Washington, John Randolph, George Mason, Richard Bland, Edmund Pendleton, George Wythe, and James Madison, as well as some other prominent Southerners such as Henry Laurens, viewed slavery with fearful misgivings and regarded it as iniquitous, dangerous, and productive of poverty. Accordingly, in preparing the Declaration, when enumerating charges against the king, Jefferson included clauses condemning him for fostering the slave trade and for frustrating numerous attempts by the colonies to curtail it. In the interest of internal harmony, the Congress eliminated those clauses when some of the New England, South Carolina, and Georgia delegates objected, the former because of the fortunes they had derived and were yet garnering from the trade, the latter because of their heavy dependence on the institution in their rice plantations.

In the north and east the war wore on. Months became years— 1776 . . . 1777 . . . 1778—during most of which the cause seemed hopeless, success impossible, except for the military genius of the great leader from Virginia who continued to keep an army, such as it was, in the field; despite an almost unbroken succession of defeats. Having failed, through more than three years of effort, to annihilate Washington's forces, in the summer of 1778, the British command again looked toward the South. In December, they gained a foothold by capturing Savannah. A year of stalemate and inactivity followed. Then, in the spring of 1780, the British moved up the coast from Savannah against Charleston, forcing its surrender after a siege of six weeks. With the fall of Charleston, the Americans lost a force of six thousand men including all the Continental forces in the South. With the key Southern city in his hands, and no appreciable opposition forces in evidence anywhere south of Virginia, Sir Henry Clinton, considering the South all but completely conquered, sailed back north to give his attention again to Washington, leaving behind an occupation force under the command of energetic Lord Cornwallis.

But there was grave error in the assumptions of Clinton and Cornwallis. Their miscalculation lay in having no more knowledge of back country Carolinians than the coastal aristocracy had displayed fifteen years earlier, during Regulator days. Although Cornwallis and his dashing but ruthless cavalry leader, Banastre Tarleton, had little difficulty in routing a superior American force under Horatio Gates, the hero of Saratoga, when the two armies met at Camden in August, their fortunes quickly turned when they began to require the active support of back countrymen. And their troubles mounted when Cornwallis began to execute his plan to march across the Carolina Piedmont to Virginia. Until then, the numerous back countrymen had been mostly apathetic to war. Relatively few had engaged in the conflict on either side. Through the years, their numbers had continued to mount sharply as they spilled over the mountains into what is now Tennessee and Kentucky, thereby precipitating new and engrossing Indian wars. With the success of the British after the fall of Charleston, bands of Tories and opportunists were emboldened to maraud the homes and farms of anyone suspected of rebel sympathy. Soon almost everyone was involved, neighbor against neighbor, in what was to become the most devastating and ruthless civil war in American history.

Beyond the mountains, in the morning shadows of the Great Smokies, many erstwhile North Carolina Regulators had purchased a vast tract from the Cherokees and settled their families in the fertile valleys of the Watauga and Holston rivers. When news of what was happening to the east drifted over the mountains, their leaders were galvanized to action. Anticipating ultimate involvement, they gathered several hundred of their neighbors into a sort of giant posse; armed only with their squirrel rifles and supplied only with parched corn in their saddlebags, they set out for the east on an indefinite campaign for the cause of liberty. Through snow in the mountain passes and cold rain in the hills, picking up recruits along the way, they pressed on into South Carolina in search of quarry. On October 7th, 1780, they had found their quarry and had it treed atop steep-sided Kings Mountain. In the fierce battle that followed, Cornwallis' main auxiliary force, a well-trained Tory army under Colonel Patrick Ferguson, well-supplied and outnumbering the patriots, was annihilated in the most glamorous battle of the war—and the most significant too, for, from that day forth, the tide of a war, which seemed all but lost, turned strongly the other way.

A few months later at Cowpens, in what has been called the most imitated battle in history, General Daniel Morgan shattered the myth that Tarleton and his dragoons were invincible. Meanwhile, patriot bands under such leaders as Francis Marion, Thomas Sumter, and Andrew Pickens, through hit-and-run tactics and disrupting supply lines, were slowly but surely stinging the occupation forces to desperation. Rendered reckless by that desperation, Cornwallis allowed himself to be sucked far into the back country, all the way to the Virginia line, by the astute Nathanael Greene, who had been sent south to succeed Gates after the latter's fiasco at Camden. Quaker Greene, masterful tactician of the war, never won a battle, but through skillful Fabian tactics rolled the British back into Charleston in the months that followed.

Meanwhile, Cornwallis had moved what remained of his army, after his pursuit of Greene and his "victory" at Guilford Courthouse, to Wilmington and thence, by sea, to tidewater Virginia, from which base he continued ravaging and raiding Virginia plantation country. However, by the beginning of fall, it was obvious that he had placed his force in a precarious position. Washington was on his way south to join Lafayette, who had been matching wits with, but avoiding any direct clash with, Cornwallis. A strong French fleet with 3,000 fresh troops had taken control of the Chesapeake Bay, cutting off all hope of escape by sea. Outnumbered and bottled up on Yorktown Neck, Cornwallis had little choice left. A few days after the first anniversary of Kings Mountain, the Earl unconditionally surrendered his entire command. The same small Virginia peninsula which saw, a century and three-quarters earlier, the British standard raised by passengers of the *Susan Constant*, the *Goodspeed*, and the *Discovery*, now saw it lowered in final defeat. A new nation had been successfully launched.

But the foundation upon which the new nation was built was one of loose sand. It lacked both foundation stones and binding mortar. The multitude and intricacy of problems confronting the young nation, added to the dearly bought experience of the war years, cried shame on the rope of sand which bound the thirteen states in union under the Articles of Confederation. It was apparent that to form a more perfect union, establish justice, insure domestic tranquility, and secure the blessings of liberty, a far more firm foundation must be provided.

The fifty-five men who gathered in Philadelphia in the spring of 1787 to lay out plans and specifications for that firmer foundation composed a remarkable group by any measure. For a raw young nation, much of it still crude pioneer area, to have produced such an aggregation of talent is remarkable—even amazing. Although there was stature in every delegation, leadership again devolved upon the Virginians. The imposing Washington, already regarded as the Father of his Country, was selected to preside. Through the tortured months to follow, the force of his dignity and prestige and his sound wisdom would serve the convention well. The brilliant legal mind of James Madison would earn him the title of "Father of the Constitution." Edmund Randolph, George Mason, George Wythe, and John Blair were also to play important roles in the convention. Outshone only by the Virginian delegation was that of South Carolina. John Rutledge, Charles Pinckney, and Charles Cotesworth Pinckney, together with the Virginians and a handful of others, notably Benjamin Franklin, Alexander Hamilton, James Wilson, Elbridge Gerry, and Rufus King comprise the segment of the fifty-five to whom history credits the drafting of the great document which was to become the Constitution of the United States.

During the war years and the postwar years preceding the Constitutional Convention, a rising sense of liberality was in evidence among Southern aristocrats. But these liberal leanings were intellectual rather than sociological. When they prepared the several state constitutions, they had not included universal white suffrage or removed high property qualifications for public office. But under the leadership of Jefferson, they had established the widest religious freedom the world had known. Primogeniture had been abolished and the institution of slavery assaulted. Jefferson and his followers sought to abolish slavery in Virgina and prevent its spread to western territories ceded to the national government. Although antislavery sentiment was growing in Virginia, it was not widespread enough to give hope of early success there. But in the national congress, their measure to close to slavery the areas west of the Appalachians was lost only by the vote of a single delegation. Looking back on his failure and at the same time foreseeing its consequences, Jefferson wrote:

> the voice of a single individual of a State which was divided . . . would have prevented this abominable crime from spreading itself over the new country. Thus we see the fate of millions unborn hanging on the tongue of one man, and Heaven was silent in that awful moment.

Although Southerners brought to the Convention a relatively high measure of intellectual liberalism, they also brought at least their share of realism. What with the states united into a nation and independence attained, their thoughts turned increasingly to economic interests of their several states. And those local economic interests were frequently in conflict with their intellectual liberalism. It was from mutually conflicting special interests and from the conflicts of those special interests with the intellectual ideals of the leading Southern delegates that the knottiest problems of the Convention came. And it was from the long drawn out and sometimes bitter battle between those interests and ideals that there emerged from Independence Hall in Philadelphia a South spelled with a capital "S."

Before, during, and for a long time after the Revolution, tobacco prices were at a ruinously low level. With immutable economic sympathy, the value of the Virginia planters' slaves had fallen precipitously. To most Virginians, slavery appeared a dying institution, to be ended completely in the state as soon as some practical means could be devised to get rid of the blacks, either by transportation back to Africa as freedmen or sale to other slave regions. On the other hand, to delegates from the Carolinas and Georgia, who in reality represented only the rice coast of those states, where the interest of back countrymen continued to be largely ignored, slavery was an absolute essential of economic survival. For the expansion of their slave holdings, they did not take kindly to being placed at the mercy of those Virginians and Marylanders desiring to dispose of their Negroes. Widely divergent were the interests of the eastern states and New England. Already their delegates saw clearly that the future of their section was bound up with manufacturing, commerce, and shipping. Ample provisions for fostering and protecting those interests became their main mission in Philadelphia. The Easterners' devotion to those objectives was offset by an equally strong fear of those objectives in the plantation states, in whose memories still dwelt the prewar bondage of the planters to British shippers and factors who always managed to skim most of the cream from planters' profits. With prescient foreboding, Southern slave masters saw themselves enslaved in turn to the commercial interests of the North.

To the talented group from Virginia, it was apparent that the problems presented by these conflicting interests would have to be faced in the Convention. It was equally apparent to them that the government the Convention devised, if it was to be enduring, would have to be strong enough to cope with these conflicting interests and their inevitable accretions through the years. To lay the ground to that end, they arrived early in Philadelphia and among themselves drew up a plan of government—a strong centralized government that would have reduced the states to little more than administrative units. When the South Carolinians arrived, they too spoke for a strong central government but with limitations—limitations that would protect their special interests. The "strong" central government they envisioned would have to be powerless to hamper Negro slavery, and its powers to regulate commerce would have to be sufficiently limited to prevent a monopoly by Eastern trading interests of the exports and imports of agricultural states. Firmly aligned against Alexander Hamilton and these men were the delegations of small states who sought equal representation with the larger, and the followers of Jefferson who, although he was then in France, was in close correspondence with many of the delegates. Drastically oversimplified, that was the lay of the land when the Constitutional Convention began its difficult deliberations in the spring of 1787. Four months later, the final draft of the Constitution was signed by thirty-nine of the fifty-five and submitted to the states for ratification.

As finally hammered out, the history-making document was a bundle of compromises. The plan for two houses, one representing the states and the other the people, mollified the smaller states. The system of checks and balances between the departments quieted some of the fears of those who sought a relatively weak central government. Through balking and trading, commercial interests got most of what they sought and Carolinians and Georgians got part of what they sought. Problems presented by Negro slavery and maneuvers of the delegates from the far South during the consideration of those problems were productive of the most arbitrary and artificial compromises among the entire bundle of compromises. That expanding plantation areas would not be placed immediately at the mercy of waning plantation sections for additional slave needs, the right to continue to import slaves was guaranteed until 1808. The problem of whether slaves were people to be represented and taxed or simply mere chattels, as any other farm livestock, brought the inherently conflicting compromise whereby each Negro slave should be considered as three-fifths of a person. Confronted with these and numerous other compromises, few if any were entirely satisfied with the document. For Jefferson, Samuel Adams, and Patrick Henry, it removed the government too far from the people. Those of the southernmost states had forebodings of what was to happen—that the national government might fall into the hands of a North intolerant of Southern rights. Hamilton, Washington, Madison, and the other Virginia delegates feared the government, erected on the foundation expediency had forced them to accept, would not have the strength to stand strains they foresaw would be its lot. However, within a few years, it became obvious that yet another giant from Virginia had come to their aid, as Chief Justice John Marshall, through a series of great decisions, enormously solidified the foundation of the central government.

Surely it was a bitter as well as a tragic Fate which watched, with wry irony, the all-out efforts of men to devise a government endowed with sufficient strength to withstand the herculean efforts of their own posterity to rend asunder their mighty work.

The Convention at Independence Hall created more than the foundation for a national government. It created another entity—the South. The conflicting interests, dissident views, jealousies, and animosities, the bitterness each compromise generated did not dissolve with the Convention. As delegates departed north and south for their homes, they carried in their portmanteaus copies of one of their creations. Full-blown in their minds, indelibly writ, they carried the other. The South as a section apart—a peculiar entity—had been created in the minds of men, North and South.

Even as the national government was being moved to its newly prepared foundation, a menacing crack, quite across it, had appeared. As the weight of the structure mounted, the rift widened. Already the wings leaned ominously apart, North and South, from threatening rupture.

The South   5

Becomes

a Kingdom: 1

B ETWEEN MASSACHUSETTS and South Carolina, between Ver-
mont and Arkansas, between Connecticut and Alabama,
there exists as great a difference in everything, except language and
style of dress and architecture, as there does between Scotland and
Portugal, England and Naples, Wales and the Ionian Islands . . ."
observed Charles Mackey, erstwhile editor of the *Illustrated London
News*, after his tour of the United States in 1857. Had Mackey made
his tour a quarter-century earlier, he would doubtless have reached the
same conclusions; for well before that time, the wide parting of the
ways, North and South, economically and socially, had opened a wide
chasm between the sections. It remained but for inevitable political
divergences, operating in an atmosphere of ever mounting tensions
flowing from those economic and social differences, to prove that that
chasm could not be bridged by peaceful means.

How had it happened that Virginians and Carolinians (and their
spawn to the west) who, but a little more than a generation earlier,
had played the major role in launching their grand experiment in
self-government, were so soon soberly considering the possibility, even

the possible inevitability, of abandoning it to their junior partners to the north? Had anything they had done brought them to the crises-ridden thirties? Or was it perhaps those things which they had not done? For even then it was obvious to all observers that the vast difference between the sections was largely the result of a dramatically changing North confronted with a relatively static South, a South which, economically and socially, was frozen in the colonial agricultural mold of an earlier age which had already become a binding strait jacket from which there was no escape. How had the people of that wide and varied section become so fettered?

Basically, the answer is inherent in the region's geography. Physically, the South is a vastly more varied land than the North, but across its whole extent there are few sections that do not possess the essential characteristics which fundamentally conspired to place the capital "S" in its compass call. It was the region's geography which was both the first and final arbiter in welding the South into a unit and molding the minds of its equally diverse peoples into more nearly a single mind than was ever elsewhere displayed in America.

In all the world, there are few extensive temperate areas with sufficient rainfall and long enough growing season to supply many of the basic commodities for which there is a world-wide demand. The South is by far the most extensive area adaptable to the production of many of those commodities for which there has long been a world hunger: sugar and rice, tobacco and hemp, small grains, beef, and timber. Consequently, until recently, all major crops of the South, except corn which was consumed in the production of its other crops, were produced mostly for export to other regions and other countries; and the returns for all its major crops, other than fruit and vegetables, were governed by a world market rather than by domestic demand. Moreover, most of these crops required enormous amounts of hand labor under oppressive conditions, so that, in their production, labor costs were the principal factor, and those labor costs were in direct competition with the bare subsistence labor in many of the starvation areas of the world. All of these conditions made growing these crops more speculative than most agriculture, the returns being controlled by conditions prevailing in the remotest corners of the earth.

Very different conditions prevailed in the North. From earliest times, its farms were supplementary to its cities and towns. There the farmer produced for domestic demand, himself and his family, the towns of his community, and cities to the east. Consequently, he had a minimum interest in tariffs, world trade, and financing facilities necessary for the production of a single cash crop and a maximum interest in the town that consumed his produce, in the roads over which he could make his frequent deliveries to the towns, and in schools and institutions. By close association inevitably he became integrated into the life of the town.

Just as the Northern farmer planted according to the demands of his community, the Southern farmer, confronted with the demand for a commodity suited to his soil and climate, answered that demand by planting that crop. So it came to pass that effects of geography, interacting with all but immutable economic laws, planted, germinated, cultivated to a showy flowering, and in turn blighted the plantation South, leaving but a withered harvest for the support of its posterity. Already, by the middle 1830's, in response to these forces, almost every section of the South, except the narrow salient of the Appalachians, was dominated by the mass production of some world trade commodity, and all across the land, from the Potomac to the Brazos, swarms of black men were laboring in fields and forests to wrest from the soil those products for which far distant consumers were willing to pay cash.

The men of the South who responded to those economic summons, the landowners and the would-be landowners, slave owners and the would-be slave owners, were basically brothers of their counterparts of the North. Such differences as existed were mostly but the products of differing environments, as were likewise their increasingly divergent views. That each was simply responding to a different summons can be amply supported by concrete illustrations.

When the Puritans turned pilgrims, determined to settle in the new world, there was disagreement among them as to whether they should head for Virginia or regions farther south. The *Mayflower* headed for Virginia. Winds deflected its course and altered history, when its passengers landed on Cape Cod and proceeded to establish their stern theocracy on a barren coast inhospitable to agriculture except on a meager scale, but conducive to the production of Mathers, Phillips, Sumners, and Garrisons. The other ship, bearing its cargo of the sternly pious and righteous, found its haven for theocracy on the island of Old Providence off the eastern coast of Nicaragua. Like their brethren in New England, and other Europeans wherever they touched in America, they early embraced Negro slavery. But here, conditions were agreeable to the establishment of sugar cane culture. Soon the colony was unsuccessfully attempting to curtail the increase of its slave population. Within a generation, it was suffering a devastating slave revolt. Weakened by the struggle with its slave population, it was unable to resist conquest by the Spanish a few years later.

Meanwhile, New England Puritans had disposed of their Negro slaves, finding them too costly to maintain; and they were selling their Indian captives, taken in the Indian wars, into slavery in the West Indies instead of employing them in domestic agriculture.

From later times and from nearer home may be drawn another example of how promptly circumstances alter men's convictions. As soon as Virginia's transmontane empire was opened, settlers streamed over the mountains into territory that would later become Kentucky, Ohio, Indiana, and Illinois. Most of those settlers came from Virginia and the Carolinas. Kentucky's soil and climate proved adaptable to the establishment of tobacco and hemp plantations. North of the Ohio such plantations failed to thrive. Within little more than a generation, the Ohio became a blaring barrier across which erstwhile Virginians glared while casting at each other epithets and opprobrium, as the region north of the river became one of the foci of uncompromising abolitionism. New England was the other.

Thus it was simply through compliance with fundamental laws of supply and demand, operating in an all but unrestrained economy, that King Cotton, in alliance with the satraps of tobacco, rice, and sugar, by 1835 held the whole South in rigid thralldom. Behind lay a long series of tempestuous years, as the North moved away in new directions from a South that simply multiplied its colonial image. Double harness had already proved as irksome to the plodder of the pair as to the deviate. Serious trouble between the fractious pair had

had its beginning only five years after their agreement on a "more perfect union," the main objective of which was to provide a stronger double harness to restrain both alike from traveling separate ways. Ironically, trouble had started with a Yankee visitor on the plantation of another Yankee turned Southerner.

In the fall of 1792, young Eli Whitney had set sail for Savannah to accept a position as tutor on a plantation in the South Carolina back country. Although he had just been graduated from Yale, he was already twenty-eight, his education having been frequently interrupted by the necessity to augment such funds as his Massachusetts farmer-father was able to furnish him. Whitney was endowed with versatile talents, not the least of which was a flair for mechanics. On the long voyage south, a warm friendship developed between him and the elderly widow of General Nathanael Greene who, after a summer in the North, was returning to Mulberry Grove plantation near Savannah, one of the several escheated Tory plantations with which South Carolina and Georgia had rewarded the General for his services in the Revolution. While visiting at Mulberry Grove before setting out for the interior, Whitney was challenged by Mrs. Greene with the problem posed by the upland cotton fiber's tenacious affinity for its seed. For a century or more, cotton had been a familiar incidental crop on most Southern plantations where its fibers were used to clothe the slaves in homespuns of their own making, but its production was limited by the difficulty of separating the seed from the lint, a pound of lint a day being about as much as a worker could produce. Many planters entertained visions of the possibilities cotton offered, visions of great wealth they might gain if this difficulty could be surmounted. When the problem and the possible returns which might be realized from its solution were being discussed by a group of guests at Mulberry Grove, Mrs. Greene urged her young guest to utilize the plantation workshop and try his hand at fashioning a machine which would speed the seed removal process. A few days later, Whitney was demonstrating his cotton engine which he had ingeniously constructed from materials found in the shop. He could little have reckoned the enormous consequences of that day.

Since England had become fiber hungry by the invention of the spinning jenny and the power loom, it can be assumed as inevitable that the development of a cotton gin would follow, but if its invention had come two or three decades later, it might not have spelled the tragedy it did, for, in 1793, the South was just approaching a critical crossroads. For a quarter of a century tobacco prices had remained at disastrously low levels. This, together with their increasingly exhausted soils, had forced many Virginia planters to turn to wheat and other crops requiring relatively little labor. In consequence, many were finding that the cost of maintaining their slaves was exceeding the return from their services and, thus, were looking for a means of ridding themselves of their bondsmen whose value on the market had dropped drastically from former times. For many years, practically all of Virginia's outstanding leaders had been openly critical of slavery. Given a satisfactory solution of the problem of what to do with the Negroes after they were freed, they were ready to advocate abolition of the institution. All the back country from Virginia southward and westward, which was the vast majority of the South both in area and population, was yeoman farmer country where slave owners were few and their holdings small and not very profitable, in those regions too far removed from shipping points to engage in cash crop agriculture. Only among the relatively few planters of the rice coast was there any dynamic advocacy for retention of slavery. And even there, where Negro labor in quantity was most essential, were indications that the system had passed its zenith. With most areas suitable for rice culture already pre-empted, rice growing in the section had no way to go in the future but down. In the light of these economic realities, it appeared likely that, unless unforeseen developments drastically changed the picture, ways and means would before long be devised to do away with the institution of slavery. Almost nowhere at the time was the problem considered from moral angles. The facets of the question were almost wholly the problems of racial integrity and economics, and, of these, that of economics was paramount, as the waning of slavery in the North had demonstrated.

Just at that critical time in the South's history, Whitney's cotton engine came as that unforeseen development which quickly reversed the flow of economic interests—setting the South off downstream on a flow of mounting turbulence, calling for ever-increasing engrossment, down to a maelstrom from which, after that moment, there was no escape.

What with England's sterling-backed fiber hunger and vast expanses of Southern soil warmly hospitable to the fiber-bearing oriental mallow, the effect of Whitney's gin was electric—at least, as electric as anything could be in pre-electric eighteenth-century times. While Whitney hurried back North to arrange for the commercial manufacture of cotton gins, the "grapevine" carried news of his invention through the plantation country. The very next season, alert planters in Georgia and South Carolina began planting cotton on a commercial scale. By 1801, they were producing 100,000 bales, a fabulous crop for those days. The lure of dollars, so rarely seen in the hinterland during the century and a half that it had remained a deep and populous, but essentially stagnant, frontier, led farmers there to embrace cotton growing. Each decade the crop doubled until, in 1859, its 4,500,000 bales comprised two-thirds of the entire world crop and King Cotton was proclaimed by his minions, supreme monarch of the entire world. As bale by bale he mounted the throne, growing ever more despotic as he rose, his realm extended ever farther abroad, beyond those who labored in his fields and their immediate overlords, to places where his showy blossoms rarely graced a field. Such a place was Virginia, fretting under its overload of blacks, which nevertheless represented much of its property heritage. To Virginians, the ever-mounting demand for more and more slaves to staff the multiplying cotton plantations burgeoning across the deep South presented a long sought opportunity to rid themselves of their surplus and grow richer instead of poorer in the ridding process. All but suddenly their slave population was transformed from a deeply disturbing liability to a highly prized asset.

Already, by 1835, King Cotton, abetted by the cash crop autocracies of the tobacco country, the rice coast, and the sugar belt, had so fixed his grip on the whole South that it was obvious, at least in retrospect, that his millions of subjects, rich and poor, master and slave alike, were bound in hopeless vassalage, and that the economic and social laws of his regime were far more inexorable than the laws men make in conventions and deliberative assemblies. As laws from assemblies of men met the fixed edicts of the King, the irreconcilable conflict between them became the "impending crisis" which, as tensions mounted, spilled over into the "irrepressible conflict."

Even while these portentous developments were getting under way in the South, equally great changes were taking place in the North. There, people were looking in other directions. At a pace comparable to the expansion of cotton growing, commerce and industry were sweeping the whole North into their orbit, generating towns at every crossroad. Nevertheless, during the two decades of diverging tendencies, relations between the sections did not reflect to any great degree their mounting differences. Overcoming qualms as to its legality, President Jefferson had reflected nationalist and not sectional interests in acquiring the Louisiana Territory where, in its settled parts, a Gallic version of the Southern slave-based plantation system was flourishing and expanding. It wasn't until the War of 1812 that any substantial measure of heat was added to sectional fires, which were kindled when the Constitutional Convention was wrestling with the problems presented by the slave trade, slave representation, and slave taxation. Although the principal cause of that war was the impressment of American sailors, largely from New England ships, New Englanders themselves preferred to swallow humiliations and continue their prosperous trade. Resentment there against the war was so heated that it fell to the South and West to fight the war for what they regarded as New England's honor. Feeling between the sections ran high, culminating in the Hartford Convention where New Englanders took preliminary steps toward secession. While a fortuitous end of the hostilities saved the union, the South's resentment against New England's role in the affair failed to pass with the crisis.

Indirectly, the War of 1812 was also responsible for the next development which increased sectional antipathies. In conformity with age-old economic laws, a business depression swept the country as an aftermath of the war's stimulation. When the Panic of 1819 struck, the South's debtor position and its cash crop economy made for far more distress there than in the North. As farmers have ever been wont to do, Southerners felt that their plummeting commodity prices were the result of nefarious manipulations by "money interests" of the North. When the Bank of the United States was forced into wholesale foreclosures of Southern farms and plantations, the natural scapegoat was again the avaricious money interests "up North." The conviction grew that a Yankeedom, jealous of the South's continuing political domination and prosperity, was bent on hamstringing the section through commercial oppression. However lacking in fact those suspicions may have been in 1820, life and substance were soon breathed into them by emergence of the tariff issue. The protective tariff's obvious sectional partiality gave retroactive foundation to the Southerner's earlier unwarranted suspicions.

At this point, the forces driving the sections apart were becoming vastly more involved. Crowding in on each other and each impinging on the others, rendering each more difficult to handle, were a flood of newly risen problems. Out of Jefferson's purchase came the red hot issue of slavery in the territories, especially in the proposed state of Missouri. There was Georgia's dispute with the government over Indian lands, culminating in a bald defiance of a Supreme Court decree. A dynamic evangelical movement was sweeping the North, fanning to flaming militancy the abolition societies which were springing up all over the region. The activities and propaganda of those societies, emancipation debates in the British Parliament, and the sensational Nat Turner slave revolt in Virginia were all conspiring to thrust to the forefront the moral aspects of slavery.

All the while, the South was in the physical ferment of the rush of cotton culture across the whole expanse of the Gulf States, which, even as it generated parlous booms in newly settled areas, left distress and depression in the older South from which much of the population and capital was being drawn. These and other critical problems of the troubled twenties and thirties contributed to the rising Southern nationalism and eventually to disruption of the union, but limits of space and the necessity of sticking to our theme preclude treatment of those problems which did not contribute substantially to the molding of the Southern mind, unless they provide a measure of guidance for problems of the twentieth-century South. By any measure, the tariff issue, the abolition movement, the slavery question, and westward expansion of the plantation South qualify for attention in some detail.

During the first twenty years of John C. Calhoun's long and contentious public career, he had consistently embraced a progressive and nationalistic philosophy of government, which necessarily included a liberal interpretation of the Constitution to the ultimate derogation of those powers reserved to the several states. Soon after his election to Congress, he was being counted among leaders of the Young Republicans. When to their advocacy of internal improvements and protective tariffs, they added ardent support for the brewing War of 1812, they came to be known as the young "War Hawks." Following the Panic of 1819, Calhoun had lent his support to a series of tariff measures of increasingly steep rates. Down in South Carolina, among his constituency, were powerful leaders who heartily disapproved. They had convinced most South Carolinians that a protective tariff was a nefarious device to rob those who produced raw materials for sale on a free market, the loot of the robbery being directed into the pockets of those who manufactured the goods the producers had to buy on a protected market. As Thomas Cooper, the brilliant English-born president of South Carolina College put it in 1827:

> Wealth will be transferred to the North, and wealth is power. Every year of submission rivets the chains upon us, ... Is it worth our while to continue this union of states, where the north demand to be our masters, and we are required to be their tributaries? The question ... is fast approaching to the alternative, of submission or separation.

When with the tariff of 1828, the "Tariff of Abominations," South Carolina's strenuous opposition was supported by the legislatures of Virginia, Georgia, and Alabama, Calhoun found himself in a difficult position. His nationalism had just failed to bring him success in his first bid for the Presidency. His state and his section were now obviously repudiating his political philosophy. After a period of hesitation for soul searching, he adopted the political expedient of following that he might again lead. Since he was one of the most severely logical figures in American political history, this flip over required that he also embrace the legal foundations for opposition to protective tariffs; this in turn required that he join the advocates of a strict construction of the Constitution. By 1832, Calhoun was leading the tariff opposition. Under his aegis the South Carolina Nullification Convention declared the tariffs of 1828 and 1832 "null, void and no law," and not binding on the state, its officers, or citizens.

Back of this impasse, created by conflicting sectional interests, one with the backing of the federal power and the other supported by a "sovereign" state, lay also a personal conflict born of the age-old sectional difference within the South itself. The principals in this conflict, Calhoun and President Andrew Jackson, were both products of the South Carolina back country. Jackson, through the years, had remained true to the frontier upbringing that Calhoun had abandoned in favor of the dominant planter class into which he had married. Personal differences and Calhoun's straying from their traditional political fold had driven the two to bitter mutual animosity.

By the spring of 1830, sectional differences within the party on the issues of the day; tariffs, internal improvements, and public lands, and the rift between the President and Calhoun, his vice-president, were seriously threatening their new Democratic party. A rapprochement between warring interests was urgent. A group of party leaders thought this might best be accomplished by a social get-together. They accordingly laid plans for a great dinner party to be held at a Washington hotel on April 13th, Jefferson's birthday. The prearranged toasts had been carefully designed to encourage the mutual tolerance and compromise needed for party unity. While the purpose of the banquet was peace and tranquility, that purpose was belied by the air of tension which prevailed throughout the evening—through the eloquent offering and solemn drinking of twenty-four of the twenty-six prearranged toasts. Then the plans of the peacemakers began to go awry. The twenty-fifth toast was the President's, and he was neither a compromiser nor a speaker of other than his mind. Rising, glass in hand, he glared down the length of the table at Calhoun and spoke his mind, slowly and emphatically, "Our Union—it must be preserved." So tense was the atmosphere that no one dared break in with a cheer or applause. The next move was Calhoun's. Shaken, pale, with eyes blazing, the tall, gaunt figure hesitated and then raised his glass, "The Union—next to our liberties, most dear."

With the memory of that evening, its atmosphere and those words, and the accretions of ill will since that evening, and of the great States' rights debates which followed in the Senate, Jackson was confronted with what he regarded as the open rebellion of his native state. True to his Jefferson Day toast, he moved decisively. He employed persuasion in a message to the people of South Carolina:

> Fellow citizens of my native State, let me admonish you—I have no discretionary power on the subject. . . . Those who told you that you might peaceably prevent [the execution of the laws] deceived you. . . . their object is disunion . . . disunion by armed force is treason. Are you ready to incur its guilt? If you are, on the heads of the instigators of the act be dreadful consequences.

To convince them that they would have to choose between recanting and armed resistance and treason, he made preparations to dispatch troops and ships to require submission under the Force Bill he had secured from Congress. Finally, he employed diplomacy and justice by setting in motion modifications downward in tariff rates.

Under these assaults, Nullification was beaten and the union preserved—for the moment. But that the illegality of Nullification under their States' rights theory was still not recognized by the Nullifiers was quickly demonstrated. As soon as the Convention had voted its recession of the Nullification Ordinance, it at once proceeded to nullify the Force Bill.

The passing of the Nullification crisis left its residuum. Part of it was that more Southerners had become accustomed to thinking in terms of disunion, albeit in the more consistent shape of secession. Also, there was the conviction planted by the crisis in the minds of Southerners everywhere, nullifiers and anti-nullifiers, that the South was being exploited by an avaricious majority for its own enrichment, and that the majority would have its way by force if necessary, that appeals to constitutional rights were fruitless, that the South had become an oppressed and exploited subsidiary of the flourishing North. The South had been thrown emphatically on the economic defensive—a touchy and sensitive defensive—as ready to see grievances imagined as grievances real.

The tariff issue was one of the few major issues of the first half of the nineteenth century which was debated on its own merits, without becoming deeply involved in the slavery question. By 1835, men were complaining that no matter what came up for discussion on the floor of Congress, the slavery question was soon involved. Although it had not entered directly into the tariff issue, without doubt, the sectional ill will which slavery had already evoked added to the bitterness of the tariff dispute.

For the first quarter-century after the establishment of the federal union, most of the discussions of slavery were confined to its economic and social aspects, and most of the long thoughts being given the problems it presented were those of Southerners intimately concerned. Many men, especially in the border areas, were entertaining doubts as to the economic worthwhileness of slavery. For some, those doubts had matured to conviction that the institution had become an economic liability, the same conviction that had brought about its abandonment in the North. As has been pointed out, most outstanding Virginia leaders and a considerable number from other Southern states were already outspoken in their opposition to its indefinite continuance. They were deterred only by the problem of the disposition of Negroes on their being freed.

A few idealists such as Jefferson, Patrick Henry, and the Quakers had gone beyond those men and were speaking out against slavery on moral grounds. Their views involved assumptions far in advance of their times in the South, and in the North as well, assumptions that blacks were not only men but Americans, entitled as other Americans to the inalienable rights of life, liberty, and the pursuit of happiness. Practical men, too, were taking long views and earnestly seeking solutions to the problem. James Madison proposed that proceeds from the sale of public lands be devoted to the cost of compensating slave owners under a gradual emancipation plan. Without dissent, the importation of slaves had been prohibited. The American Colonization Society had been established in 1817, with strong support in Virginia and Kentucky, and with the co-operation of another high placed Southerner, President James Monroe; its objective being the establishment of Liberia to receive freed slaves.

Stimulated by those leaders and reflecting a growing antislavery sentiment, the American Colonization Society was quickly endorsed by the Georgia and Tennessee legislatures. Auxiliary chapters sprang up all over the South, especially in Virginia, Kentucky, and Tennessee. Of the hundred and thirty antislavery societies organized in the country, more than two-thirds were in the South. People could freely speak their minds on the subject. Several antislavery publications were launched in Tennessee and Kentucky. The president of South Carolina College, without risking his position, could question the advantages of slavery. Governor Thomas Randolph of Virginia recommended that funds be provided for the purchase and deportation of the slaves of his state.

To add to this more hopeful atmosphere, the South was at the same time experiencing a rebirth of religious fervor. Rural living had long conspired with widespread poverty, poor roads, and natural barriers to isolate Southerners, not only from the means of mass education but also from active affiliation with any church. In 1830, not one Southerner in ten was a church member. In the thirties and forties, a new burst of religious enthusiasm swept across the whole nation, North and South. In the South, church affiliations almost tripled. Camp meetings and protracted revivals flourished, although this new awakening was characterized by more dignity and far more conservatism than earlier Southern revivals. To the north, on the other hand, the new burst of interest in religion was characterized by greatly increased liberalism, especially in New England. Before the force of the wave was spent, the sections were well on the way toward swapping their traditional religious bents. Thereafter, liberalism would be more often found in the North and religious austerity and its accompanying intolerance in the South.

All in all, in the early thirties, there were many hopeful signs in the South indicating that it might be at least on the road to an ultimate solution by peaceful and orderly means of its incalculably difficult economic and social problems. But outside the South, things were already happening and developments were already under way which, in an amazingly short time, would halt Southern progress, undo it all, and finally reverse the current completely; putting in its place, retrogression against the whole mainstream of the nineteenth-century western world.

There is bitter irony in the source of much that induced the South to turn back from its forward path. It was mostly good men, men of good intent, but intolerant and possessed of narrow vision, who played the major role in widening the chasm between the sections to hopeless proportions. Whipped to fanatical enthusiasm by preachers more dedicated to their ultimate aim—the abolition of slavery—than to maintaining peace on earth, they provided the mainspring for most of the forces which drove the sections farther and farther apart in the years after 1830.

The major rift prior to then had been political, and the slavery issue merely a convenient political instrument. From its establishment until 1820, the national government had remained under almost exclusive control of the South. Virginians had occupied the presidency for all but four years. The chief justice for all but five years had been a Southerner. The legislative branch was likewise dominated by men from the South. A North which had become the more populous region was naturally resentful of this long control which they had come to regard as an unwarranted hierarchy. By 1819, when the question of the admission of Missouri as a new state came up, Northern political leaders saw an opportunity to tip the political scales in their favor, if Missouri could be admitted as a free state. The issue promptly widened to involve the right of Congress to deprive the people of one section of the country of the right to transport their constitutionally recognized property into the territories owned in common by all the people. The long debate which followed and the Missouri Compromise, by which it was composed to almost nobody's satisfaction, had brought jealousies between the sections to a new high. It was against the backdrop of this ill will that the "good men" began to play their roles.

While Southerners were beginning to rediscover the solace of that old-time religion, Northerners were more often finding an outlet for their new religious fervor in social reforms. Along with such movements as those for prison reform and temperance, the eradication of slavery soon became a popular major aim, both because of the extent of its evil and because it involved a minimum of immediate sacrifice on the part of reformers themselves. The antislavery movement rapidly assumed ascendency over all the reforms sought, as hundreds of thousands in the North dedicated themselves to plucking the beam from the eyes of their brothers to the south. The first fruit of this rising dedication was one of the last fair and completely sane moves to be made in the entire slavery controversy. At the behest of reformers in 1824, the Ohio legislature adopted a resolution inviting Congress and the several state legislatures to consider a plan for the gradual emancipation of Negroes and their colonization abroad, at the expense of the Federal government. Eight other states promptly endorsed the Ohio movement. With a lack of foresight difficult now to comprehend, the planter-dominated Southern legislatures either ignored or rudely rebuffed the suggestions. Although the Ohio plan was much the same as those which the great Virginians had urged not long before, except that it was more generous in placing the expense on the whole country, Southerners generally construed it as uninvited meddling in their own affairs. Resented, too, were the "holier than thou" attitudes surrounding adoptions of the resolutions.

After that rebuff, little or nothing would be heard again of any plan which would place on the nation as a whole, the enormous expense of doing away with an institution which the nation as a whole had had a part in establishing and from which the nation as a whole had garnered such profits as the institution produced. Thereafter, conceptions of justice in the North became increasingly one-sided, justice for the Negro crowding out any consideration of justice to the slave owner or to the Southern states, in some of which, slave property constituted the bulk of taxable wealth. Now, with the Federal government out of the picture, the fiscal problems involved in emancipation were quite beyond solution. Certainly, no state could eliminate from its tax books the majority of its taxable wealth and simultaneously assume the payment of a debt greater than all the property remaining on its tax rolls, mostly the property of non-slave owners.

After the Ohio Resolution, every event seemed to fall into place in a fateful conspiracy to widen the breach between sections. When, in 1829, in Savannah, a pamphlet couched in violent terms, urging slave revolt, was found in possession of slaves, the whole white South was thrown into unreasoning fear. The immoderate pamphlet was the work of a free North Carolina Negro named Walker who had moved to Boston where, presumably with the aid of some of the "good" men of the city, he had arranged for the publication and distribution of his *Appeal*, which accused slave owners of killing their slaves for the fun of killing and urged the blacks to take their revenge, to "kill or be killed," assuring them "twelve black men . . . well armed for battle" would "kill and put to flight fifty whites." In terror, men associated themselves and their families with their yet fresh memories of the horrors and brutalities of the slave revolts of Santo Domingo and Haiti, as copy after copy of the *Appeal* came to light in the possession of slaves from Virginia to Louisiana. Reactions were both responsive to the threat and immediate. The laws, often honored by their breach, prohibiting the teaching of slaves to read, were given new life and more rigid enforcement. New devices to keep printed materials from slaves were effected. Laws prohibiting free Negro sailors from going ashore in Southern ports were enacted and enforced, even though the South Carolina prototype of these laws, which had been adopted when a slave plot was discovered in that state in 1822, had already been declared unconstitutional by Federal judicial decree.

Before the excitement caused by the *Appeal* had had a chance to subside, the British Parliament began its historic slavery debates. Their influence on this side of the Atlantic was deep and telling. As they followed the debates, slavery men and antislavery men alike were reinforced in their opinions. Finally, England's decision to abandon slavery stirred its American opponents to greater action. In the South, it enhanced the section's feeling of isolation and put it further on the defensive.

Inspired and encouraged by what had taken place in England, a few months later, William Lloyd Garrison brought out his first copy of the *Liberator*. Although he disavowed the spirit of the *Appeal* and spoke "submission and peace," the tone of the *Liberator* soon belied its avowals. Although it addressed its appeals to the conscience, its unrestrained indulgence in invective, its carelessness with truth through gross distortions of fact, and its savage attacks on slaveholders could have been calculated to provoke only violence. One of its early issues carried a song "to be sung by slaves in insurrection" which urged them to "strike for God and vengeance now." By pure coincidence, so far as is known, within a month after that challenge, the most terrible slave revolt in Southern history occurred in Virginia. Led by Nat Turner, a slave preacher who professed to voices and visions, the brutal slaughter in a single night of almost sixty persons, mostly women and children, and the mutilation of their bodies in orgiastic rites, was, in microcosm, confirmation of the worst fears entertained by Southerners everywhere of what might result if Northern agitators persisted in their course. It further strengthened the conviction that white men could not live in their own country unless Negroes were kept under severe restraint or removed entirely.

The Nat Turner revolt caused Virginia squarely to face its unhappy predicament. In open and candid debate, the Virginia legislature in January, 1832, weighed grave alternatives. Disturbing realities of the problem were confronted. Blacks outnumbered whites east of the Blue Ridge by 81,000, and there was every indication that this disproportion would increase. Louisiana and Georgia had already prohibited further imports of slaves, and it appeared likely that other states would follow their lead and thereby close Virginia's outlet for the surplus of her fecund black population. They faced waning economic returns from the system and the enormous cost of its abolition. With the support of the governor and leading newspapers, antislavery forces pitched their arguments on humanitarian principles, on the conviction that slavery was a serious impediment to progress, and on the ever-present danger to whites which the Negro masses represented as long as they remained among them. Slavery men pointed to the long demonstrated superiority of Virginians, attributing the eminence of her leaders to the slavery system. They emphasized the prevailing happiness and well-being of the blacks under the system.

They questioned also the legal right of the legislature to interfere with slave property.

When all was finally said and the vote taken, the influence of tidewater planters and their disproportionate representation proved strong enough to defeat the abolition forces. Again, by a narrow margin, Virginia was left with her traditions to become the capstone of the Confederacy. The Virginia debate marked the last Southern attempt to abolish slavery. It also marked the last free and open discussion of the pros and cons of slavery. Thereafter, most Southerners with antislavery views discreetly kept them to themselves. Even then, deeper South, feeling against antislavery advocates was running so high that life in Charleston had become intolerable for the more outspoken abolitionists, many being forced to move north, among them the famous Grimké sisters, one of whom would become the wife of Theodore Dwight Weld, who would soon be the foremost leader of the antislavery forces.

Even while the slavery problem was being debated by Virginia lawmakers, a group of men, under the sway of the dynamic religiosocial revival in the North, who had been finding philanthropic outlet in the American Temperance Society, seeing wider worlds to conquer, were organizing the American Anti-Slavery Society. Under the driving force of the irrepressible Weld, they were launching a crusade that would play a major role in developments which followed. Their efforts were concentrated on Northerners, on whipping up in them extreme animosity toward slavery and slave owners, tactics more appropriate to preparation for war than their proclaimed Christian and peaceful aims. These tactics were sometimes questioned even in the North. Some asked for "facts pertinent to . . . the effectiveness of Northern abolition on the South." And their program was negative—ignoring completely the means whereby slavery might be brought to an end in an orderly and peaceful manner and ignoring the effects of emancipation and the problems which emancipation would inevitably present. Most of Weld's subordinate leadership, his "ardent host," was made up of crusading ministers of unquenchable enthusiasm. Soon they were flooding the country with immoderate tracts. An unending stream of antislavery petitions descended on Congress, millions of them. In the South, resentment mounted with each new attack.

In the face of these fierce and abusive attacks, Southern opinion hardened toward all abolitionists. Southerners did not distinguish between the militant Christians who, however biased, intolerant, and impractical, were motivated by devotion to an ideal and not by personal ambition or politics and those abolitionists who were using the issue for less lofty motives. Their recollections of the Missouri issue, protective tariffs, and the public works issue blinded them to all views but that the only object of the abolition movement was to crush the South's long standing but waning control of the national government —to reduce the South to political impotency so that it might be exploited at will by Northern money grubbers. Neither could they understand the "holier than thou" attitude of the abolitionists, an attitude they resented enormously. Were not Southerners then the most devoted churchmen in America? How could they, faithful Christians and law-abiding citizens, be charged with moral depravity and gross ignorance of the teachings of Christ, for merely retaining a traditional social and economic institution inherited from their fathers? Men who would make such charges must, of necessity, be mad fanatics or self-seekers, with a larger than usual endowment of traditional Yankee cupidity. And men of that stripe deserved nothing better than a good horsewhipping. For some, lynching would be more appropriate; weren't they trying to inflame the Negroes to murder them in their beds?

Leaving the mounting slavery issue on that distracted note, let us turn aside for a moment and take a quick look at other aspects of the South of the 1830's.

The South Becomes a Kingdom: 2

6

T HE FIRST FOUR DECADES after invention of the cotton gin had witnessed the greatest changes in the Southern scene in all the quarter-millennium of its ante-bellum history. But those changes were almost exclusively quantitative rather than qualitative. Within a score of years after Whitney's visit to Mulberry Grove, cotton culture had captivated the old southeast. The long cleared fields and patches that had been devoted to producing the needs of farmers' families were already giving their substance to the voracious new crop. By then, small but relatively populous, South Carolina was already exporting more of the vegetable fleece than any other political entity in the world. The novelty of dollars in the pocket, the exhilaration and optimism resulting from having, for the first time, something more than the barest necessities of life, quickly produced a boom atmosphere in the land. And no infection is more contagious than the boom spirit. It mounts in intensity as it moves out from its point of origin. A veritable cotton mania gripped the region. On the crest of a wave of optimism, cotton culture swept westward across the lower South. The result was a greatly magnified version of what happened to the northward in tobacco land, where culture of the aromatic weed had marched west to newer and stronger soils, over the mountains into the Ohio and Tennessee valleys, bringing temporary prosperity to the newer regions while leaving behind abandoned fields, exhausted soils, and economic stagnation.

Possessed by the cotton mania, thousands soon turned their faces westward in search of new lands suitable for the cosmopolitan plant, adaptable to almost any well-drained Southern soil. Since the capital demands for starting a cotton farm were but a draft animal, a few simple tools, and land; available land became the only problem of consequence for the would-be cotton planter. To the west lay millions of acres of fertile public domain to be had cheaply and on credit, and great rivers, traditional highways of the still almost roadless South, to carry produce to deep water ports. True, much of that vast territory still belonged to the Indians under treaty arrangements with the government, but that situation had often been encountered by frontiersmen and still the frontier had rolled steadily westward. Much of the Gulf coast was still in Spanish hands, but Old Hickory, flush from his postwar victory at New Orleans and as conquest-minded as ever, was just then chasing Indians in Florida, probably with ulterior designs on weak Spain's colony, thereby shaking the tree from which Florida would soon be easily plucked, through a nice balance of "big stick" and "dollar" diplomacy. With all the Gulf rivers freed from Spanish control, the region became even more attractive and the thousands trekking westward soon swelled to tens of thousands. As word of the new El Dorado spread, Georgians and South Carolinians were joined by North Carolinians and Virginians, Kentuckians, and Tennesseans, and their numbers swelled to hundreds of thousands. As an impressed, on the scene observer saw it, "The stately and magnificent forests fell. Log cabins sprang as if by magic into sight."

Figures graphically document King Cotton's westward rush. From a mere 40,000 people in 1810, the population of the Alabama-Mississippi region jumped to 200,000 by 1820, to 1,377,000 by 1840. By 1830, the territory west of Georgia was already producing half the cotton crop, becoming two-thirds by 1840. Land prices spiraled, inviting wild speculation. In the face of mounting land values, the pressure of settlers and speculators to possess themselves of the vast estates of the Creeks, Cherokees, and Choctaws became irresistible. Through the persuasive power of bullets, through illegal purchases, and invalid treaties, and finally in defiance of the United States Supreme Court itself, the Indians were steadily pushed into ever narrower confines, although they would not be completely ousted from all the territory King Cotton was claiming in the Gulf region until little more than a decade before the Civil War.

The rapid expansion of cotton culture soon reflected itself in falling prices for the staple. But the burden of lower prices fell mainly on the older cotton regions to the east. The bountiful yields of rich new lands of the Gulf regions made fabulous returns possible even at lower prices and the boom continued. Fortunes were quickly made and as quickly lost. As always with booms, the all-pervading optimism stimulated a vast expansion in credit at ruinous interest rates, inviting, all too frequently, overextension and bankruptcy. It was rough and tumble business, rife with fraud and chicanery, fraught with unfortunate social consequences.

The new cotton El Dorado was attracting immigrants from all sections and from all classes but most heavily from Virginia and the Carolinas. In the migration years, South Carolina gave up two-fifths of its population while Virginia and North Carolina each lost about a third. In those states, planters and patchers alike were bitten by the westward urge. Among the migrants, there was at least as high a proportion of planters to patchers as there was in the older regions, and these planters brought with them, to the raw frontier, their slaves, their education, and their fine manners. But always, it must be remembered, the proportion was extremely small. And, once they were in the frontier country, it soon grew much smaller, for the old aristocrat with his ingrained principles of strict integrity, liberality, and trustfulness in business dealings, and his disdain for aggressiveness, more often than not was worsted in his competition with equally clever but less scrupulous fellow entrepreneurs in the "no holds barred, tooth and nail" climate of the rough-and-tumble frontier boom. So for the planters, the frontier casualty rate was particularly high. The slaves they had brought with them and the plantations they had purchased were often very soon in the hands of parvenus or speculators—who invariably set about aping the manners and customs of the defeated, including, generally, a full complement of suddenly discovered ancestors among the Virginia or Carolina planters, as they bounded up the social stair bale by bale. Thus, pretensions to the contrary notwithstanding, most of the mansioned planters and most of the leaders of the lower South in 1861 were but one, or, at most, two generations removed from the log cabin patcher.

Of course, any categorical discussion of an area as vast as the Gulf States, Tennessee, and Arkansas involves inaccuracies in detail. Here and there, through the region, were islands of aristocracy such as Natchez, Jackson, and Montgomery, with valid and living continuity with the coastal planters of old states. These were usually in the more fertile areas, earlier seized upon by wealthier migrants. Around those islands, the disorderly boom swirled without engulfing them. And there was also New Orleans and its satellite sugar plantations which were just then coming into full flower with aristocratic traditions of their own. In 1840, there were nearly seven hundred great sugar estates averaging more than fifty slaves each. True, forty years earlier there had been less than a hundred of them, but their expansion had not been as frantic as that of the new cotton country. There was a measure of stability there which only time can lend, more akin to Virginia than Alabama, for example. On the other hand, there was the even rawer Texas into which only the most daring ventured, and they well-armed, aware that they would eventually have to "shoot it out" for their lands and political convictions. So cocky and self-confident were those early Texans that few hesitated to carry with them their slave property, with full knowledge that slaveholding was illegal in Mexico. For a considerable while, those brash daredevils were outnumbered by a substantial colony of slavery-hating Germans, who were earlier on the scene. The early history of Texas, where only the most intrepid dared settle, is a fitting tradition for the proverbial Texan of the twentieth century.

As a concomitant of all this movement in earlier decades of the nineteenth-century South, there was a parallel quantitative development in that primary ingredient of Southernism—slavery, and hence a Negro population of formidable, unassimilable proportions. The extent to which slavery had been developed on the Louisiana sugar plantations has been touched upon. In the Alabama-Mississippi region, many counties were as overwhelmingly black as the coastal regions of Virginia and South Carolina. A man's property and prestige were measured largely by the number of slaves he owned. Acquisition of them on a steadily rising market usually consumed the major part of the cotton grower's capital and often involved him in heavy credit operations. Observers reported that the acquiring of more and more slaves had become, with many, a veritable obsession. Travelers complained that no matter what the conversation was about, it soon turned to "niggers and land" but mostly to "niggers." Ever-mounting demand for them was supplied, in part, through the widespread activities of smuggler-importers, but mostly they were purchased in declining older regions to the east. Virginia was already being charged with being a Negro-breeding farm. In truth, its slave sales played a substantial role in sustaining its failing economy. South Carolina, committed to cotton growing on soils which could no longer profitably compete, had to keep more of its blacks, but its economic distress was no less severe.

This distress in the older regions was having political repercussions. In Virginia, many leaders ascribed their troubles to slavery itself. The fruit of that conviction was the effort, which has already been noted, to abolish the institution. Among South Carolinians, whose cotton production had already dropped from first to sixth among the states, the conviction was general that the protective tariff was to blame and nullification was their reaction. Georgia more clearly perceived the real cause of distress and began thinking of ways to encourage industry. The old, once promising cities of the older section were stagnating. Their shipping had already dropped sharply. Norfolk had lost half its commerce. Charleston had plummeted from sixth to twelfth place among the nation's cities. A South Carolinian observed:

Our merchants are bankrupt or driven away, . . . our ships are all sold! . . . our mechanics in despair; the very grass growing in our streets. . . . Fields abandoned; the hospitable mansions of our fathers deserted; . . . our slaves, like their masters, working harder and faring worse. . . .

And yet, even then, cotton was the nation's richest export and four of the other five leading exports of the nation were the products of Southern soil.

So in the 1830's, the pattern of the later South was complete. The metamorphoses of gestation had run their course and the old South was born—the old South of book and song, romance and tragedy, of adulation and castigation, of nightmares and dreams. Yes, already in 1835, it was true that South Carolina differed from Massachusetts, and Alabama from Connecticut, as greatly as England from the Ionian Islands. Thereafter, the South was fixed by its pattern. The only changes which would occur in the remainder of the ante-bellum period were changes of quantity and degree.

The earlier issues between the sections had been primarily economic—a struggle for economic dominance of the nation. Gradually, that struggle had been transformed into a political struggle as men grew to realize that the government is a powerful force in economics. The issues then became mostly incidental to a struggle for political dominance. A rising struggle for moral dominance, led largely by men little interested in politics, had been embraced by political opportunists to advance their objectives. After this merger, the South found itself on the negative side of almost every domestic issue.

The only exception to that was the Texas-Mexico affair. The positive force behind the issues of Texas annexation and the War with Mexico came mainly from the South, and expansion of cotton culture played a major role in originating them. But the charge that the whole affair was but a Southern scheme to expand slave territory was unjust. Many leading Southerners opposed the War with Mexico and many Northern leaders supported it. The South had also been the driving force behind the War of 1812 to avenge indignities to New England shipping, and certainly no hopes had been entertained that new slave territory might be found in the expected acquisition of Canada. Yet in that conflict, no less than in the Mexican War, Southerners had shouldered the major burden of the conflict. So, although King Cotton's claim to Texas played a part in developments, the South's traditional propensity to combat and Americans' waxing imperialism were basic factors. The announced objective of the President, Southerner James K. Polk, was the acquisition of California, scarcely a potential slave land. Nevertheless, vehement charges in immoderate terms were leveled against the South, charging that the sole objective of the affair was to expand slave interests and more firmly saddle the hated institution on the nation. The fruit of those charges; a new high in bitterness, a new low in understanding.

The western subcontinent seized from Mexico brought up again the old question of slavery in the national territory which had been patched up in the Louisiana Purchase by the Missouri Compromise. Few, if any, Southerners saw in the arid plains and mountains of the West a land which might be adaptable to slavery, but they resented slaveholders being treated as pariahs and legislated out of any territory owned in common by all the people of the nation.

In 1850, yet another Southerner was in the White House, but cumulative differences between the sections seemed further than ever from solution. Talk of disunion was heard in high places. The theory of the paramount sovereignty of the individual states was more frequently expounded by Southerners. An ever-increasing number of effusions on the subject of the positive good of slavery was convincing many Southerners but few Northerners. These were the South's responses to Northerners' appeal to the higher law doctrine when confronted by sound constitutional arguments, responses to the branding of slavery as a crime and slave owners as criminals, responses to a growing minority demanding immediate emancipation by whatever means necessary. Into the breach again came Henry Clay with plans for a grander Missouri Compromise to dispose of all areas of dispute. From that last great effort of the famous compromiser came the Compromise of 1850; replete with concession matching concession, it undertook to dispose finally of every major issue between the sections. But it was too late. The sole fruit of its adoption was a temporary lull in the rising storm, a lull which was shattered within three years by a reopening of the whole dispute, in more violent form, with the Kansas-Nebraska bill.

It was too late to save the nation. The sections, save for their artificial lashings rapidly chafing away, were already separate entities. The old feeling of unity was gone. The government was all but paralyzed by the persistence of the slavery issue, injecting itself into every issue discussed on the floors of Congress, regardless of the subject. Even spiritually the sections had parted. A universal God had been replaced by sectional gods who bitterly disagreed. Both the Methodist and Presbyterian churches had already broken apart along sectional lines under the strain of the irreconcilability of Northern clergy, who were the leaders of those branding slavery as a horrible crime, and Southern clergy, who were equally busy justifying the "positive good" doctrine of slavery with ample scriptural support drawn from the slavocracy of ancient Israel.

Emotionally, the sections had grown equally alien. That the North could be stirred by *Uncle Tom's Cabin*, which appeared in 1851, that it could accept it as gospel and hang on its every word and tear; whereas the South regarded the novel as a libel and a travesty on its way of life is ample illustration of that emotional divergence.

The Kansas-Nebraska bill, which shattered the short but tense quiet which followed the 1850 Compromise, was none of the South's doing; but antislavery forces, refusing to recognize that, laid the blame at its door and charged the South with breach of faith. With motives still not clear, a group of Northern and border state senators proposed in that bill that the Missouri Compromise be repealed to permit the settlers of each new state to decide for themselves whether the new states should be slave or free—the subsequently famed "squatter sovereignty" doctrine. Although antislavery forces regarded the measure as a diabolical scheme to extend slavery into free territory, Southerners looked upon it as a generous if belated offer to rectify past injustices concerning the rights of slave owners to enter the territories. When the bill was enacted, there was a rush by both pros and antis to settle Kansas and thereby determine its future. There were clashes and brawls, fraud, chicanery, and finally guerrilla warfare all over the scene, the confusion culminating in rival governments and rival constitutions. Although Kansas bled in Kansas, it bled far more in the partisan statements which swept the country and in the press of the day which was far more interested in propaganda than in factual reporting.

No sooner had the Kansas excitement subsided, with yet another Northern victory, than new crises rolled in ever closer succession, like mounting waves of a rising storm. The papers of the day tell the fury of the atmosphere. Said the *Liberator* of Southern aristocrats:

> Their career from the cradle to the grave is but one of unbridled lust, of filthy amalgamation, of swaggering braggadocio, of haughty domination, of cowardly ruffianism, of matchless insolence, of infinite self-conceit . . . of more than savage cruelty. . . . monsters, whose arguments . . . [are] the bowie knife and revolver, tar and feathers, the lash, the bludgeon, the halter and the stake.

And according to the New York *Tribune*:

> The Southern Plantations are little less than negro harems. . . . Of all the Southern presidents hardly one has failed to leave his mulatto children. . . . The South is a perfect puddle of amalgamation! [there] lynch law is inevitable . . . [and] we must look for hideous savagism worthy of original Africa in crime and punishment. . . .

Apropos those quotations and by way of illustrating the extremity of propaganda of the day, those editors, in accusing the South of amalgamation, were accusing it of embracing what has been and yet remains its greatest phobia, the fear of which is even now the section's greatest deterrent to granting full acceptance to its Negro minority.

Southern papers at the same time were charging the North with a determination to free the slaves and force amalgamation upon them, a disaster which could be prevented only by independence from Northern domination. More than that, the South emotionally retaliated with the conviction, according to a British observer:

> . . . that the New Englander must have something to persecute, and, as he has hunted down all his Indians, burnt all his witches, and persecuted all his opponents to the death, he invented abolitionism as the sole resource left to him for gratification of his

favorite passion. . . . whose wisdom is paltry cunning, whose valor and manhood have been swallowed up in corruption, howling demagoguery, and in the marts of dishonest commerce.

With tempers at such a pitch there is little wonder that emotion provoked incidents should be common, and so they were. One of them, however, became a national scandal. Senator Charles Sumner of Massachusetts delivered a speech before the Senate which was as irresponsible and arrogant as it was insulting to some of his Southern colleagues, among them Senator Andrew Butler of South Carolina. A few days later, Representative Preston Brooks, a relative of Senator Butler, entered the Senate chamber and with his walking cane severely beat Sumner. Overnight in the North, the narrow and fanatical Sumner, a man who could never have been successful in politics except for the intensity of the day, was a hero and a martyr, whereas Brooks was said to have demonstrated the well-known Southern propensity to resort to violence when cornered by reason and righteousness. In the South, some deplored the Brooks' act, but he was generally wined, dined, and presented with canes in gratitude for administering a small measure of the whipping Sumner deserved.

Even while the dispute over Kansas raged, the Supreme Court handed down a decision which further enraged the North. In an opinion written by its Southern Chief Justice, Roger B. Taney, a former slaveholder who had freed his bondsmen, the Court held that a slave, Dred Scott, who had resided in free territory was yet a chattel and not a citizen and therefore could not legally entertain a suit in Federal courts. At the same time, the Court declared the Missouri Compromise unconstitutional, sustaining the long standing Southern contention about territories. Although the decision was in accord with the wording of the Constitution and well-established principles of constitutional construction, the North was in no mood to accept cold reasoning and "antiquated" laws. That the rising doctrine of a higher law had not been recognized by the Court as taking precedence over the Constitution brought down on the Court, especially on its aged Chief Justice, abuse and widespread defiance which took the form of a stepped-up flouting of the Fugitive Slave laws and increased support for the "Underground Railway," whereby escaped slaves were spirited across the North to Canada where they would be beyond recovery by their owners.

The setback suffered by antislavery forces in the Dred Scott decision was matched, at about the same time, by a blow which befell the opposing camp. A young back country North Carolinian, Hinton Helper, possessed of a full measure of his region's twin hates, the Negro and the aristocracy, published *The Impending Crisis of the South*. Helper used census statistics showing the greater prosperity of the North to back his contention that slavery was an economic drag. He wanted the slaves freed and transported. To depose the power of the aristocracy, he called for a slave revolt through which he hoped non-slaveholders would secure dominance. For his pains, he was driven from his native state by the ire he inspired in slaveholder and non-slaveholder alike—and he sold 200,000 copies of the *Crisis* as a campaign document for the Republicans in the 1860 campaign.

In at least one respect, Helper's thesis was sound; and it touched the South on a sensitive nerve, one that would be repeatedly touched for years to come, by reformers seeking to prod the South to change its ways. Wrote Helper in a frequently paraphrased paragraph:

. . . we are . . . subservient to the North every day of our lives. In infancy we are swaddled in Northern muslin; in childhood we are humored with Northern gewgaws; in youth we are instructed out of Northern books; at the age of maturity we sow our 'wild oats' on Northern soil; in middle-life we exhaust our wealth . . . in giving aid and succor to every department of Northern power; in the decline of life we remedy our eyesight with Northern spectacles, and support our infirmities with Northern canes; in old age we are drugged with Northern physic; and, finally, when we die, our inanimate bodies, shrouded in Northern cambric, are stretched upon the bier, borne to the grave in a Northern carriage, entombed with a Northern spade, and memorized [sic] with a Northern slab.

There was yet another brief lull—a year and a half, in which crisis-frayed nerves began to relax a bit and the more optimistic spoke of seeing some glimmer of hope. Then, suddenly, even they saw not the faintest glimmer.

The faintly rising hopes of that uneasy lull were suddenly shattered on the night of October 16, 1859. That night, John Brown, at least half-mad with fanatical zeal, suddenly played his small bit. It was a brief part, but, played against the backdrop of long accumulating distrust, its effect was electrifying. Of even more effect was the discovery of what lay behind the insertion of the part, how it came to be included in the tense drama. In the first place, John Brown was an experienced performer. He had gained his reputation back in "bleeding" Kansas, where he had played a major role, augmenting substantially the flow of blood on its tortured plains. With the flow staunched there, Brown's deranged zeal for emancipation soon drove him to search for other bloodlettings in the cause. With that in view, he enlisted the support of such prominent abolitionists as Gerrit Smith, Samuel Howe, George Stearns, Thomas Higginson, and Theodore Parker, men included in our encyclopedias as noted philanthropists and clergymen. Whether these men knew what John Brown was planning may be open to question, but they certainly knew his reputation and his propensity to violence. With their financial backing secured, he enlisted and armed about twenty kindred spirits and repaired to the neighborhood of Harpers Ferry, Virginia, where there was an arsenal from which he intended to seize arms in quantity, to augment the nine hundred and fifty pikes and one hundred and ninety-eight rifles he had already accumulated with which to arm the slaves he expected to recruit.

Finally, with his long laid plans complete, on October 16th, he crossed the Potomac, entered Harpers Ferry, and seized the arsenal as planned. With his augmented supply of arms, he anticipated that all that was needed to bring slaves into revolt was to supply them with arms; and that a revolt, once well-started, would rapidly spread until the whole South was rendered a grand scale Santo Domingo. But the slaves did not revolt, even with the proffered arms. Brown's net success was a few murders, after which he and his followers were all killed or captured. Brown was shortly brought to trial and duly executed.

In itself, John Brown's raid was little more than a sensational incident motivated by an unbalanced mind, but its symbolic connotations shook the country. In the North, by many, he was quickly enshrined with a martyr's halo. There he became the very symbol of a more aggressive campaign against the South and slavery. In the South, especially after the names of his prominent supporters were revealed, Brown symbolized the ultimate development of all abolitionists and the extent to which they were willing to flout established law and order to gain their objective. If John Brown were mad, they, his backers, were only a little less so. Most terrifying was the conviction Brown had planted that abolitionists would stop at nothing, not even murder on a grand scale, to gain their objective. And those contrasting symbols would persist. Within two years, men in blue would be singing:

> *"John Brown's body lies a-moulding in the grave,*
> *But his soul goes marching on."*

And men in grey:

> *"We'll hang John Brown to a sour apple tree,*
> *As we go marching on."*

But sooner, those symbols would compel men to action. It was just the sort of thing that Southern extremists, such as Edmund Ruffin of Virginia who had sent one of Brown's pikes to each Southern governor, Barnwell Rhett of South Carolina, and William L. Yancey of Alabama, needed to fire the populace with indignation, to whip it into line on the secession issue. Years of suspicion and antagonism had prepared the ground. With the help of John Brown and the florid oratory and endless harangue of these "Fire-eaters," there was soon more unity of purpose, more determination that the limit had been reached, than the South had previously known. A wartime atmosphere spread across the land. Dissent was intimidated into silence. The British consul in Charleston reported:

I do not exaggerate in designating the present state of affairs in the Southern country as a reign of terror. Persons are torn away from their residences and pursuits; sometimes "tarred and feathered"; "ridden upon rails," or cruelly whipped; letters are opened at the Post Office, discussion upon slavery is entirely prohibited under penalty of expulsion, with or without violence, from the country.

The Northern merchants and "Travellers" are leaving in great numbers.

On the surface, at least, all internal issues disappeared from the South save the *modus operandi* and the timing of the break.

Since most of Brown's backers, most of those who were enshrining him and, in fact, the overwhelming majority of all militant abolitionists had aligned themselves with the new Republican party and were comprising its most vocal segment, Southerners generally regarded the whole party as an abolitionist political organization bent on giving their "higher law" precedence over the Constitution. Even more judicious heads, observing the rising power of abolitionists in the party, foresaw abolitionist domination of the party as inevitable. More and more, as these convictions hardened in the months that followed, the determination spread abroad that a Republican victory in the 1860 elections should be the signal for leaving the union. With the signal agreed upon, the "Fire-eaters" set to work with new vigor to prepare the popular mind for the fateful step.

The minds of many were already prepared. Under the impact of recurring crises, many had grown accustomed to the idea of disunion. Many had already privately transferred their prime allegiance from the government in Washington and its civil laws to the court of King Cotton and his economic and social laws. Many thought his regime would prove both more partial to, and more powerful in, the protection of their special interests. They had widely embraced the famous words of Senator James H. Hammond when he publicly acclaimed on the floor of the Senate the South's choice of allegiances and dared defiance of its power:

> Without the firing of a gun, without drawing a sword, should they make war upon us, we could bring the whole world to our feet. What would happen if no cotton was furnished for three years? . . . England would topple headlong and carry the whole civilized world with her. No, you dare not make war on cotton. No power on earth dares make war on it. Cotton is King.

As the campaign of 1860 got underway, Southern suspicion of the Republicans seemed to be confirmed. The sounds emanating from its campaigners sounded similar indeed to those that the abolitionists had been making for years. The changes were rung on the moral apostasy of slavery and the "higher law" that forbade its continuance. Little or no thought or consideration was given the mountainous consequences which would inevitably flow from immediate abolition. Northerners seemed not to comprehend that slave property constituted the major item of Southern wealth. It was a major collateral of the section's banks and other financial institutions. The race problem which would be created by emancipation would be momentous. New institutions for the support, education, and welfare of ex-slaves would have to be established to replace those functions which had devolved upon slaveowners. The very states and their sub-units would face bankruptcy, and entirely new fiscal policies would have to be discovered and developed. The results of summary abolition would amount to a revolution. Nevertheless, abolitionists and Republicans ignored these problems and drove relentlessly toward their objectives. At least, that was the appearance Republican campaigners created. Of course, the party had its less extreme segment, but it was also less vocal. Probably candidate Abraham Lincoln himself was among the more conservative but, as his statements were commonly susceptible to different interpretations, no one could be certain.

Contending with the Republicans for national control was a broken-down Whig party seeking to reverse its eclipse under a new banner, the Constitutional Union party. Major opposition, however, lay with the Democrats, a party long riven with internal dissension. At its convention in Charleston, there was immediately an impasse on platform statements. The wrangle which followed, culminated in the secession of its "Fire-eating" Southern wing under the influence of Yancey, resulting in a split party with two sets of candidates. Dissension had opened the door wide for Republicans, enabling Lincoln's election by a mere forty percent plurality.

Lincoln's victory was the long appointed signal. The chips were down; it was the South's next play. It became South Carolina's lot to be the next player, despite plans of the secession men that the first break should be made by a Gulf state, since Southern leadership had already moved westward with cotton just as national leadership had earlier moved north with wealth and population.

South Carolina's move was prompt and decisive. With her long background of dissatisfaction born of economic distress and increasing political eclipse in national affairs, she was already looking back on the glories of her past and with bitterness comparing it with her diminished power, a change blamed on Northern policies. As the conviction grew that the state would act in the event of a Republican victory, the state's unionist minority rapidly evaporated—at least ostensibly. The conservatives either fell into line or ceased to speak out any longer for fear of popular disapproval. There was an air of unanimity abroad as the convention gathered in Columbia to consider secession—a unanimity substantiated on December 20th, when the convention, having meanwhile adjourned to Charleston, adopted the Ordinance of Secession without a dissenting vote. At long last dissension had become disunion.

The South
Becomes
a Kingdom: 3

7

U P TO THIS POINT, this account has been little more than a summary of the elements of the framework of the South—the geographical and historical, the political and social elements of its structure—all bound together into a cohesive unit by its commercial-agricultural economy. On that framework, the South of 1860 was built. To give the picture more semblance of life and blood, more of the living vitality which history was to prove the South possessed to an amazing degree, it is necessary to look beyond mere geography and events, to look at the people who vitalized that geography, were modified by it, who were both the makers of and the products of those events, and to examine their social system which was likewise the product of that geography and the creator and product of those events.

In 1860, some 9,000,000 people were living in the South. Of these, 3,500,000 were Negro slaves. Of all these people, only about one in twenty lived in even a small town. In all the vast extent of the South, there were only about twenty-five towns of over 4,000 population and only two of more than 100,000. More than that, nearly all those who did not live in those few towns, lived on farms and gained their livelihood through agriculture. Rural living as an urban adjunct was all but nonexistent in those days. Thus composed, the South was perhaps, relatively, the most rural area of any size ever occupied by western civilization. Normally, in most societies, the urban centers guide and dominate the fashions and thinking of the whole, rural and urban. In the old South, however, the reverse was the rule. The section was so overwhelmingly rural that the mere force of rural numbers imposed ruralism on even those few of its towns which might rank as cities.

If one is to know the historical background of Southern thinking, if one is even to begin to understand the South, one must realize that its extreme ruralism is one of the two essential keys to the vault that has held, for more than a century, its Pandora's box of prejudices and predilections that so baffle the urban mind. The presence of the Negro in massive numbers is, of course, the other essential key.

Mention of that second key calls for some statistical background relative to it. A dominant five and a half million whites shared Southern living with three and a half million black bondsmen. But by no means did those whites share equally the ownership of those blacks. Only about one in sixteen owned a single slave. These, together with their wives and children, about one in four additional, made up the entire slaveholding society. In using the word "society," no social distinction is implied, for although ownership of slaves was frequently a stepping stone to social distinction, the vast majority of slaveholders never attained the social distinction which usually accompanied those classed as planters. They were small farmers who acquired by purchase rather than "rental" the one, two, or even four farm hands needed to help out with their crops. Five out of seven slaveowners belonged to that small farmer class owning less than ten slaves. Such farmers were comparable to farmers in a non-slave society who employed from one to four helpers, for there would normally be but three field hands available from the ownership of ten slaves.

Of all the nearly 350,000 slaveowners, less than 8,000 were in the traditional planter class, those owning fifty or more slaves, productive of fifteen or more field hands. What is truly remarkable is the enormous influence of that mere handful of 8,000 out of 1,250,000 Southern white families, both in the events of the day and on a latter day South, peopled by a similarly small percentage of their actual posterity.

In all the South in 1860, there were but 1,733 planters owning more than a hundred slaves, about $100,000 in value at the time. However, there is no gainsaying that among a relatively tiny group of planters, there were ample wealth and elegance to foster in the mind's eye enhancement and multiplication of the Southern planter in generations to follow. The opulence of that group is implicit in the statistics of one authority on the prewar distribution of agricultural income in the cotton country. Of the 667,000 families deriving their income from cotton, 1,000 received almost half of the gross or about $50,000 each, leaving the other 666,000 families with an average of but $100 each as their gross money income. And the small slaveholder fared little better than the average small farmer. The average income of farmers owning five slaves or less was about $125, those with ten slaves about $300.

To round out this statistical background of the agricultural South, something should be said of the distribution of capital involved. The total prewar value of all the slaves was about $3,000,000,000. That was substantially more than the value of all the farms and plantations. The market value of lands in slave states was then much below that of comparable lands in free states, a situation partly accounted for by the continuing soil robbery of plantation crops and partly by the lower productivity of slave labor. Most authorities, both Northern and Southern, generally agreed that three free laborers produced as much as four slaves—and cost less when the support of slaves during bad weather, illness, and old age was taken into consideration, not to mention interest on the investment the slave represented. Many of the South's economic deficiencies flowed directly from its heavy capital involvement in slave property. There was little money left to form banks, build railroads, buy merchant ships, or construct factories. There was not even enough to buy the slaves deemed necessary, so it was borrowed in the North.

Those are the essential statistics of an agricultural system which, in spite of its deficiencies, was enormously productive of wealth, more for the North, however, than for the South. More than half of the nation's exports were products of Southern soil—and in every instance, their production made the section poorer by diminishing the resources of forest and mine, or by depleting the soils and subjecting them to devastating erosion. Virtually all of the nation's tobacco, sugar, rice, and cotton came out of the South. Cotton alone comprised forty percent of the country's exports. But out of every dollar received for it, forty cents stayed in the North in the form of factors' commissions, interest charges, freight, and insurance. The sixty cents remaining had to take care of the cost of growing the crop, its ginning and delivery to port, and, if anything was left over, the profit of the farmer. Beyond that, it had to cover the hazards of crop failures and of short crops and to provide for the maintenance of the planter and his slaves through fairly frequent periods of disaster. Even greater were the North's profits flowing from Southern commodities through their fabrication in the North: the spinning and weaving of cotton, fashioning of lumber into usable articles, the making of rum from molasses, and ropes from hemp.

Beyond that, the North further profited from the South's plantation economy. Of the sixty cents which went South to the producers, a good part was soon on its way back northward. Plantation crops, especially cotton, had an all but inexorable tendency, as with mass production generally, to monopolize all the better lands of the grower, leaving neither labor nor land for production of other crops. Even before 1845, diversified farming had almost vanished. For its staple foods, the agricultural South had become heavily dependent on the North. Corn and pork, the standard fare of its slaves, and to a large extent of the masters, too, were mostly imported instead of being raised. More than ninety percent of the South's corn requirements and eighty percent of its pork were shipped into the cotton region from the North. Cotton had even crowded out that traditional adjunct of every Southern farm, the still. Its homemade applejack, peach brandy, and corn whiskey now made up but five percent of its alcoholic consumption. Ninety-five percent was sent South in return for what remained of the ever restless cotton and tobacco dollars.

Under such an economy, there is little wonder that the South grew poorer and more resentful as the North grew richer and more arrogant.

The society that made this a way of life, the society that made those statistics, the society which was in turn molded by that economy was in many respects unique. It was a society the diversities of which were welded firmly together by its overwhelming dependence on agriculture, its all but exclusively rural environment, and the all-pervading presence of the Negro in great numbers. Most of all, it was the presence of the Negro in every facet of Southern life that made for that uniqueness. Everywhere in the South, except in the mountain regions, he was present in substantial numbers, but he was most numerous in what is known as the Black Belt, a strip beginning in tidewater Virginia and extending with increasing width southwardly to Florida and westwardly along the Gulf coast to beyond the Mississippi, in most of which his numbers greatly exceeded the white population. The fact that this area of the preponderance of the Negro was identical with that from which almost all of the early Southern leadership came, further enhanced the influence of the Negro on the whole South, even beyond the Black Belt.

Colonial leadership had come almost exclusively from the slave-based society of coastal Virginia, the Carolinas, and Louisiana. In later days, much of the South's leadership was drawn from the earlier settled portions of Georgia, Alabama, and Mississippi; the Black Belts of those states. And that old time leadership was not only political and economic, it was also social. It was thus inevitable that large scale slaveholders should have become models of the ambitious and newly successful throughout the whole agricultural realm. If a farmer in the hill country of Carolina or in Tennessee or Texas lacked the slave investment to justify the cry of one slaveholder, "Give me slavery or give me death," he hoped to have it; and in the way King Cotton had been elevating his devotees from barefoot plowboys to planters, in the decades between 1820 and 1860, he figured that his chances were good, even if he was still behind the plow.

Cotton had always made gamblers of his minions. Any year they might hit the jackpot, regardless of how long they had played for it and how much the game had cost in sweat, in soil, and in hard living.

That, to a considerable degree, explains the remarkable uniformity throughout the South of the reaction to the Negro. The pattern was set where there was an overwhelming race problem, where there was a real fear with a real basis, and that pattern of the leadership class was copied over and over by lesser men elsewhere, even where it did not necessarily fit their environment and circumstances. Thus, Virginians migrating to Kentucky, even if they failed to bring their proportion of Virginia slaves, brought their more easily acquired and more easily transported fears of the blacks, their prejudices against them, and laws for their circumscription.

Among those prejudices the migrant carried west with him was the conviction that the Negro was subhuman, or at best markedly inferior to the white race. He was confident that the Negro could never be trained to take a place in modern democratic society. In consequence, he harbored no doubt but that means would always have to be provided to keep the Negro in a subservient position, subject to the direction and dominance of the white man. Today, such opinions are regarded as shallow prejudices harbored only by the most ignorant. How then could intelligent men, some even outstanding leaders in the ante-bellum South, have maintained such views? There are two answers to that question. In the first place, few men are reasonable and objective under fear. And always in the Black Belt was a background of fear—fear of the overwhelming numbers of their semi-barbarian "internal enemy." The second source of that conviction was the Southerner's uncritical observations. He had seen the blacks at simple and menial tasks and doing them poorly. Unlettered and confined by force to a simple and highly restricted environment, they gave every appearance of being dimwitted brutes. The success and obvious intelligence of some free Negroes confirmed rather than challenged those prejudices, for most of the freedmen were mulattoes and it was thought that only their white blood gave them their intelligence and industry.

Consequently, the migrant carried with him a conviction of the inferiority of the Negro. He handed it on as gospel to his neighbors who might not have had the same opportunities for first-hand observation. He inculcated it in his posterity, not malevolently but rather in the firm belief that he was teaching them truths he had himself observed. And unless they were taught otherwise by more objective teachers, they continued, through the years and through the generations, to act and react according to the time-honored lessons which had been taught them.

The other motivating prejudice of the ante-bellum white Southerner in relation to the Negro was no product of the Black Belt plantations. It was of far more ancient lineage, so ancient, in fact, that its origins are shrouded. Although it was then and is even today part and parcel of the emotional equipment of the overwhelming majority of Southern whites, it is Southern only to the extent that the Southern white is more Anglo-Saxon, Celtic, and German than is the Northerner. It is the prejudice of people of those origins against dark skins wherever they come in contact with them, whether they be Negro, Chinese, or Indian. It's the prejudice of the Boer and the Briton in South Africa, the Englishman in India and Hong Kong, and the American confronted with red men and imported blacks. It's the old Othello prejudice. While it baffles explanation, it cuts deep wherever the whites of those origins come in contact with people of a different color. To brand this prejudice as Southern was unjust and still is. The only reason that it appeared to be Southern is that whites in the North had never been put to the test. The average man in the North had had but incidental contact with men of color. His absorption with the Negro problem had been intellectual, objective, and at a distance. More recently, face to face with realities, he has demonstrated that the Othello prejudice is no monopoly of Southerners.

In 1860, faced with a population consitituency of more than one Negro for every two whites, and with a black majority in the home regions of most of its leaders, the South was deeply concerned with this race problem. Southerners had no way of securing a sympathetic understanding of their concern from whites in the North who had, as yet, not been confronted with the problem.

Southerners, with their racial prejudices stimulated to a high degree by the formidable mass of black skins in their midst, were filled with indignation by abolitionist charges of interracial concubinage. The abolitionist claim that the South was "a cesspool of amalgamation" made them fighting mad. Incidentally, the very wording of abolitionist charges, convicts the abolitionists themselves of a replete stock of the racial prejudice in their own emotional makeup.

Actually, in the old plantation region, the eastern Black Belt, the Southern system had performed remarkably in keeping amalgamation at a minimum through two centuries of blacks and whites living together in closest contact. There is ample proof of that in ebony skins of the vast majority of Negroes of that section to this day. But barriers were not so great outside the Black Belt. Not infrequently, the back country frontiersman—and the South beyond the eastern Black Belt was in the main a deep, persistent frontier throughout its ante-bellum history—even after he became a slaveholder, was often as uncouth, illiterate, and amoral as his slaves. And there is ample proof of that en evidence in those regions today.

Although conviction of the innate inferiority of Negroes and the aversion to skin of a different color were motivating prejudices which gave rise to much of the South's bent of mind, there were other Southern traits in the development of which the Negro played an important role.

To the friendly observer, planters of the old South usually seemed proud men, born leaders with a natural air of authority, men who would brook no crossing, men confident of their standing. To the unfriendly, they appeared arrogant, overbearing, haughty, short of patience, and easily provoked to violence. In the final analysis those are but two sides of the coin, a coin minted by the accustomed right from childhood to command obedience and service from others. Understandably, the tendency to command and the easy manner of doing it were ingrained attributes of those who always had subjects to command. Thus, the Negro no doubt played his humble role in producing the South's preponderance of national leaders as long as slavery existed.

Ever aspiring to that position of command, as a farmer grew more prosperous, he commonly gave first thought to acquiring more slaves. The more slaves he acquired, the less physical labor was necessary on his part. A minimum of physical labor became at least one of his major objectives in life. From that aspiration it was but a step to regarding physical labor as a badge of failure. It was just as simple as that, and just as inevitable, too, that physical labor lost in the South the dignity the earlier American frontier had given it; historically a symptom of decadence in any society.

At least partly related to the planter's disdain for physical labor was his almost equally strong aversion to mercantile vocations. Perhaps, however, his mercantile aversion had most of its origin in his usually unhappy dealings with his factor, who ordinarily performed most of the business essentials of the plantation, from supplying the necessary operating capital to the marketing of the crop, as well as many personal errands for the planter and his family. Helpless in the toils of the distant business world, the planter held a lofty disdain for the mercantile world and a fixed opinion that business was a line of endeavor into which no true gentleman would direct his talents.

Although most of what has been said so far of the effect of the Negro on Southern thinking, applied largely to the planter class, his effect on the section was actually all-pervasive. Since most yeoman farmers and small slaveholders were kinsmen of some planter or aspired to a planter's status, they generally seconded the planter's views on slavery and the Negro.

But what about the poorer yeoman farmers whose small holdings and poor lands put them beyond such aspirations, and what about the million odd "poor whites" living out their miserable existences in a standard no better than, if as good as, the lot of the slaves? From one end of Dixie to the other, miserable shanties of the "poor whites" should have been as much a hallmark of the section as the plantation homes they so vastly outnumbered, except for their being all but hidden behind the glamorous façade of planters' mansions. What stake had those people in a social order, which left them economically perhaps worse off and educationally little better off than slaves? Why should not they have nurtured a jealous hate of the planter and joined their numbers to the "internal enemy?"

To a considerable extent, the answer again is the old Othello prejudice. Those people were all but universally of the Anglo-Saxon world, albeit the jetsam of that world. Having little but the color of their skins in which they might take pride, they pushed their Othello prejudice far beyond the suasion it held with other classes. Whereas the upper classes were convinced that the Negro was incurably inferior to the white man and racial integrity should be preserved at all costs, the "poor white" harbored a real hatred of the black, a hatred which was nonexistent in upper classes. The basis of that hatred was a fear more insidious than a fear of revolt. If the Negro were given equal status with him, his only pride, his pride of color, would become much less ego warming. But more than that, he feared the potential competition, social and economic, of the Negro in a free society. The "poor white" was discerning enough to realize that if slaves were freed, his class would bear most of the brunt of their competition. So "poor whites" became the staunchest supporters of slavery and gave Southern racial prejudice most of the animus with which it has been charged through the years.

Fairly commonly, non-slaveholders, interviewed by observers of the ante-bellum South, spoke out against slavery, but always they conditioned their disapproval on a solution of the race problem and always their solution was to send freed slaves out of the South. Here are samples from the 1850's:

> I wish their warn't no niggers here. They are a great cuss to this country. . . . I reckon a majority would be right glad if we could get rid of the niggers. But it wouldn't do to free 'em and leave 'em here. I don't know anybody, hardly, in favor of that. Make 'em free and leave 'em here and they'd steal everything we made. Nobody couldn't live here then.

And:

> . . . I'd like it if we could get rid of 'em yonst. I wouldn't like to hev 'em freed, if they was gwine to hang round. . . . they is so monstrous lazy; if they hadn't got nobody to take keer on 'em, you see they wouldn't do nothin' but just nat'rally laze round, and steal, and pilfer, and no man couldn't live, . . . now suppose they

was free, you see they'd all think themselves just as good as we; of course they would, if they was free. Now, . . . how'd you like to hev a nigger steppin' up to your darter? . . . but I tell you I don't think it's right to hev 'em as slaves . . .

In homespun language, and on a more personal basis, those were the same hard rocks of opinion that wrecked the efforts of Jefferson, Madison, and Mason when they made their moves to rid the country of slavery. Likewise, they represent realities which the abolitionists never saw but which every Southerner, regardless of his sentiments as to slavery, knew intimately and to which he saw no solution. Whether the fear was as real as imagined was beside the point.

That uniformity of opinion among Southern whites of all classes, that wide "white peerage" of the South, is what gave the section its basic solidarity, a solidarity in the face of wide diversities; social, economic, and historical, within itself. It gave it a solidarity that overrode all other economic and political considerations, dwarfing all other issues. The best illustration of the truth of this statement lies in the wreckage of the often and ardently sought political and economic partnership between the agricultural South and the agricultural West, an economically sound alliance, ephemerally achieved in early decades of the nineteenth century, only to be wrecked in the priority the South (faced with realities of the problem) gave to its racial convictions, convictions with which the agricultural West, aloof from these realities, could tolerate less and less.

Rivaling the effect of the omnipresence of the Negro on Southern thinking was the effect of the South's extreme ruralism. The extent of that ruralism has already been mentioned. In a region where ninety-two people out of a hundred lived isolated in the country by incredibly poor communications with such towns as there were, as well as between themselves, in a region containing areas as vast as North Carolina, Florida, Mississippi, Arkansas, and Texas without a single town of 10,000 people, it would be impossible for that almost total ruralism not to have a great effect on the views and thinking of its people. And this was especially true in the South where ruralism acted on its subjects in concert with the frontier conditions which still prevailed, even in 1860, over much of its expanse. The effects of urban living upon urban dwellers are by no means all found on the credit side. But there were some virtues and advantages usually inspired or enhanced by urban living that the South of 1860 sorely lacked.

The impact of mind on mind through urban living makes for a greater degree of liberalism, of thinking in accord with the times, in contrast to the tendency of those who are isolated by rural living from the impact of other opinions, to ossify the views and opinions inherited from their forebears. Urban centers are generally fountainheads of liberalism and progress; rural communities, the strongholds of conservatism and social stagnation. To a considerable degree, the South's extreme conservatism was the product of its extreme ruralism, but not wholly so. Its agricultural economy also played an important role in producing that conservatism. Agriculture is one of the most primitive of human enterprises. Manufacturing, communication, transportation, and business call for alertness for new developments and a readiness to adopt new ideas if one expects to survive competition. Plantation agriculture even lacked most of the stimulus of competition. Such competition as existed was largely impersonal, between sections and nations. Certainly neighboring planters had no such conscious competition as existed between their merchant or manufacturing counterparts. All of which made for a much more relaxed and easygoing living among the South's planters and farmers. But for their gain on that score, they paid the price of a lack of any vital identity with the mainstream of social and economic developments in a rapidly changing world.

That physical and psychological isolation of the overwhelming majority of ante-bellum Southerners was responsible for several characteristics commonly regarded as earmarks of Southerners even to this day.

Lacking towns which might be the nuclei for some organized social and cultural organizations, most Southerners were thrown largely on their own for ways and means to relieve their lonely isolation. In consequence, those few organizations that functioned in their rural environs, the church and political gatherings, were embraced with special ardor.

Most reporters of the customs surrounding the rural church were struck especially by the social aspects of church attendance. They tell of the congregation gathering long before service time to visit together in groups about the church grounds, gossiping and discussing news of the day, talking endlessly of their restricted but consuming interests: land, crops, politics, and slaves. After interruption by the service, this diversion was resumed with most of the congregation hanging around, visiting and picnicking long after services had ended.

In fact, churchgoing was so attractive that regular scheduled services left an unfilled demand. That unsatisfied hunger, especially in the long, dull summer months, together with the practical difficulties of getting to and from the often distant church, gave birth to protracted meetings and camp meetings, where thousands camping together for days were not only whipped into religious fervor by the unrestrained, extravagant, and emotional exhortations of accomplished revivalists, but were also given the opportunity, rare for them, to feast and carouse under the stimulation of a carnival-like atmosphere. Since the staid and ritualistic Episcopal church was not adaptable to this sort of mixture of emotional religion and social stimulation, the overwhelming majority of Southerners gave their loyalties elsewhere, generally to the less conventional Methodists and Baptists.

The fact that tradition usually associates the planter with the Episcopal church is but another part of the planter myth. Among the nine million Southerners in 1860, there were less than sixty thousand Episcopalians, most of them living along the Virginia and Carolina coast. In addition to emotional appeal, the Southerner sought the stability and comfort of "that old-time religion," unadulterated by modern liberalism. For him to desire any other sort would be inconsistent for one who had shunned the mounting progress of the world, eschewed industrial progress, and forgotten Jeffersonian democracy. Under the influence of that rigid "old-time religion" the South embraced Puritanism a hundred years after it had begun to relax its hold on New England. It was that fundamentalist Puritanism which had become the vanguard of secession. Twenty years before political secession, this Puritanism had found its bonds with the growing liberalism of the Northern wings of the Methodist and Baptist churches so chafing that Southern wings seceded. Free then to apply the sociology of the slaveholding Israel of Biblical times, the Southern clergy supplied much leadership in expounding the positive good arguments for slavery and eventually in encouraging political secession.

Among the other social outlets to which the Southerner turned to relieve his rural loneliness were the community militia and political gatherings. Consequently, both of these were given more attention and devotion than they received in the North.

Everywhere in the South, military organizations prospered beyond those of other sections. As a matter of fact, in ante-bellum years, the South continued military minded while interest in the military waned in a distracted and busy North. No doubt because of the section's long continued dependence on the military against both its constant internal and external threats, a military career was given the dignity and respect accorded only to planting and politics.

At political meetings, the Southerner came to expect a show of real entertainment, florid and colorful oratory, and clever debate. The politicians gave him what he wanted. Given such widespread interest and unfeigned adulation, there is little wonder that politics attracted so many of the best talents of the South. Here was a rare field of real competition in the South. No more proof of its effectiveness is needed than the section's disproportionate share of outstanding political leaders of the nation. The sad feature of the story lies in the fact that for so long, so much of the region's best talents were diverted from other fields of endeavor where talent and leadership were greatly needed; in its economy, its industry, and in letters and arts. From a neglect of those other fields came a disrespect for them which in turn further crippled appreciable advances in them.

Ruralism was the source of other traits and bents which came to be regarded as Southern. One of the most famed was its traditional hospitality, the fondness of the Southerner for social entertainment. A guest relieved the host's loneliness and mitigated his feelings of isolation from the world. More guests were even better antidotes. The latchstring on the outside was therefore the answer to a great need of the host and, because of the paucity of public accommodations, it was also the answer to an equally great need of the wayfarer. But the South's traditional hospitality was not widespread through the classes. It was almost exclusively confined to the few of the real planter class, and generally it was extended only to the better class of traveler. Among other classes, limitations of homes and poverty of provisions prevented emulation.

Yet another fruit of isolation was the extent to which home and family became the focal point of the Southerner's life. In his day to day existence, that was the only place where his social needs could find sustenance. His daily routine on the plantation provided few social contacts other than with his slaves. Home at the end of such a day was far more gratifying than to his urban counterpart who would have had stimulating contacts with people throughout his working hours. More than that, the planter's home was not only the heart of his family, it was also the heart of his business. It was the seat of an authority over his labor force. It was his office as well as his home. It and his church were the only foci of his social life. The Southern home was, in fact as well as in fiction, enhanced in importance beyond those elsewhere.

The aggrandizement of the home naturally reflected itself in the aggrandizement of the mainspring of the home, the mistress of the house. On a Southern slave plantation, the assignment of the woman of the house was much more than that of wife, mother, and housekeeper for her family. Among the blacks, most of the women, the children, and the sick were also her special responsibility. By that extension, her household responsibilities were often multiplied. Beyond that, she was expected to be an ever ready and accomplished hostess who could gracefully add frequent guests to her teeming household. Her importance to the household and the plantation's operation was proportionate to the immensity of her assignments. Partly in recognition of that and partly by way of compensation, the mistress of the Southern plantation and, through emulation, Southern womanhood generally, was exalted as in no other society in the world. And Southerners talked of it endlessly. The purity, the nobility, the bravery, the beauty and charm of its womanhood became a favorite subject, regardless of the occasion, for the oratory of politicians, ministers, and after-dinner speakers alike. Thus was myth piled on top of fact until, in the minds of most Southerners, their women came to be a special breed apart and above women elsewhere. Their superior endowments became one of the favorite defences of slavery. The most feared menace of abolition centered likewise in them.

The South

Becomes

a Kingdom: 4

8

A T THIS POINT, to develop other traits of Southerners, it becomes necessary to emphasize a condition which prevailed in the South which was only a little less influential than ruralism and the Negro. The frontier conditions under which the great majority of Southerners lived up to 1861 has been referred to several times already. The need now is to develop and emphasize the importance of those conditions in creating Southernism. Although there is no way of determining when a frontier ceases to be a frontier, essentially frontier conditions prevailed almost up to 1861, from within one or two hundred miles of the Atlantic Ocean westwardly for a thousand miles to the deserts and western prairies, excepting in a few long settled regions near the Gulf and those areas within the influence of such towns as Nashville, Memphis, and Louisville. Although in 1861, the Gulf states were already the central domain of the Cotton Kingdom, they had mostly been settled for only half a lifetime or less. Since the Virginia and Carolina back country had been settled for more than a century and Kentucky and Tennessee only a generation later, one may ask why the frontier label is placed on all that vast territory, while the western reaches of the North, settled later than Tennessee and Kentucky, had already ceased to be regarded as frontier country. The answer lies in the towns of the North and their relative absence in the South. From the orbit of each town, as it sprang into existence, the frontier was pushed out until those orbits met and overlapped and the frontier was no more. Back from the coast in the ante-bellum South, those orbits were few and isolated and rarely overlapping, resulting only in infrequent islands of a more mature society.

Across that thousand mile expanse, most of the inhabitants had been raised in log cabins, on farms where they had to make do with what they could grow or manufacture on the place. A goodly percentage of the elders could recall the Indian wars by which they had gotten their farms. Rivers and streams remained their most important means of transportation. Few roads had been built and most of them were difficult for even wagons to negotiate. Although almost 10,000 miles of railroad had been built in the South, much of it was in the coastal sections and little of it could be called a railroad system. Much mileage was laid with the sole object of getting plantation produce to seaport or river port rather than as a communication system through the region. Most of the people were new to the country in which they lived. For example, not a single leader of Mississippi in the Civil War was a native of the state. And usually, they had been too busy carving their farms from the wilderness and providing their families with roofs to develop the social orderliness that marks the end of the frontier.

In the horse drawn era, rural conditions alone placed a serious obstacle in development of a school system, even in a mature and well-ordered society. In regions all but roadless, lacking the nuclei of towns and villages, where society was embryonic and the thin-spread government new and hesitant in face of the distrust of many who had long gotten along without it, obstacles standing in the way of establishment of an effective public school system were formidable indeed. And so it proved in the South.

Counting slaves, about half the people in the South in 1860 could not read and write. Although most states of the region had some provision for a public school system, schools remained rudimentary or existed only in theory, except for the few in or near larger towns. That failure to establish a public school system was largely owing to a lack of support from the public. The planter looked after his own children. The masses regarded public schools as an impingement on their personal freedom and an expense not justified by any practical usefulness of education in an agricultural society. The paucity of public schools, however, was partly offset by hundreds of private academies which were established in more prosperous neighborhoods. These academies were usually conducted by a single schoolmaster who emphasized Latin, Greek, and oratory. However, the fee charged for attendance prevented general use of them by the masses. It is not surprising that only one white child in seven was in school in 1860, that about a fourth of the adult population could not read and write, and that Southern illiteracy was about three times as great as that of the North, despite the great influx of European immigrants into that section.

In education, as in every aspect of Southern life, for the true planter class, the field was far more roseate. Its scions were usually schooled in the neighborhood academy sponsored by planters of the community, or by a tutor employed for the household or, through concerted action, for several neighboring households. Beyond that schooling lay the only part of education in which the South excelled the contemporary North. In 1860, the South had half the colleges of the nation to cater to a fourth of the country's white population; it had three times its proportion of students in attendance in both Southern colleges and those of the North. This was in marked contrast to the general education picture, even after taking into consideration the fact that many Southern colleges were small denominational schools, permitting education only within a very restricted horizon.

With the masses so poorly trained and so little inspired intellectually, with few towns to facilitate intellectual exchange, with the upper classes distracted from things intellectual by politics, planting, and soldiering, and with those vocations given a social prestige which was not accorded those who wrote or delved in the arts, it is understandable that the South showed little interest in and contributed almost nothing to the literary and intellectual flowering which was taking place in the North, especially in New England. Nevertheless, although few Southerners were willing to give themselves wholly to things cultural and few were willing to assume the obligations of culture, the planter class greatly desired the reputation of being cultured. Its spokesmen endlessly argued that through slavery they had attained the most cultured society the world had ever known. If they failed to convince the world of that, they succeeded in thoroughly convincing themselves and most of their posterity. The disparity between their claims and the facts as weighed in retrospect seems to lie in their confusion of leisure with culture.

The planters' claims of superior culture were based on the concomitant of ample leisure and the presence among them of a higher ratio of college-trained men than in upper classes elsewhere. But if a society fails to inspire its members generally with a desire to add to their cultural heritage and fails to arouse in them any sense of obligation to use their cultural attainments for something more than personal consumption and enjoyment, it is scarcely a cultured society. Beyond that, on other scores the planters fell far short of claims made for them. While they devoured Scott's romantic novels, associating themselves with his heroes and heroines and their society with feudal England, apparently without seriously wondering if theirs was not an unsupportable atavism, their consumption of more realistic fiction and of serious books and periodicals fell far below that of the North. Literary and philosophical journals flourished in the North, but they were all but nonexistent in the plantation realm. And the score was even worse in the more practical arts, in science, invention, and architecture. From urban centers of the East came most of the scientific advances of the day. Whitney's invention of the cotton gin had been symbolic. Southerners in the years of the Cotton Kingdom all but stopped inventing, even to solve their own special problems. Their architecture was frozen in the neoclassical mold which Jefferson had fashioned, so that plantation houses (except the majority which were still hewn log structures) and public buildings from the James to the Mississippi were stereotyped by columned façades.

More basic than those deficiencies was that of the climate of the Cotton Kingdom—not the climate of sun, wind, and rain; but the human climate, the mental, moral, and social climate. In the days of Virginia titans, men could ponder on the long term future of their native land and express grave concern; they could disapprove of its economic strait jacket and its social structure and freely express their disapproval; they could agree with the criticisms leveled at their section by outsiders and remain respected and beloved at home. Jefferson, Madison, Randolph, and Mason felt no compulsion to hide their disapproval of the slave-based plantation system. They remained Southern heroes. Even in the 1830's, the governor of Virginia and Richmond newspapers could roundly denounce slavery and lead a serious effort to be rid of it; and even in slavery-wedded South Carolina, a Joel Poinsett could still freely speak his disapproving mind on the subject.

But in 1850, in a South driven to the defensive by immoderate and unsympathetic criticisms leveled at it from the North and abroad, that atmosphere of freedom of thought and expression was gone. By then, most Southerners had curbed their thoughts to the narrower field of the immediate future; and of those few who had continued to concern themselves with an indefinite future, under the frowns of moral disapproval directed at their homeland from every quarter, even fewer had the temerity to speak their thoughts in a land where it had become both social and public policy to present an undented solid front in the face of outside opposition. By then the taboo against unconventional thinking, as measured by the Southern standards of the day, had become so powerful that a James L. Petigru could become an all-time hero among his fellow Charlestonians because of the bravery he displayed in continuing to speak his disapproving mind even after secession. But the number of those as morally and socially daring as Petigru was negligible. The taboo was far too powerful. Nor was it confined to the slavery issue alone. It covered a wide field; from opposition to the States' rights doctrine, or approval of mercantilism, manufacturing, and the protective tariff to innovations or even liberalism in religion, in fact to everything that wasn't Southern. Under the force of such taboos, one is led to ponder what would have become of Thomas Jefferson in his native region had his time been a half-century later. In such a stifling intellectual climate, there is small wonder that while the old South was proclaiming itself the most cultured civilization the world had known, it was, in fact, culturally vegetating behind a superficial but attractive façade.

Along with intellectual and personal freedom and a high degree of education and culture, one of the prime measures of a mature and successful society is the extent of the orderliness of that society, the extent to which it has attained the ideal of functioning peacefully under a rule of law rather than of men, or of economic interests and crops for that matter.

Under the pressure of their economic interests and their abiding fear of their "internal enemy," the Southern states frequently showed little hesitation in defying the rule of law. They had settled Tennessee and Kentucky in defiance, first of the crown, and later of the laws of Virginia and North Carolina. They had seized the lands of Creeks and Cherokees in defiance of solemn treaties and Federal court decrees. On a larger scale, they had seized Texas from a weak but unoffending Mexico. They had continued to enforce and even continued to enact Negro Seamen Acts, quarantining free Negro sailors in Southern ports, in the teeth of a declaration of the unconstitutionality of such acts by the Federal courts. And all across the plantation country, men persisted in giving full rein to their emotions, taking the law into their own hands and substituting lynch law for the rule of law. And Negroes were seldom the victims. While they made up a third of the population of the section, only ten percent of the lynching victims in the old South were blacks.

In addition, the section's record of personal violence, whether elegantly performed in strict observance of the Code of Honor or in the form of eye-gouging in a circle of cheering ruffians, is unsurpassed by the record of any other section in all American history. The presence of the Negro was unquestionably a factor, but there were many other significant sources for the South's record of violence. Primarily, it was the natural product of frontier life, which, even in 1860, persisted as the environment of the majority of Southerners.

Among other inducements to violence, climate, of course, was foremost. Heat shortens tempers and increases irritability. Another source was ethnological. Celtic peoples, who formed the dominant strain among white Southerners, have always had a propensity to violence; in Scotland, in Ireland, or on the Iberian peninsula. Also, history had ennobled the violent background forced by circumstances on the colonial deep South. Its exposed position, confronting the perpetual enmity of the power of Spain and France, and its interminable Indian wars, which continued long after the Northern frontier had moved far to the west, made a readiness to resort to arms a habit of thinking in that region. And ruralism played a significant role in enhancing the South's propensity to violence. Country living in relative isolation has few contacts with the laws of society and consequently tends to reduce to a minimum the country dweller's awareness of the restraints of law. When country men, lacking such awareness, meet in taverns or towns, a high incidence of violence is likely to result.

Finally, there was the Negro's contribution to the propensity to violence of the ante-bellum Southern white. In making that contribution, the Negro was simply the tool of circumstance. The unceasing, underriding fear of the "internal enemy" always called for an ample store of arms and a thorough training in their use among the whites and an ever-present awareness that they might, at any time, be called upon to use them against human beings. From that came the all but universal custom of "gun toting," a Southern habit of long standing which in itself increased the section's toll of violence. That was part of the Negro's contribution to the old South's violence; but more important was his part in making the South callous to violence. On every hand, wherever there were large plantations, there were field gangs at work under the supervision of a Negro driver whose badge of office was a rawhide lash. And behind the scenes, everyone knew that it was only the lash in the hand of the overseer or owner that kept many of the slaves in bondage. Such observations, and that awareness of the power and prevalence of violence, inevitably inured even the non-slaveholder to an acceptance of violence as a means of obtaining one's ends. And in the slaveholder himself, those means inculcated an uncommon arrogance and a high degree of readiness to resort to violence to enforce the authority he had come to think of as supreme in himself.

The South   9

Becomes

a Kingdom: 5

BECAUSE OF THE ROMANTIC MYTH in which it has been enshrined by its protagonists, mention of the old South brings to the popular mind visions of an old, mature society with long-established and well-ordered customs, traditions, and institutions. That vision would be true, or at least substantially true, if it were confined to tidewater Virginia or even to eastern Virginia and coastal Carolina. The myth in the popular mind lies in seizing upon the reflected light from those regions and ascribing it to Southern society in general. Certainly there was little that was long-established and mature in ante-bellum society of the heart of the Cotton Kingdom. When Whitney invented the cotton gin, Florida, including all the Gulf coast to Louisiana, was an all but uninhabited colony of Spain. Except for a few sparse settlements in Tennessee and Kentucky, all the rest of the South, west of the mountains and of central Georgia all the way to the Mississippi, was a wilderness inhabited only by the Indians. The territory which would later become Louisiana, Texas, and Arkansas was also vested in Spain but occupied only by Indians, except along the river in the environs of New Orleans. In a period of less than seventy years after Whitney's pregnant contrivance, the ante-bellum Cotton Kingdom had seized for itself that territory, peopled its vastness, built its fabled glory, and closed its books. A single Biblical lifetime, three score years and ten, is scarcely a sufficient period to justify any assumption of antiquity to the society of the heart of the old South. Much less so is forty years, the period between 1820 and 1860, during which most of the settlement of the deep South occurred. Thus, in popular conception of the antiquity of the old South there is, in fact, as with most popular conceptions of the South, a handful of truth in a peck of myth.

In the popular mind, the old South and the plantation South are all but interchangeable terms. But in that popular identity, there is only a nonexclusive accuracy, for if the old South was the land of the great plantation, it was far more the land of the little farm. Although five-sixths of white Southerners were engaged in farming, less than one in thirty-five owned farms of more than five hundred acres, the very minimum area which could usually be dignified with the term "plantation." And a substantial portion of those holdings of plantation size were not plantations. They were holdings of swamps, mountains, barren sand, or woodlands. Of course, in truth, there were thousands of extensive, well-ordered, and prosperous plantations in the old South, and by their extent, they dominated for the casual observer the scene of the day, as they still do in retrospect for the romantic of today. The error is only an enormous error of degree. The real plantations were so few among so many farms.

Likewise, mention of the old South brings to mind alabaster mansions, adorned with pillared façades, standing in groves of moss-draped live oaks planted by the hands of generations long gone. To document that mental picture, where are those storied mansions today? Yes, Sherman burned quite a number of them, but actually his flaming ribbons of destruction across the South comprised but a tiny portion of the total area of the plantation South. Many, of course, met with later disaster. But if they were once so ubiquitous, they would not now be so strangely few and far between that they have usually become tourist shrines, while in the North, where a greater growth of population should have exerted more pressure for their destruction, country houses as old as those in the ante-bellum South are fairly commonplace.

The truth is that the real plantation house of the mind's eye was rare indeed, even in its day. The usual description of plantation homes, given by travelers in the ante-bellum South, west of the old Atlantic seaboard strip, is of commodious but modest hewn log dwellings, commonly much added to and given more durability and tidiness by an overlay of clapboards. In the 1850's, Frederick Law Olmsted reported often traveling a whole day through the hill country of Mississippi, Alabama, and the Carolinas without seeing any structure of other than logs. Another account of the rich Yazoo river delta, in 1857, says that at that time all planters' homes were of logs and such seems to have been the rule in all the newer western reaches of the old South, excepting only a few islands of elegance such as Natchez and the Mississippi River sugar region. Only a few years earlier, Albert Sidney Johnson, who was to become one of the most brilliant Confederate generals, was clearing fields with the help of a single slave and building a log cabin for his family on his newly acquired fifteen hundred acre "plantation." In the face of such conditions, there is but one reasonable conclusion, our romantic mind's eye peers back to glory through rose-colored magnifying glasses. It sees things that truly were, but it greatly exaggerates them.

To draw such conclusions as to the realities of the old South, to pare its mansions down to proper size and number, is not to belittle the Southern heritage. It should rather enhance it. The log cabin was the supreme symbol of a vital and expanding young America, a proper symbol of pride. What is bad is only the tendency of the South, with considerable help from outside, to eschew that inelegant symbol and pervert the fact of its origins, to have it appear that its noble society of yesteryear was born without toil, sweat, and travail; like Minerva full-blown from the brow of Jupiter. Such a struggle-free creation would reflect less credit on the South than she justly deserves.

Of the majority of the planters themselves, it is much the same story. However, the South did have enough great planter-aristocrats to inspire the aura of respect with which tradition has surrounded them all. These few were the ones who utilized the leisure provided by their prosperity under the slave system to acquire culture for themselves and render able and self-denying public service as well. Generally, they amply repaid their obligation to a society which had been generous to them. Most early Virginians of note and many early Carolinians were men of that stamp. Their imprint was so heavy that the far more numerous *nouveaux* of later and lighter imprint, deceiving by ostensible similarities, were confused with the originals. Those prototypes of the accepted stereotype of the cultured and refined Southern planter-aristocrat were often of such stature that, for generations, many others with the same outward trappings found it easy to walk in their long shadows.

The glorification of that stereotype of the planter-aristocrat persisted. It persisted as long as there was an old South, which was long after the leadership of planter-aristocrats had been supplanted by newer, more vital, and more realistic blood from below. It persisted in Virginia, even as a succession of seven out of eight of its immediate ante-bellum governors were drawn from the lower classes. It persisted through the era following the end of the Virginia Dynasty, during which period most Southerners of national note, most Southerners who aspired to the presidency, were drawn from the farmer-masses, such as cabin-born Andrew Jackson, Andrew Johnson, and Abraham Lincoln, or products of the yeoman farm such as James K. Polk and John C. Calhoun. It persisted on into the years of the Confederacy, which nevertheless gave its highest offices to cabin-born Jefferson Davis and Alexander Stephens. The South's fascination with the glory of its planter-aristocrat stereotype, as often as not led these newcomers to surround themselves with its accoutrements. Rough old Andrew Jackson gave up the law, built his traditionally styled Hermitage, and turned planter. Calhoun did the same and more. From his Fort Hill he became spokesman for his adopted brethren of the top echelon, just as Jefferson Davis did a few years later from Brierfield in Mississippi.

That the old school planter-aristocrat would lose out, in the insidious revolution which was going on throughout ante-bellum years, without changing the outward appearance of Southern society, was to be expected. His training and gentlemanly traditions had so curbed his aggressiveness and ruthlessness that he was no match for less restrained ambitious men across that wide frontier which embraced most of the South. There, thousands quickly rose to planter status by long strides at a running pace, but they were seldom of the original planter-aristocrat imprint. The pace of that surging up from the bottom gave rise to numerous "cotton snobs," whose arrogance of wealth and personal power coupled with their uncouth ways irritated their contemporaries. But, and this is important, as soon as the evidence of his uncouthness was safely interred with him in his grave, the "cotton snob" was invariably, posthaste, enshrined by his posterity in that special niche always reserved for planter-aristocrats in democratic America.

Thus, although it is true that the old South had many planter-aristocrats with all the traditional virtues, it was also true that, in retrospect, many more are counted among the élite solely on the basis of their ownership of slaves and land; because of the stubborn belief, which had its origin in the deep frontier of the old South and has grown ever since, that, if a man owned sufficient acres and slaves, he was, ipso facto, cultured, courtly, generous, and brave beyond other men and, hence, an aristocrat.

By way of footnote, it is interesting to note an ignored corollary of that assumption of the identity of gentlemanly standing and sufficient property in land and slaves. There was a grave difficulty presented by the Negro slaveholder of Negroes, especially the larger holders. In Charleston in 1860, a third of the numerous free Negroes owned slaves. There were some Negroes in South Carolina and Louisiana owning fifty to two hundred. If owning slaves and being a planter automatically made an aristocrat, the situation presented grave difficulties.

The glamour of those plantation mansions which actually were in essence, and the wealth and prestige of the masters of those mansions, so focused attention upon them that the reputed opulence of the ante-bellum South grew from an ill-founded assumption to a firm conviction. Supported by statistics showing that the bulk of the nation's export materials were the products of Southern soils, that conviction became an unshakable fixation. Most Southerners have no doubt that, before the ruin of "the war," the South was prosperous and wealthy beyond any other section. That conviction is tenaciously held, despite reliable available figures showing the smaller per capita income of the old South as compared with the North, figures showing that, although its population was nearly half that of the North, it had but one-seventh the financial resources, and figures showing that even its great pride, its agricultural lands, had values far below comparable lands in the North. Moreover, the South was the locale of the nation's two most poverty-ridden classes, the propertyless slaves and the almost equally propertyless "poor whites," scarcely indicia of a prevailing wealth.

And, inherent in the South's massive production of raw materials, was the old story of selling one's substance. Not only was it a case of poverty following the producer and wealth following the fabricator and fashioner, but in the South's case, much of its production was gained through soil mining. All the clean-tilled plantation crops of the South, tobacco, cotton, and sugar cane, were voracious soil consumers. Soils in eastern Virginia were worn out in colonial times. Eroded hills and abandoned farms were commonplace in older states of the South by 1830. The poverty produced by soil mining followed in the train of King Cotton and followed closely, too, even into the cotton frontier. Writing of his home county in 1850, Senator C. C. Clay of Alabama described it as "a county in its infancy," but one of abandoned farms, depleted and given over to broom sedge and already "exhibiting the painful signs of senility and decay apparent in Virginia and the Carolinas. The freshness of its agricultural glory is gone, the vigor of its youth is extinct, and the spirit of desolation seems brooding over it." That is a picture of the "heart of Dixie" and the core of the Cotton Kingdom, and there is in it little of imagined ante-bellum wealth and prosperity.

Carry Me Back to Old Virginny and *Massa's in de Cold, Cold Ground*, with a multitude of assists from romantic writers of the old South, have planted an ineradicable impression of the mutual devotion of master and slave. Unquestionably, such relationships were common between good masters and good slaves. But equally unquestionable were exceptions. Overwhelming evidence points to the conclusion that the vast majority of slaves, even those of kind masters, ardently desired their freedom, but in most instances not enough to strike to secure it, as is proved by their prevailing loyalty when so many men were away serving with the Confederate army. Although comparatively few slaves escaped or revolted, the desire for freedom is evident in the "jubilee" celebration of emancipation and the alacrity with which erstwhile slaves left the scenes of their bondage and set out for "sum'airs else."

How devoted to slavery were even the devoted masters of devoted slaves? Whenever the slavery question was in issue, which was during most of the ante-bellum time, the South gave every external appearance of solidarity on the point. But for one to be terrified by the prospect of emancipation and willing to fight to prevent it was something very different from approving of slavery, a difference which the prevailing opinion in the North stupidly and persistently failed to recognize and understand. The majority opinion in the South throughout ante-bellum times was probably positively proslavery, but there was always a substantial minority, at times and in places perhaps approaching a majority, who disapproved of slavery, but not as much as they feared and dreaded the consequences of the only alternative they were offered—emancipation with free Negroes remaining among them.

Beneath the gathering war clouds of 1860, most of those internal contrasts and most of those diversities were concealed by an overwhelming external unity. The many diverse Souths, the South of the great plantation and the South of the little upland farm, the South of the arid plains and that of the humid fields of rice and cane, the mountain country and the miasmic swamps, the fertile South and the barren South, the South of the well-educated and refined and the South of the ignorant and crude, the austere Calvinist South and the romantic, unrestrained, hedonistic South, that of the very rich and of the incredibly poor, of the haughty aristocrat and the democratic yeoman, all those Souths under the long succession of mounting blows from without had been welded into an amazing appearance of solidarity. Although the South always had been, and to this day remains, a land of contrasts, under the overwhelming influence of a few common bonds of unity, its agricultural economy, its ruralism, and the presence of the Negro, internal divergencies were pushed into the background by the very threats of external enemies who would tamper with any of those common bonds.

That surface solidarity, born of a few powerful similarities among a multitude of less powerful diversities, so effectively concealed those diversities that they have continued to be generally unnoted and neglected by outsider and Southerner alike, seeking to solve the riddle of the South, by reliance on the myth of the old South instead of on the facts. Only through a preoccupation with its few common bonds and the neglect of its numerous diversities can the assumption be made of a mind of the South in place of millions of minds of the South. No one would suggest that there was a mind of New York or of California. And only through that preoccupation with a few common characteristics and the omission of all variations from an assumed pattern could the romantic stereotype of the myth of the old South come into being.

The myth of the old South was a defensive creation of the old South, designed to convince its attackers that it was not the benighted and atavistic realm they charged it with being. Millions accepted the myth as fact, but most of them were Southerners themselves. In the face of relentless attacks, most Southerners became sincerely and profoundly convinced of the truth and merit of their defense—of the genuine superiority of Southern institutions and Southern ways, regardless of their merit on any objective scale. And it was the myth, rather than the facts of the old South, that was of such transcending importance; for it was the myth rather than the facts which so enormously influenced the conduct of the South in 1860, and it was the myth rather than the facts that has held the South in a bondage of preconceptions and prejudices for a hundred years, a bondage that is being loosened only by the dynamics of a mid-twentieth century world. As long as that myth persists, it will keep the South a region apart. Meanwhile, it has been costly to the region's leadership and progress for, in the face of the stereotyped ideal requiring its every loyalty, the South has had to deny itself the stimulus of thinking in the presence of conflicting ideals and interests.

To support that fixed ideal of the old South and to avoid the awful consequences of facing realities in a partisan 1860, when justice lay with neither side, Southerners made their tragic decision to disrupt the Union they had played such a major role in creating. With full knowledge that they were probably swapping "the ballot box for the cartridge box," as one North Carolinian put it, they prepared to defend, even with their lives, the section's rights against an aggressive external enemy which persisted in ignoring those indisputable legal rights by resorting to an appeal to a higher, unwritten law which that enemy had discovered for the salvation of the South. The issues had at last boiled down to a trial by fire and ordeal between old rights, written and defined, and what was the right, in the eyes of the Lord, as interpreted by people in the North, far removed from realities in a South of which they had as little understanding as they had appreciation of its problems.

The South Becomes a Nation

10

I<small>N THE WINTER</small> of 1861, with symbolic appropriateness, Charleston, the social capital of Southern planter society, was again the focal point of the nation's bitter internal dissensions. This time, it was obvious that what happened there would be more decisive than those events the city had witnessed in the previous year —the disruption of the Democratic party along sectional lines and the ratification of the Ordinance of Secession. Now, with awful predestination, human puppets, armed with instruments of death, their strings manipulated by economic interests, had been danced in opposing groups onto the quiet stage of the city's wide but sleepy harbor, helplessly to await the puppeteer's next whim.

Sixty years of ever-increasing economic conflict between the commercial North and agricultural South had inexorably directed the guns of General Pierre G. T. de Beauregard's shore batteries in the direction of Fort Sumter's bulk, above which yet floated the Stars and Stripes, a symbol of alien defiance to the new seven-state Confederate States of America. Through most of those years of economic conflict, the political power of the South had succeeded in placing road blocks in the way of the North's efforts to use the national government to enhance its economic interests, and in return had reaped a bountiful measure of ill will from the North. In more recent years, after the growth of the North had wrested political control from a South now helpless to frustrate the employment of the government as an economic auxiliary of the North, there was a reciprocal flow of ill will northward. Bereft of their political control, their protests unheeded, Southerners had overwhelmingly concluded that they should abandon a government that was being prostituted to the economic interests of a preferred part of its realm. Few entertained any doubts as to their legal right to take such a step. The states had always been sovereign. They had voluntarily joined in a union under a document which enumerated the powers surrendered to the union and nowhere did that instrument state that their surrender was permanent and irretrievable. For Virginia, the Carolinas, Georgia, and Texas that was sound constitutional theory, but for other states, which eventually seceded, the theory broke down badly, for those later states had been creations of the union itself, carved from territories owned by all the people of the Union in common. But that failure of the theory was little heeded. The moral obligations implicit in the union had been cancelled by the North's practical nullification of fugitive slave laws, guaranteed by the Constitution itself, and its readiness to use its numerical majority unconstitutionally to bar slaveowners from territories and enact protective tariffs, which had the effect of enriching the commercial North at the expense of an agricultural South.

It was with a feeling of high and righteous indignation that South Carolina, Georgia, Florida, Alabama, Mississippi, Louisiana, and Texas had, in rapid succession, marched out of the irksome union and set up their own confederation with special safeguards for the sacred sovereignties of its several states. To vitalize their paper union, they had hastily organized a government of men; a congress, president, and cabinet.

Although the planter class, through the decades, had led the movement which had culminated in the organization of this new nation, it found itself once the government was set up, no longer guiding the section's destiny. The new Confederacy was the embodiment of the whole white South, not just the planters. The origins of the president and his cabinet reflected that truth. President Jefferson Davis, a first generation planter, and another member of his cabinet were the only representatives of the planter class in the executive top echelon. Three members of the cabinet were foreigners. The vice-president and the other members of the cabinet had risen from humble origins. Their common denominators could be found only in their all being moderates (some until recently unionists), their determination to secure and maintain political and economic independence, and their ardent hope that those ends might be attained without bloodshed.

An immoderate and blindly partisan press and the incendiary orations of "Fire-eaters" had convinced most Southerners that the Yankees would not fight, that their money lust had made dastards of them all, that they would not tolerate a war which might interrupt their insatiable moneygrubbing. However, President Davis and his official family entertained no such illusions. Consequently, they were handling the situation at Charleston harbor with utmost finesse, both at the scene and through sub rosa talks in Washington, for the belief was general that if possession of Fort Sumter could be peacefully attained, there was every likelihood that the seceded states would be permitted to depart the Union in peace. But winter passed into spring and still the Stars and Stripes continued to fly over the sea-girt fort.

Historians have long debated without conclusion whether the tense quiet which had hung in the air about Fort Sumter for four months was shattered by a blunder on the part of President Lincoln or through his deliberate cunning. If it was the former, it must be numbered among the most costly blunders in history. If the latter, his cunning was eminently successful, for the Confederacy was thereby tricked into assuming the onus of striking the first blow in a purely aggressive war deliberately launched by the North. Whatever his intent, the firing on Fort Sumter was precipitated by Lincoln's determination to provision and reinforce Major Anderson's command in Fort Sumter and his message to Confederate officials that the relief force was on its way to the beleaguered fort.

Across the North, the cry went out that the Confederacy had

launched an attack on the Union. To defend the flag which had been assaulted, Lincoln called for 75,000 militiamen to be provided by the states on a quota basis. The call brought defiant refusals from Maryland, Virginia, North Carolina, Kentucky, Tennessee, Missouri, and Arkansas. In Virginia, North Carolina, Tennessee, and Arkansas, the realization that if they stayed in the Union, they would be expected to furnish troops to march against their fellow Southerners sufficiently consolidated opinion to break the stalemate in movements toward secession. Thus Lincoln's move to forestall further disintegration of the Union had just the opposite effect and soon added four more stars to the Confederate emblem. The more parlous situations which developed in Kentucky and Missouri, although they fell short of authentic secession, were seized upon as sufficient indications of pro-Confederate sentiment for yet two more stars to make the thirteen which appear on the traditional Confederate banner.

Almost everywhere throughout the South, the news of action in Charleston Harbor was greeted with enthusiasm and rejoicing. It marked the end of decades of frustrating tension which had all but monopolized the section's best talents. It brought relief from long months of high tension which had held it in a paralyzing grip. At last there was opportunity for action and few entertained any doubts as to a favorable outcome of that action, despite insuperable statistical odds in favor of the Union. The Southern press and the Fire-eaters had so belittled the Yankees that a mere four to one in man-power odds was not in the least frightening. Nor was the paucity of the South's operating mines and manufacturing establishments to produce the materials of war, nor was the fact that two Northern cities alone had more financial resources than the entire Confederacy, where several states had not a single bank. The world-wide power of King Cotton, the old sacred cow of the plantation South, would more than take care of those deficiencies. The world would have to have cotton and the material of war would be the exchange. The assumed superiority of the fighting qualities of Southerners, superior morale, and cotton were the triumvirate upon which they pinned their optimism.

In the summer when the invasion of Virginia ended in the pell-mell flight of the Yankees at Bull Run, that optimism seemed vindicated; so much so, in fact, that the easy victory proved almost as demoralizing to the Southern war effort as it was to the enemy. The victory distracted the Confederates from the necessity of an all out war effort and valuable months were lost, months which were utilized by the Union in launching its Mississippi valley invasion, the very move which was to spell ultimate doom for the Confederacy. Although throughout the war, the South kept its attention mostly focused on the struggle in the east, she was not only to be ultimately physically subdued through that western assault, but the early Federal victories at Fort Henry, Fort Donelson, and Nashville set in full motion the bitter internal dissensions which ultimately ate the heart out of the Confederacy.

Only at the outset was President Davis widely popular, and his cabinet never was. Even at first, the President was handicapped by antagonism of the extremists of the Barnwell Rhett, Edmund Ruffin, and William Yancey school, because of his past record of moderate unionism and by the jealousies resulting from the disappointment of such powerful leaders as Howell Cobb and Robert Toombs at their failure to receive the coveted nod. Although Davis was honest, intelligent, and ardent in the cause, he was also inflexible, arbitrary, and hypersensitive to criticism. He lacked essential qualities of successful leadership in adversity and his cabinet compounded that lack. Although the South's main strength lay in its esprit, in modern terms its superior morale, the Southern press generally failed to recognize or at least to assume its obligation to foster and maintain that spirit. Instead, even in 1861, a substantial segment was seizing upon the vulnerable President and his cabinet and making them the scapegoat for every failure and mishap, whether in the field or on the home front. After the fall of New Orleans in the spring of 1862, vituperations directed against the Confederate government by an unbridled and individualistic press rivaled criticism leveled at the enemy. From then on, the Confederate morale, its main hope for victory over a superior enemy, faltered and then steadily sank.

Meanwhile in the eastern arena, in Virginia, under the inspiring leadership of a group of superb military leaders, Confederate morale did not materially deteriorate during 1862 and early 1863, and the result was a series of resounding victories over vastly superior Union forces. It was only those victories that sustained the dissension-riven Confederacy in face of defeats in every other area. The first crack in the high esprit of Lee's command followed the failure of his Northern invasion, which was checked at Antietam in the late summer of 1862. This was the high-water mark of the Confederacy. After that, spirits flagged and final disintegration of the Confederacy became inevitable. It was the high esprit of Lee's Army of northern Virginia that wrote the most glamorous chapters in the annals of the most glamorized war of all time. That esprit, as long as it was sustained, resulted in a magnificent effort that deserved both a better cause and a better fate.

Since, confronted with overwhelming odds against it, ultimate defeat of the Confederacy was inevitable from the beginning; the war brought developments in the South which were of more lasting significance than campaigns and battles, victories and defeats. Early in the conflict, it became obvious that undue confidence had been placed in the influence of King Cotton and that even such potential power as he had, was not being made available to the Confederacy through the bungling of its "cotton diplomacy." At the outset, the extent of the world-wide cotton hunger had been greatly over-estimated. Large surplus stocks of both cotton goods and raw cotton were on hand in England and in the North. Bumper crops of grain on Northern farms were coinciding with wheat failures in Europe. Physical hunger abroad suddenly had given Northern wheat more weight in the diplomatic tug of war than Southern cotton could command. The cotton policy of the Confederate government compounded the situation. Hoping to induce an insatiable cotton hunger and European intervention to alleviate it, all exports of cotton were forbidden. As a result of this policy, great stores of cotton which might have been shipped out, before the blockade became too effective, and exchanged for war materials were left to be either seized by the invading Yankees and shipped north to supply enemy needs, or to be eventually destroyed by the Southerners themselves to keep it from the enemy.

It was the failure of the Confederacy's cotton diplomacy, and the pinch of necessity it placed on both the home front and the section's war industries, that was of considerable and lasting significance. When the fighting started, the North had eight times as many industrial workers as the South. Almost all the industries which produced the essential needs of an army were concentrated in the Northeast. Textiles, leather, iron and steel, chemicals, glass and porcelain, firearms and munitions, coal and oil were almost exclusively Northern products. So were the ships which brought to America those products which were not domestically produced. As soon as imports were cut off, critical shortages in all these lines quickly developed in the South.

On the domestic front, the result was a sudden reversion in most homes to the frontier subsistence living that, for most of the South, was of recent memory. Out came the old spinning wheels, hand looms and cards, the flints, steels and tinder boxes, and the ash hoppers to recover potash for soap making. "Bee-gums" and sorghum "sweet'nin' " replaced sugar. A caffeine-bearing wild holly substituted for tea. Ersatz coffee was made of a variety of things; parched rye, acorns, beets, and sweet potatoes. Candles were made by dipping string in a mixture of mutton suet and beeswax, cork from cypress knees, needles from hawthorns, shoe blacking from chinaberries, and rope from Spanish moss. Wallpaper was removed from the walls and bleached to supply writing paper needs. Old folks were asked to recall their all but forgotten formulas for making ink from oak galls, red dye from figs, black dye from pomegranates, and browns from walnuts, or, chemically, by soaking scrap iron in brine and vinegar to produce "copperas," which was long the prevailing color of the Confederate soldiers' "uniforms" rather than the harder to come by traditional grey. Farm homes were also the source of supply of other critical war materials. Beds of oriental poppies were widely planted and children employed in the painstaking task of puncturing seed pods and recovering the resulting opium-bearing medicinal droplets for the use of the troops. To relieve the critical shortage of nitrates, cabin sweepings and the earth from privies were treated to recover their nitrogen content. Niter beds were widely established as adjuncts of domestic units to receive human and animal offal and the carcasses of dead animals, that their nitrates might be leeched from the residue. Home tanning was revived to utilize the hides of everything from squirrels to dogs to alligators.

But the most drastic change of all which the war brought to the home front was in its agriculture. Although the shortage of manpower gave extensive areas over to rampant Southern weeds, most other areas, which had long been devoted to cotton growing, were now planted in corn, beans, potatoes, and small grains. When Sherman was marching through Georgia, he sardonically sent his compliments to "Jeff Davis" for the bountiful forage with which Georgians had provided his army.

With shocking suddenness, the impact of war had thrown Southerners back to the hard realities of frontier living. Meanwhile, a war-born prosperity was sweeping the North. Few there were feeling the pinch of necessity. Many were growing rich. Understandably, the contrast did not enhance the affection of Southerners for their "money-mad" enemy.

Tightened belts and improvised substitutes for the ordinary requirements of domestic living were not enough to offset the North's enormous industrial advantage, and it was soon apparent that cotton was not going to perform the miracles which had been expected of it. Such industries as the South had would have to be greatly expanded and a multitude of new ones established. To direct that phase of the war effort, President Davis named Josiah Gorgas, father of William C. Gorgas who would later add lustre to the name, by his success in eliminating yellow fever and malaria from the Canal Zone. Although Gorgas was Yankee-born, he had long resided in the South and was married to the daughter of a former governor of Alabama. Gorgas immediately set about performing, on a more modest scale, the miracles which had been expected from cotton. The Confederacy had within its boundaries ample quantities of the raw materials essential to the conduct of the war, but mostly they remained as undeveloped as nature had left them. Under Gorgas' stimulation, Southerners were urged to bestir themselves from the position "to which elegant indolence and aristocratic conceit had assigned" them.

Under pressure, old lead, copper, and coal mines greatly increased their production. New mines were opened. Salt works were established both on the coast and at several salt springs in the mountains. Cave floors were worked to secure saltpeter from the accumulations of the ages of bat droppings. The production of the South's few iron works and textile plants was greatly increased and new ones were established. Clothing plants, glass works, gunpowder works, arsenals for the manufacture of rifles, shoe factories, hat factories, wagon and railroad car works, paper and pencil factories, match factories, chemical works, and medical laboratories were established and brought into production.

Although many a Confederate soldier continued to march along the frozen roads of Virginia ill-clad and barefooted, although short rations were chronic and ammunition scarce, although conditions in improvised hospitals were revolting, and although the pitifully few ships available to run the strangling blockade were mostly foreign built to reap the great speculative profits involved; the people of the agricultural South had demonstrated under pressure an unsuspected adaptability. Under Gorgas' leadership, they had performed, to an amazing degree, the miracles they had expected of King Cotton. More surprising still was the enthusiasm they demonstrated in "Yankee-izing" their land, a development on which they had long frowned.

As surprising as was the South's readiness to adventure into manufacturing, its wartime attainments in a related field were even more so. Few suspected that there were latent in the agricultural South, mechanical and inventive abilities that would outsmart the touted mechanical genius of the Yankee. Nevertheless, nearly all mechanical innovations in the art of war, which appeared during the conflict, came out of the South. Most notable of these were the development and employment of marine mines, torpedoes, and land mines, the almost submerged torpedo boats of the *David* class, the first successful submarine attack, and the iron-clad *Virginia* (*Merrimac*). Only the latter was matched in the North by its *Monitor*.

Reverting for a moment to military aspects of the struggle, it should be noted that the South entered the war with other advantages which, when added to its superior morale, enabled the

Confederacy almost miraculously to stave off its inevitable defeat for more than four years in the face of the overwhelming total of advantages enjoyed by the North. Not the least of these Confederate advantages was the long standing military tradition of the South, its dignifying of the military career to equal standing with planting or a political career. That tradition, together with the self-reliance which naturally resulted from rural living on semi-self-sufficient plantations and farms, gave the troops of the Confederacy, especially at first, a great qualitative advantage both in its officers and its common soldiers.

Allied to Southerners' military tradition was the glamour with which they had imbued it and their fascination with chivalry as viewed through Sir Walter Scott's imagination. They had entered the war generally, with the feeling of embarking on a high adventure—a trial of battle skill circumscribed by limiting rules of proper conduct—rather than the soul-searing trial of brute strength it became. With those predilections, there would be every expectation that the Confederates would conduct the war on a higher plane than their more realistic enemy. And so it was. For concrete evidence of that difference, one need only compare the conduct of Lee's forces in their invasions across the Potomac with the utter ruin left in the wake of the marches of David Hunter and Phil Sheridan up the valley of Virginia and Sherman's swathe of holocaust across Georgia and South Carolina. Except for the fantastic atrocity stories which were commonly purveyed by the newspapers of both sides, no serious charge of needless brutality on the part of the Confederacy has been made, except in connection with its treatment of war prisoners. And it now appears that those charges were generally made for political purposes and pensions and were largely undeserved. Considering the average number of prisoners held by each side, there is little or no significant difference between the death rate among the prisoners of war of either side. When the plenty which prevailed in the North is considered against the stringency in the South, it appears likely that the Confederacy really did better by its prisoners than did the Union. After all, hardship and disease had been almost twice as lethal to the Confederate troops themselves as had enemy action.

Another advantage which the Confederacy had at the outset turned out to be costly indeed. Since its sole intent was to fight a defensive war, its supply lines would lie entirely within its own territory. There was also the great morale value of fighting to defend one's home. On the other hand, the Federals would have to muster the preponderant forces necessary to dislodge the defenders and every success they might gain would require an extension of their supply lines deeper and deeper into unfriendly territory. But this initial advantage became disastrous when enemy forces drove deep into the Confederacy, with the result that almost all the material destruction of the war was of Southern homes, towns, and industries.

It was the devastation resulting from the South being four years a battlefield, the loss of its property in slaves, the devaluation of its currency and bonds, and the staggering loss of life and limb which resulted from the high percentage of its available manpower engaged in actual combat, that seared the souls of its people. It was those grievous wounds and the shockingly brutal treatment those wounds were given in the years that followed, while they were yet raw, that rendered the whole South a war casualty, a cripple needing help and understanding which was rarely given, a cripple which only now, nearly a hundred years later, is beginning to regain its health.

Most crippling of all, of course, was the war's cost in human life. About half of the Southern white men of productive age saw service in the Confederate forces, a ratio almost twice as great as in the North. By 1865, half of those were dead or incapacitated. Every third household, on the average, had seen the name of one of its members on the death lists, a rate four times as great as that suffered in the North. Among the classes from which its leaders were usually drawn, relative losses were even greater. For example: the University of Virginia with but four-sevenths as many students as Harvard, had lost five hundred and three as compared with Harvard's losses of one hundred and seventeen. The cadet corps of the Virginia Military Institute and the Citadel had marched out to war as units.

Relatively, the economic cost of the war to the South far exceeded its manpower losses. Its slave property, the taxable value of which exceeded that of all its lands, was gone in history's greatest act of sequestration. Two-thirds of its livestock was gone. Much of its arable land was high in weeds. Almost everything which was usable by an armed force had been impressed by one side or the other, generally without compensation except for worthless receipts. Its railroads, roads, and bridges were in shambles. Many of its towns and cities such as Jackson, Atlanta, Columbia, and Richmond were in ashes, as were also thousands of farm homes and more thousands of farm buildings. Its money and most of its securities were worthless. All of its banks, insurance companies, and financial institutions were ruined. And there was no foreign aid program in the modern manner to help the vanquished enemy to his feet by repairing the physical devastation which lay like a pall across the land. Instead, there were indemnities in the old manner, indirectly levied but as real as any indemnity ever required of a foreign foe, and so vast in amount that they became a further staggering burden on a ruined land.

Every two days, the Union had spent on the war as much as the Confederate government spent in a year, exclusive of its purchases with Confederate currency and other paper which had become worthless in the hands of its holders. Of course, with the end of the war, the South had to assume its share of the Federal obligations incurred for those expenditures. To that was added its share of the pensions for Union veterans which would eventually amount to a multiple of the cost of the war, whereas the states of the former Confederacy had to assume the entire burden of pensions for their veterans. Finally, there was the more directly levied indemnity in the form of the vindictive special cotton tax through which $100,000,000 was wrung unconstitutionally from the poverty-ridden region.

There were other losses equally serious although less tangible. Relatively, the education of many more Southerners than Northerners had been interrupted by military service. Many of the South's universities and colleges had been destroyed. Its rising public school system was a war casualty, being practically non-existent at the war's end.

Adding substantially to the distress caused by the Confederacy's enormous losses in human life, property, and institutions were its internal dissensions which, long before the fighting ceased, were all but paralyzing the government and its war effort. The popular glamorous treatments of the Civil War generally give the impression that the South fought through the war with a single heart and that, almost to a man, Southerners were ardently engaged with a notable singleness of purpose in winning the war. On the contrary, from the very beginning there was trouble between the states and the Confederacy. For those who had battled for states' rights for generations and had become so imbued with the feeling of the sanctity of the doctrine that they not infrequently named their sons "States Rights," the several states were the recipients of their primary loyalty. When, under the stress of war, it became necessary to do things on a national scale, conflicts with the states were numerous and bitter. Most of the states, for example, refused to turn over to the national government the arms which they had seized from Federal forts and arsenals within their bounds and instead, insisted on keeping them for their own militia, with the result that critically needed arms were in effect hoarded at home unused, while battles were being lost at the front for the lack of them. When conscription was instituted, several of the states displayed a similar lack of co-operation and, in some instances, almost nullified the effectiveness of conscription acts.

Bitter disputes between the states and the central government, and nullification resolutions, followed the suspension of the writ of habeas corpus. Relations between North Carolina and the Confederacy were chronically strained. Between Georgia and the national government, they were much worse. There, in the home state of such prominent anti-Davis leaders as Vice-president Stephens, the Cobb brothers, Robert Toombs, and particularly Governor Joseph E. Brown, they frequently verged on open treason and, at times, serious consideration was given proposals that the state secede from the Confederacy. Conscription acts were widely resented. That the studiedly loose-knit, power-limited Confederacy would undertake such an unprecedented procedure as the mass conscription of its citizens was shocking to many. The employment of substitutes by conscriptees who could afford the price became a widespread scandal, especially when it developed that many of the conscriptees were worthless mercenaries who promptly deserted to collect another substitute fee from another reluctant conscriptee. The resentment which resulted from those practices and from provisions in the conscription laws, which granted exemptions for government officials and for anyone having in his charge as many as fifteen slaves, gave substance to the complaint often heard among the non-slaveholding masses that they were engaged in "a rich man's war and a poor man's fight."

With each defeat on the field of battle, with each new bungling of the "cotton diplomacy," with every rebuff from abroad, with each new spiral of ever-spiraling inflation as the presses continued to pour out fiat currency, with every new scandal of unconscionable war speculators, with every new seizure of private property by the "pressmen," with every new posting of the terrible casualty lists, the disaffection mounted in every corner of the land until there was little love left for the Confederacy. Long before its final downfall, the Confederacy had become widely unpopular with most of its citizens and positively hated by many. It was years later, after those multiple bitternesses had been forgotten, that Southerners, inveterate romantics that they are, in retrospect gave the Confederacy the devotion it had desperately needed in its struggle to take its place in the family of nations.

However chary Southerners were in devotion to their national government, few were disloyal to its objectives. Except for consistent Union sentiment in Tennessee and among many in the mountains and the abortive secession movements in North Carolina and northern Alabama, there was little active disloyalty in the Confederacy. People hated the Union and Yankees too much for that. It was a question of an old, deep hate, the product of years of building, against a new resentment; and everybody was passionately devoted to his own state which was part of the resented Confederacy. Thus, dissension ridden and divided within, there was still a common front against the opposition from without. The emotional resultant of those forces of hate and devotion drove the struggle on and on, far beyond the time when reason could see only ultimate defeat.

It was internal dissension and disaffection, more than anything else, which had spelled the Confederacy's fall. Had the high esprit of its early days persisted, nothing would have been impossible. When internal difficulties began to wither it, disasters began to occur; and each new disaster accelerated the withering. Thus the South lost its main reliance, its most potent force for victory, and the fatal handwriting was on the wall. By the time Lee was making his last desperate maneuvers in the face of Grant's overwhelming forces, desertions from the Confederate forces had climbed to an estimated 150,000, more than twice as many men as he had ever been able to field at once and many times more than remained to him then. The embittered and war weary masses had given up the fight long before then. For them, the war was already over and the surrender at Appomattox simply made it official for them as it did for that handful of die-hards who had continued the fight by sheer force of their emotions, long after all hope for victory was gone.

Back at home, those who had survived the ordeal were greeted by scenes of desolation and ruin on every hand. Even if a town or farm had escaped destruction by the invaders, years of stringency and neglect had taken their toll. Most of them found their fields in weeds and their livestock gone—a major loss in itself and an irreparable loss where there was neither money nor breeding stock to replace that farm essential. There was little food and no money. Everyone was penniless, erstwhile rich planter and "poor white" alike, for there was no money in the land. Neither were there securities which might be redeemed, nor banks from which to borrow, nor the means to pay former slaves that crops might be grown. They had nothing to sell but the precious land, and there was no one with money to buy that single wealth which alone remained to even those who had been rich. In short, the South in 1865 was a land, decimated, prostrated, and all but paralyzed by the blows which had befallen it. In effect, the vast majority of Southerners had been thrown back through centuries of progress to the frontier status of their ancestors who had first wrested their fields from the Southern wilderness. With a more battered hope and an even more parlous future, they, like their forebears, faced that uncertain future with only the bountiful rains and warm sun of their Southland, their land, and their own hands to strive forward once again from a state of social development which had existed far back in American history.

The Confederacy and the war graved its marks on the South in high relief, marks that yet stand out bold and clear through the overlay of almost a century of distractions, fusion, and accelerating change.

By far, the most drastic and lasting mark made by the war on the South resulted from its being cast back in history, back to a frontier society and economy, back to a phase of social development and a way of life most of the North had not known in a hundred years or more. Southerners in the region's wide anachronistic frontier, which the Yankee had created, reverted naturally to provincialisms, crudities, violence, and individualism, those natural concomitants of frontier living. In the face of that, it was unrealistic thereafter to expect the South to react as if it were contemporary to the stimulus. And even now, it continues to be unrealistic to expect of the South the advanced current reactions of the most advanced sections of the modern world, as typified by population centers of twentieth-century America. Moreover, that lag will surely persist into the future, until the South has had the full measure of time necessary for it not only to recover the century or more of progress which was taken from it by the disaster of its defeat but also time to catch up with its sister regions as they continue to move forward at an accelerating pace. Meanwhile, the North, with a completely conscienceless failure to assume any responsibility for the creation of the anachronistic frontier it forced on the South, continued to show, and yet shows, little patience and even less understanding of the natural consequences of that frontier.

The twin brother of the frontier the war brought back to the South was poverty, stark and all pervading. It was not only a poverty in worldly goods, but also a poverty of manpower, which long crippled all efforts to relieve the economic distress which blanketed the region. As mortified as Southerners were at their fallen fortunes, they were yet more mortified by, and resentful of, the mounting affluence of their victors. Very soon, by way of defense, Northern wealth became the fabled sour grapes of Southern eyes. A high disdain of wealth was widely feigned. All ardent pursuit of it was proclaimed declassé and unbecoming to a gentleman. Worse than that, it was Yankee. Notoriously, the lot of the poor relation in the wealthy family is an unhappy one. It warps his views and affects his personality. He affects great pride even as he becomes hypersensitive, defensive, and resentful. At the same time, he is ever alert for the opportunity whereby he may channel a bit of the resented wealth of his kinsmen into his own flat pocket. Thus it was also in the South, suddenly become the one poor section in a nation of fabulous wealth. Pride was embellished and fed by exaggerations of glories of the region's past and by espousal of the nobility of poverty. But the South could rarely bring itself to admit that any of its evils and short-comings were simply the incidents of poverty, for how could evils flow from noble poverty? Southerners' defensive bent, which had become a habit of mind under the prewar moral attacks on slavery, was now turned into a hypersensitivity to criticism under the frustra-tions of their unrelieved poverty. Even self-criticism from the most devoted sons would be angrily received as rank disloyalty; and men like Walter Hines Page, who sought but to relieve that blighting poverty and the ignorance it inevitably bred, would be frowned out of the land. But, however much lip service they gave the nobility of poverty, Southerners nevertheless enormously resented it and that resentment was ever directed against the Yankee who had visited it upon them.

In the economic realm, something else came out of the war. It was a lesson that Southerners learned, only to be soon forgotten by most of them, but well noted by a few who would long afterwards turn it to use in rebuilding their ruined land. When, during the war, Southerners had turned with enthusiasm to remedying their section's manufacturing deficiencies, they proved to their own satisfaction, and to the satisfaction of many others who never dreamed that any such potential was latent there in the agricultural South, that Southerners were surprisingly adaptable and reasonably skilled in manufacturing. More than that, Southerners had evinced great pride in their ac-complishments in the area of Yankee prowess. Although few of the seeds sown in that field in the days of the war continued to grow and bear fruit during the years that followed, the soil, at least, had been proved suitable.

Through the years since the Union was formed, friendly com-petition with the Yankee had developed into suspicion and dislike and then into bitter antagonism and even hatred on occasions. War propaganda, the ruthless destructions perpetrated by invading forces, and the bitterness of defeat, ripened Southern feeling toward the Yankee into a blind and indiscriminate hatred, which was extended to everything associated in their minds with the object of their hate; to business as typified by bankers and symbolized by Wall Street, cities and urban dwellers, immigrants and foreigners in general.

The war had yet another effect of permanent import in Southern society. The slavery issue had led Southerners of all classes to the discovery of a common denominator among themselves, which was more powerful than their long-standing internal schisms. Old political rivalries between the coastal aristocracy and back country yeoman and the economic resentment of "poor whites" against the planter had been gradually submerged by the social, economic, and political power of that common denominator—the problem of the Negro in vast numbers among them. Although many slaveholders may have felt that they were fighting to retain their wealth in slaves, and many of the more prosperous yeoman farmers may have been fighting to retain a system which they aspired to enjoy, even the poorest whites, without any such aspirations, were nonetheless ardently interested in retaining a system whereby they were being spared the economic, social, and political competition of masses of the blacks, a competition the brunt of which they instinctively knew would fall on them. To that common denominator, the war had added a powerful camaraderie, cemented with the emotional bonds of a great common experience. For a long time to come, simply having been Confederates together was a sufficient common bond to transcend a multitude of internal conflicts.

In retrospect, the Confederacy became the sacred standard around which white Southerners, regardless of class and station, rallied at every threat from without, whether physical, economic, ideological, or legal. Time failed to close the grave of the short-lived Confederacy, nor, for a long time, did it diminish the mourning for its death. Instead, mourning increased as people began to forget the things they hadn't liked in the deceased in its vital days. It and "the war" would become the subject of literally thousands of books (which accounts for the sketchy factual treatment in this chapter) and tens of thousands of emotion-charged addresses, ever feeding emotional flames, until, eventually, the dead Confederacy would be given a devotion and loyalty far beyond that which was accorded it when it so desperately needed devoted support, until, at last, for many Southerners, the Confederate battle flag would become a formidable emotional rival of the Stars and Stripes, and "Dixie" more stirring than the strains of the "Star-Spangled Banner."

The South

Becomes

a Conquered Province: 1

11

Look to the South, and you who went with me through that land can best say if they too have not been fearfully punished. Mourning in every household, desolation written in broad characters across the whole face of their country, cities in ashes and fields laid waste, their commerce gone, their system of labor annihilated and destroyed. Ruin, poverty and distress everywhere, and now pestilence adding to the very cap sheaf to their stack of misery; her proud men begging for pardon and appealing for permission to raise food for their children; her five million of slaves free, and their value lost to their former masters forever.

Those are the words of William Tecumseh Sherman who had left a trail of ashes and a thousand mile long line of blackened chimneys, which had come to be known as Sherman's sentinels, across and through the heart of the South. They were spoken more than two years after he had given General Joseph E. Johnston his terms of surrender and had received their acceptance, only to have his more vindictive civilian superiors in Washington break faith with both him and the Confederate general and repudiate them after the surrender had been effected.

That disgraceful breach of faith was but an early illustration of a tendency, which was to become commonplace in the bitter years to follow, on the part of the military men, among the victors, to regard their vanquished foe through far more kindly eyes than those who had stayed safely at home and waxed rich or powerful through opportunities offered by the booming business and political upheavals of war years. Among those who had been men of rank in the Federal armies, only a few such as Philip Sheridan and Benjamin F. "Beast" Butler would find it in their hearts to match the hatred and vengeance which was to be vented on the South in postwar years. Those who had opposed Southern armies in the field had generally acquired a sincere respect for their foe. They had seen the South and Southerners and had gained a measure of understanding of them and their problems. They had seen with their own eyes, as Sherman was reminding his listeners, that their Southern brethren already had been "fearfully punished" simply by the war's devastation. While that was sufficient for most of those who had marched with the conquerors across the blighted land, it was far from sufficient for many others.

It was nowhere near sufficient for that relatively small, but highly vocal, group of vindictive bigots of the stamp of William Lloyd Garrison, Charles Sumner, Wendell Phillips, and many of the top prelates of the Northern Methodist Church. If they were to have their way, the South's retribution had just begun. For railroad promoters such as Jim Fisk, insatiable in their hunger for ever more princely gifts of the public domain, for industrial magnates and men of finance such as Jay Cooke, ever seeking higher and higher protective tariffs to pyramid their profits with the least possible effort, and for such spokesmen for those ruthless business interests, as Horace Greeley, it was essential that the South be rendered impotent to resume the opposition it had displayed toward those interests in prewar years. During Confederate years, with representatives of the conservative agricultural South gone from Washington, those men who regarded government as little more than the handmaiden of business, through the good offices of the vital young Republican party had audaciously taken practical control of the national government, and they now had no intention of permitting their field day to be brought to a close by the return of Southern Jeffersonianism to the halls of Congress. The best grist for their mills would be a South of subservient colonial status to produce raw materials only and at the lowest possible price. Finally, there were those of carpetbagger bent, typified by the ruthless Thaddeus Stephens, who saw boundless opportunities for power and profit, if the conquered region could be subjected to their control.

For those men of hard purpose, the suffering and desolation of the war had not been sufficient punishment for the South's audacity in its effort to resist conquest by aggressive forces of the dominant section. For them, it was not sufficient that half the South's white manpower of productive age was dead or maimed, that so many were crippled that in the year following the end of the war, a fifth of all the revenues of Mississippi was devoted to the purchase of artificial arms and legs for the maimed veterans of that state. It was not sufficient that many of its cities, many of its educational institutions, and tens of thousands of homes were in ashes, nor that the South's few manufacturing establishments had been systematically sought out and destroyed. It was not sufficient that the section's always inadequate railroads were in shambles, bridges gone and rails removed from countless miles of track; painstakingly heated and wrapped corkscrew fashion around nearby trees, so that on some lines, no trains would run for five years after the war.

It was not even sufficient that the whole South was practically destitute, that there were no money, no banks, no securities, and no credit, that only the good earth itself was left to its people; and even that good earth, without the means of production, had not forestalled actual want for millions of Southerners, for even its agriculture, although the simplest of men's pursuits, had been so crippled that it would take almost a generation after 1860 to even approach again the production of that year.

For those on vengeance bent, none of these were sufficient to satisfy. Even the abject misery which the sum of them connotes was nowhere near enough to serve their purposes. As the breach of faith in connection with Johnston's surrender to Sherman indicated even before the weary armies turned homeward, plans had been carefully laid by those for whom the South had not yet suffered enough. In fact, revolution was abroad in the land and its leaders, as usual in revolutions, were plotting with little squeamishness about means, so long as the means might contribute to the ultimate ends they sought.

Superficial anomalies have largely concealed the whole canvas of that revolution which reached its climax in the years immediately following the Civil War. It was a revolution in which most of the rebels were numbered among the Yankees. It was a revolution which had commenced insidiously, well before the war and did not end until the Fourteenth Amendment to the Constitution had been duly ratified. To turn traditional tables and dub the Yankees as "rebels" and regard Southerners as "loyalists" certainly calls for the marshaling of supporting facts.

A revolution is a fundamental change in a government or constitution. It usually contemplates the renunciation of an existing government by the governed and the substitution of another. It may be violent or simply a coup. It may be sanguinary or bloodless. But in any instance, it connotes the effecting of substantial changes in an existing government by extralegal means. The American revolution of the mid-nineteenth century, this "Second American Revolution," embraced all those elements. It disposed of the Jeffersonian republic which the Virginia titans of the eighteenth century had sought firmly to mold and definitely limit by a Constitution which could be legally altered only by an overwhelming mandate from the people. It disposed of that government of strictly limited powers and relatively few functions and substituted one of almost unlimited powers, with functions nearly as wide as society itself. And it accomplished the change without resorting to the amendatory procedure prescribed in the Constitution and without the consent of the majorities required by its terms.

Despite the fact that the first overt acts of the armed phase of the revolution were committed by the South, there are few historians who fail to regard the North as the actual aggressor in the conflict, those ostensible overt acts being but incidents in a revolutionary conflict which in its bloodless stage was well under way; and although technically the Southern states moved out of the existing government, their movement out was simply the machinery by which they elected to stand pat in loyal support of the form of government as established by their forefathers. Theirs was simply a movement designed to resist revolutionary changes in the government they had inherited in common with Northern rebels. The fact that the North retained the bulk of the machinery of the pre-existing government was little more than fortuitous. Had the secession movement in Maryland succeeded and Washington fallen into Confederate hands at the outset, it is likely that there would have been almost as much continuity between the pre-existing government and that of the seceding states as developed in the North when it succeeded in retaining the capital.

At first, the revolution seemed to be merely evolution. That was in the early days of the great debates on the tariff, internal improvements, and national bank issues. With burgeoning industrial and commercial interests in the North, in prewar years the pressure mounted to bend the government, regardless of Constitutional limitations, better to serve those interests, with the conservative South always in opposition. As the influence of commercial interests became more widespread and its sway in government circles increased, determination mounted to be rid of that thorn in the side. They would force the South to fit into the frame of the commercial pattern they were intent on designing. Protective tariffs, regardless of their adverse effect on an agricultural economy dependent on free trade abroad, centralization of financial control through a national banking system, and finally an attack on slavery itself, the foundation of the South's agricultural economy, were but aspects of that mounting revolution. Since the conservative, plantation South would not voluntarily fit into the scheme, it would have to be forced into it. The practical nullification of the fugitive slave laws, guaranteed by the Constitution, and the unconstitutional exclusion of slave property from the territories were evidential of that determination. When pressure to force the South into the North's Procrustean bed became unbearable, secession had followed.

Freed during war years from the statesmanship that had been its main deterrent, the revolution moved forward at an accelerated pace.

Enlisting a motley crew of social reformers, prelates, abolitionists, opportunist politicians, and corrupt politicians, commercial and industrial interests climbed into the saddle and rode with a free rein toward their objective, transformation of the government into the handmaiden of business. Necessarily, many restraints of the Constitution would have to go. To remove those restraints by the amendment procedure prescribed was both too slow and too uncertain, since it involved securing the consent of the masses. It was deemed better to ignore or defy it and at the same time seek a subservient Supreme Court to co-operate in the revolution.

The aggressive onslaught of those revolutionary forces against the government which had been inspired by Virginia planter society had, by the end of the war, wrought vast changes in it, although mostly, it is true, by indirection; but more than that, it had succeeded in drastically changing the popular attitude toward that government. Thereafter, it would be generally regarded as omnipotent, and no field would be beyond reach of its newly multiplied tentacles.

Although the revolution had not then even reached its crest, when the men in grey returned to their homes to view with distress the changes which the war years had wrought there, the government to which they were returning was, although less obviously, at least as changed, as manhandled, and as inhospitable as their ruined homes appeared. And its incompatibility and inhospitality were to increase.

Although the essence of those revolutionary changes was already a *fait accompli*, they would become obvious only gradually, as the revolution found it unnecessary to maintain much of its subterfuge. Not the least of the elements, which tended to conceal the extent of the progress of the revolution, was the occupancy of the White House during the war years and the early years of Reconstruction by native Southerners. Although both Lincoln and Andrew Johnson were possessed of a passionate hatred for slavery, they were also imbued with a loyalty for the Constitution and a respect for constitutional processes far more agreeable to Southern loyalists than to Yankee rebels of their constituency. And both were to display an understanding of the South and a sympathy for its people which would bring down on them ire and contumely from powerful radicals of their party.

The war on the seceding states had been launched on the premise that no right of secession existed. Consistent with that premise, there had been no declaration of war and no announced war aim other than the preservation of the Union. Both Lincoln and Johnson remained faithful throughout to that premise. Consequently, in 1863, when Federal forces had gained at least a foothold in every Confederate state and had occupied almost all of Arkansas, Tennessee, and Louisiana, and Lincoln was faced with reinstating the seceded states in the Union, his only problem was to prescribe a method by which they might reinstitute their civil governments within the Union. He did this by a proclamation which granted pardons to all who took an oath of allegiance, save a few Confederate leaders, and further provided that when one-tenth the number who had voted in the election of 1860 established a loyal government, it would be recognized.

Relying on the President's proclamation, the three occupied states proceeded to set up civil governments and duly elected representatives to Congress. But before they arrived in Washington, radical revolutionists had gained control of Congress. The radicals had little respect for the announced premise upon which the invasion of the South had been predicated, or for the Constitution, or for the plighted word of the President. The equally ugly faces of power politics and blind vengeance were already rearing their heads. To serve their purposes, Congressional leaders resorted to "higher laws" again, laws over and beyond the Constitution. According to the radicals, those "higher laws" provided that, by attempting to secede, the Southern states had committed suicide and reverted to territorial status, or that they had gone into suspended animation. In any case, regardless of the particular theory contended for, it was generally agreed that the seceded states were beyond protection of the Constitution until Congress itself decided to admit them to the protection of its mutilated remains. Confronted with Congressional defiance of the announced objective of the war, the President's proclamation, and the Constitution itself, their request for re-admission to the Union rejected, Arkansas, Tennessee, and Louisiana continued under military rule, awaiting the pleasure of the now all-powerful revolutionary clique.

Meanwhile, Lincoln had issued his Emancipation Proclamation

purporting to free slaves in portions of the Confederacy not in Union hands. Although it was ineffectual and was made primarily for its propaganda value, especially for its effect in European diplomatic circles, President Lincoln had long hesitated to make it because of his doubts as to whether its unconstitutionality was redeemed by its being a war measure. That he believed that was its only legal justification is borne out by his subsequent veto, as unconstitutional, of an act of Congress freeing the slaves in areas not covered by the Proclamation.

This veto and a pocket veto of an act providing more rigid specifications as conditions for re-admission of occupied states were evidence of the growing breach between the President and Congress, with the sanctity of the Constitution at stake, when an assassin's bullet saved him from obloquy and persecution that were to be the lot of his successor, who so closely resembled him in everything from his origins to his political theories. For the revolutionary conspirators in Congress, the bullet of John Wilkes Booth was a godsend. It saved them the necessity of contending with the prestige of a successful wartime president and in his place, delivered into their hands a man more vulnerable to their attacks, a man not only born a Southerner, but one who had risen to power in the Southern political arena despite his hatred for slavery and aristocrats.

Even before Lincoln was laid in his grave, the curtain was raised on the most corrupt and disgraceful period in the entire epic of America, a period which was to prove essentially more damaging to the South than the war itself, a period the evil fruit of which is still being garnered and will inevitably continue to spread its poison for many years to come.

Lincoln's exit from the scene and the accession of Johnson were greeted by unfeeling conspirators on Capitol Hill with unconcealed delight. The assassination itself greatly augmented a highly vocal minority calling for sterner measures against the conquered South. Ordinary citizens in increased numbers were now adding their voices to the clamor which had often been heard in Congress, demanding the hanging of President Davis and other leading Confederates and the disposal of General Lee by a firing squad. This echo from the public was sweet music to radical ears. As for Johnson himself, the radicals assumed him to be one of them because of his well-known hatred of slavery and aristocrats. Beyond that, they calculated that if he were to prove recalcitrant in effecting their schemes for a more complete destruction of the South, he, a Southerner, could be easily sacrificed on the altar of sectional prejudice.

It soon became apparent, however, that they had judged the new President wrongly. His first official moves came as a rude shock to their assumptions as to his attitudes, for they indicated that, however strong his hatred of slavery and aristocrats, his devotion to the Constitution, to justice, and to his own integrity was far stronger.

With only a brief hesitation for stock taking and counsel, he assumed his great burden where it had fallen from Lincoln's shoulders. Retaining his predecessor's cabinet, and with the added prestige of Grant beside him as advisor, he was soon moving forward with Lincoln's humane plan for reconstruction of the beaten region. That was in the late spring of 1865 and Congress would not meet in regular session again until December. Provisional governors were appointed for the seceded states, to administer them while the machinery of civil government was being constructed. By mid-summer, most of them had held constitutional conventions, repealed their ordinances of secession, adopted new constitutions, elected state officials and representatives to Congress, and duly ratified the Thirteenth Amendment legally abolishing slavery.

Despite the confusion and overwhelming destruction wrought by war, remarkable progress was soon made toward establishment of stable and respectable civil governments. Consideration was even being given the possibility of enfranchising the newly freed blacks with, of course, proper safeguards in the form of property and educational qualifications, a right not then accorded Negroes in most of the Northern states. In accordance with the Constitution, Johnson had left that problem to be handled by the individual states. However, at least a step in that direction was made by the so-called "Black Codes," which were soon adopted by most of the newly formed legislatures.

The mere freeing of slaves did not make them citizens nor give them most of the rights, privileges, and protections accorded citizens by existing laws. As soon as emancipation became a reality, it became obvious that detailed provisions would have to be made for the protection of whites from the masses of freedmen and for the protection of Negroes from those whites who might take advantage of their ignorance and poverty and for their protection from themselves. As soon as they became aware of their freedom, multitudes of them had set out to roam to "joy freedom." They were soon aimlessly roaming the countryside in bands, subsisting by petty thievery. Tens of thousands flocked to the towns and cities attracted there by their innate gregariousness and by rumors, usually false, that there they would be taken care of by the army or by the Freedmen's Bureau; where, instead, they found themselves destitute and homeless, as was evidenced by their death rates which frequently jumped from a prewar rate comparable to that of the whites to double or more.

The Freedmen's Bureau had been set up by Congress shortly before Appomattox for the purpose of aiding freedmen in their transition to free status. However, the support given it was insufficient to scratch the surface of the need and it soon became a refuge for grafters and politicians who turned most of its energies to political and propaganda purposes, stultifying to a large degree its original purposes. It became apparent that the real burden for tutelage of erstwhile slaves and for care of them during their transition to their new status would devolve upon Southern whites. But they were in no position to help by direct handouts. Almost all of them were themselves in distress, and a half million were destitute. The Black Codes constituted a realistic and practical approach to the problem.

Modeled on the vagrancy and apprenticeship laws extant in the North, on the regulations of the Freedmen's Bureau, and on the codes adopted in the British West Indies after emancipation was affected there, these codes dealt with vagrancy, apprenticing, and labor contracts. Although they granted basic civil rights to the freedmen, they did not grant them suffrage, the right to sit on juries, or the right to testify in cases involving whites. Those provisions of restrictive intent were a serious blunder, as we shall see. Viewed in the light of the day, these codes represented a giant step forward from slavery, and now that the heat and smoke of the times have cleared away, historians generally regard both the codes and the intent that brought them into being as sincere efforts to help the Negro to move forward in a strange new world in which he would no longer have his master to guide him.

If the codes were stern and shocking by today's standards, so also were the apprentice laws which were in effect in Northern states. If they were grossly discriminatory, it must be borne in mind that there were few people then who were not sincerely convinced that the Negro was an inferior being, usually endowed with but the mentality of a child and with even less moral discrimination. But there were some, mostly Negrophiles and reformers in the North, who did not share that commonly held opinion. They generally had had some acquaintance with educated Negroes in the North and little or none with the masses of ignorant field hands who composed the bulk of the black population of the South. From those men and from radicals in Congress, who were looking eagerly for any excuse to frustrate the President's plan of reconstruction that they might proceed further against the South, the Black Codes brought a storm of protest, especially those clauses which specifically limited the Negroes' civil rights. They charged that through them, the South was snatching victory from defeat and that, if the codes were permitted to stand, slavery would thereby be re-established.

As farfetched as were their charges in truth, radicals used them effectively as they gathered ammunition to proceed against the President's reconstruction plans. They found more ammunition in the tendency of reorganized Southern governments to place former Confederate heroes in high positions. Congressional radicals seized upon that tendency as indicating improper humility and repentance on the part of the vanquished and used it effectively to block the seating of newly elected congressmen and senators from the seceded states. By twisting, magnifying, and multiplying the amazingly few racial incidents which were occurring here and there in the South, as it adjusted itself to its suddenly altered social system, the radicals manufactured more ammunition for their campaign of vengeance and hate.

However, more persuasive than anything else in the radical revolutionaries' efforts to whip together a militant majority in both houses of Congress was the strength shown by the Democrats in the elections in the South. Five years of struggle against a Republican-led enemy had largely erased the traditional bitter cleavage between southern Whigs and Democrats. Galvanized to action by the prospect of having the opposition enhanced by the representatives of eleven states, the radicals launched their new war on the South with a heartless determination to cut it to their pattern or "make a frog pond" of it.

The South had no shield against this new onslaught. With the surrender of the armies of Lee and Johnston, hostilities had simply ceased. There was no armistice or peace treaty spelling out the limits of the fate of the vanquished. It was a surrender based on faith, faith in the announced program of President Lincoln, sealed by the steps he had already taken to carry that program into effect. It soon became apparent that, under the leadership of Sumner and Stevens, revolutionaries in Congress had no intention of keeping faith with the martyred President. The refusal of the House and Senate to seat congressmen and senators from the former Confederate states was notice to that effect.

With conservative Southern delegations denied admission, the radicals remained in control of both houses of Congress. By unsparing use of the party whip, by excluding unsympathetic representatives on any technicality which might be discovered, and by continuing to keep the doors of Congress closed to representatives from the South until radicals could be substituted for those who first knocked at the doors, the revolutionaries, during 1866, pushed their preponderance in both houses to the two-thirds necessary to enact legislation without the president's approval.

The opening salvo of the new campaign against the South, the third phase of the ever-mounting national revolution, came in the form of the Civil Rights Act of 1866. This act, in clear defiance of the provisions of the Constitution before the adoption of the Fourteenth Amendment, undertook immediately to make freedmen citizens of the states, reduced the states' representation in Congress if they were not permitted to vote, and forestalled any attempts to apply literacy requirements for voting or any requirement that voters should be taxpayers. More than that, it undertook to disfranchise almost all prominent white leaders of the South and required repudiation of wartime obligations of the states. Knowing full well that even a partisan court could scarcely avoid declaring most of this act unconstitutional, the radicals embraced most of its terms in a proposed constitutional amendment, offering it for ratification as the Fourteenth Amendment.

With the offering of the Fourteenth Amendment for ratification, the intent of the radicals began to unfold. With malice aforethought, they had weighted the proposed amendment with terms which they fully expected Southern legislatures to reject. That was part of the plan. Another part of the plan required of Congress an absurd inconsistency, which nonetheless does not appear to have bothered the plotters at all. In refusing to permit the representatives which the Southern states had sent to Congress to be seated, Congress had refused to recognize the seceded states as being states of the Union, in barefaced conflict with the wartime contention that they were never out of the Union. Now they were being recognized as states for the purpose of amending the Constitution. Congress was being placed in the position of denying former Confederate states the protection of the Constitution which it was now asking them to assist in changing.

As hoped for and anticipated, all except Tennessee indignantly rejected the proposed Amendment. Those rejections were the signal for an all out campaign to reduce the South to a proper degree of humility and subservience.

Meanwhile, even as plans for this new campaign to subjugate it were being fomented, all across the devastated South, men were struggling with a multitude of mounting problems. The steps taken to re-establish civil government have already been mentioned. Although they were faced with the gargantuan task of repairing the damage inflicted by the war on their communications systems, public buildings, and private property, there was more urgency in the necessity of getting their fields into production again. Upon that their very survival depended. The prime essential to accomplish that was to get former slaves back to the land, back to some productive effort, and to check their discouraging tendency to roam and exist by pilfering and marauding. The Black Codes had been their first effort in that direction. An entirely new production system had to be devised to replace that which had been swept away. The whites still had their land, despite the threats which kept rolling down from the North that it would soon be confiscated and divided among freedmen. The blacks had only their brawn. Both were penniless, but their needs were equal. Both must eat or perish.

From those realities share cropping was born. Using his land as security, the white man obtained credit from the North, then the only source of that essential, to make necessary advances to the freedmen that he might survive while he tilled the land for a share of the crop which was produced. Thus was born a new sort of peonage with the master far removed from the scene, sitting behind his desk in a Northern bank, counting the ten, fifteen, or even twenty percent interest he was garnering from his dealings in human misery. All the while these patchworks for survival were being complicated and made more difficult by the fretting of human emotions.

First lack of civil government, and later the distractions incident to its re-establishment, greatly complicated the Southerners' efforts to rebuild. The Freedmen's Bureau offices, which were soon to be found all over the region, were lodestones everywhere attracting freedmen from the land upon which they would of necessity be dependent for survival, attracting them far more by promises than by performance in supplying their needs. Many Bureau agents appeared to believe that their prime mission was to foster, in the freedmen, a hatred of their former masters and a conviction that they were the subject of great injustices at their masters' hands; for which injustices great restitutions were due. At least as many Bureau agents were cruelly leading their ignorant clients to believe that that restitution would soon be made in the form of a division of their former masters' lands among them, with a free mule thrown in to work the land.

To the disrupting influence of those overzealous agents of the Freedmen's Bureau, the even more disrupting activities of the Union League were soon added. Financed by the money power which was behind Congressional radicals, League men were soon organizing the blacks into secret societies everywhere that numbers could be gathered together to hear their harangues; inculcating in their ignorant victims the conviction that the year of jubilee was at hand awaiting only their gaining the ballot and using it to vote Republican. Their forty acres and a mule would surely follow.

All the while, in many places occupation forces were proving as demoralizing as the Union League. There was a tendency for the better elements to be mustered out earliest, leaving the worst to man the occupation units. Many of those were undisciplined Negro troops who delighted in humiliating helpless whites. Many proved as adept as the League men in spreading hatred, suspicion, and false hopes among the freedmen, and a reciprocal hatred among the humiliated whites.

Even before the fighting had stopped, treasury agents began invading the South, ostensibly in search of Confederate government property that might be confiscated. There was little of value left in the stricken land but several million bales of cotton, which was then bringing more than a dollar a pound. Operating under commission arrangements, with commissions running up to twenty-five percent, cotton agents were soon searching out cotton in every corner of the cotton country, laying claim to almost every bale they came across, unless the owner made it worth-while for them to certify that his bales were not enemy property. Only a small fraction of the proceeds of the millions of bales confiscated ever reached the treasury; but agents accumulated fortunes in a matter of months.

Another millstone around the cotton grower's neck was the punitive cotton tax. Levied in 1865, in the very teeth of the provision of the Constitution prohibiting that sort of taxing by Congress, it drained from the impoverished region more money than was sent to the South in relief, both public and private, and all the cost of the military administration of the South during the whole fifteen years of Reconstruction, before it was finally repealed at the behest of Negroes and carpetbaggers, as they got into cotton growing on their own.

Inevitably, all these impediments, which appeared in the path of Southerners as they bent their efforts to make a new start from all-pervading ruin, went a long way toward souring the "spirit of Appomattox." That the spirit of Appomattox, the magnanimity which was displayed at Lee's surrender, had been accepted in the South with a faith that deserved a better fate is borne out by the observations of Whitelaw Reid, who was to succeed Horace Greeley as editor of the

New York *Tribune*. Reid traveled through the South a few months after the surrender. Summarizing his impression for publication a few months later he wrote:

> Here was an opportunity for a statesman to grasp. . . . The people wanted civil government and a settlement. They asked no terms, made no conditions. They were defeated and helpless—they submitted. Would the victors be pleased to tell them what was to be done? Point out any way for a return to an established order of things, and they will walk in it. They make no hypocritical professions of a new-born Unionism. They had honestly believed in the right of secession. The hatred of Yankees . . . had grown and strengthened with the war. . . . . Filled with hatred to the Negroes, nearly always inspired in any ruling class by the loss of accustomed power over inferiors, they nevertheless yielded to the Freedmen's Bureau, and acquiesced in the necessity for according civil rights to their slaves. They were stung by the disgrace of being guarded by Negro soldiers; but they made no complaints, for they felt they had forfeited their right of complaint. They were shocked at the suggestion of Negro suffrage; but if the government required it, they were ready to submit.
>
> The whole body politic was as wax. It needed but a firm hand to apply the seal. Whatever device were chosen, the community would at once be molded to its impress. But if the plastic moment were suffered to pass—!

The plastic moment did pass. Treachery, perfidy, and persecution firmed the wax. Southerners had been told by Lincoln and Johnson what should be done to secure the blessings of peace and civil government, but Congress had reneged on the President and they had been rejected. No statesman had risen to grasp the opportunity Reid delineated. Instead, only the ugly heads of vengeance, of fanaticism, bigotry and political venality had raised themselves to grasp the opportunities each saw in the condition of the beaten region.

The South

Becomes

a Conquered Province: 2

12

THE FIRST GREAT CRISIS of the nation had produced an amazing coterie of ageless stature: Franklin, Adams, and the Virginia titans, Washington, Jefferson, Madison, and Mason. Their combined genius had created the republic. Except for Lincoln and Lee, both of whom left the scene before its most critical period, and possibly Johnson; the second great crisis brought to the fore as leaders a motley crew, all of whom, for one reason or another, were intent on destroying much that the earlier group had built. Except for those mentioned, none of them added a glimmer of lustre to the nation's history.

Most powerful of those into whose hands the destiny of the nation passed when Congress seized control from President Johnson was Thaddeus Stevens, party leader of the radical Republicans in the House. Ruthless and unscrupulous in the means he employed to gain his objectives, he was driven by a bitter and unrelenting hatred of aristocrats and a blind devotion to Negroes, one of whom lived with him, reputedly as his mistress. To gain his objectives, he openly defied the Constitution, maintaining that the South had forfeited all rights under it and that only the rules of war and conquest now governed. Only death quieted his fanatical drive for the execution of Confederate leaders, disfranchisement of all who supported the Confederacy, and confiscation of their property for distribution among the freedmen, who were to be made the masters of a re-made South by their immediate enfranchisement, with ample assurances that they would be loyal Republicans to perpetuate the revolutionaries in power.

In the Senate, the rebels were led by Ben Wade and Charles Sumner. Wade's sentiments were like those of Stevens. Distrusted by his fellow radicals and openly referred to by one of them as "that scalawag," he missed being elevated to the presidency by one vote in the Senate when the ballot was taken on the impeachment trial of President Johnson, he himself voting for the conviction in hopes that he, as president of the Senate, would thereby be elevated to the presidency. Sumner was of a different stripe. Although narrow and intolerant of those who did not share his views, he was honest and sincere. However, his unrestrained hatred of slaveholders and his ardent Negrophile attitudes led him to a viciousness toward the defeated South fully matching that of Stevens and Wade. In his later years, when he softened a bit toward the South and openly disapproved of the blatant corruption of his party, he was renounced by it and driven from power.

With Stevens in the inner circle of conspirators in the House were the depraved J. M. Ashley of Ohio and William D. "Pig Iron" Kelly, both of whom were to become involved in bribery scandals, and Benjamin "Beast" Butler of Massachusetts, whose wartime ruthlessness, as field commander and military governor, carried over undiminished into his career as congressman, during which he was President Grant's spokesman in the House, even as he was involved in a series of corruption scandals. Of the same circle, who for years controlled the destiny of the nation and especially of the South, were two more Massachusetts congressmen, both of whom were, like Stevens, extremists and both of whom were to be involved in bribery scandals, only to be rewarded by the radicals with yet higher offices. They were George S. Boutwell, who would become Secretary of Treasury under Grant, and

Henry Wilson, who would become Grant's second vice-president. Another of the House conspirators who was to be richly rewarded for his proficiency in climbing to power on hate, graft, and perfidy was James G. Blaine, whose soubriquet "the continental liar from the State of Maine" yet lives. His involvement in the carpetbagger railroad scandals of Arkansas in no way hampered his promotion by Grant to Secretary of State and, later, the nomination of his party for the presidency. Also in the House, serving as its Speaker at the war's end, but destined soon for higher positions, was Schuyler Colfax who, despite the infamy of the numerous bribery scandals in which he was involved, was rewarded by his fellow radicals with the vice-presidency in 1867.

In the Senate, assisting Sumner and Wade in forwarding the revolution, was the venal Simon Cameron of Pennsylvania. Master politician and crony of the grafters, as Secretary of War under Lincoln, he had, by his favoritism in awarding war contracts to the unscrupulous, made fortunes for many, including himself. He himself showed his standard of political ethics when he described an honest politician as "one who when he is bought will stay bought." Consequently, he was presidential material in the eyes of his fellows and once narrowly missed the Republican nomination. There were three more men in the Senate who were high in the party councils, Roscoe Conkling, Oliver Morton, and Zack Chandler. Although not thoroughly of the spirit of the times, in that corruption was never charged against them, they were no more scrupulous in forwarding their political careers by joining their fellow radicals and by dealing cruelly with the South to the end that it might be rendered a secure political satrapy of the Republican Party.

Beyond the halls of Congress were other high-placed radicals equally intent on revolution. There was E. M. Stanton, the Secretary of War whom Johnson inherited from Lincoln, who, while leading Johnson to trust his confidences, was all the while acting as a spy for the conspirators bent on destroying the President—an example of the ethics of the revolution. Another exemplar of those ethics was General Grant. Starting out as Johnson's top advisor and a strong supporter of presidential reconstruction policies, Grant, on having the presidency dangled before him, suddenly skulked out of the presidential circle and flopped over to the radical camp, where he would find the company vastly more to his taste, as his presidential years would prove, when he persisted in protecting and defending the Constitution defiers and grafters alike, to the end that his administration became the most corrupt in American history, a corruption which eventually involved numerous members of his family and even the President himself.

Although those were the ostensible actors as the revolution moved towards its climax, the real power behind them was the money of those in whose interests the revolution was being staged; the Jim Fisks who were interested in ever bigger land grabs in connection with their railroad promotions and who hesitated not at all in their market corners to swindle the helpless public, the Jay Cookes who made millions through government favoritism in the sale of government securities and in government contracts, and numerous high tariff manufacturers shamelessly seeking greater personal profits at the expense of consumers by means of ever higher tariffs. It had been their money "invested" freely that had put many of those politicians in high offices. It was their money that was keeping them there. It was their money that was buying the votes necessary to forward the revolution. As the revolution rolled on, as tariffs were pushed higher, as land grabs became more bold, as swindles increased in size and number, as the climate was made more hospitable to money interests, the age of the "robber barons" was ushered in—and there was still more money ready for "investment" in the cause.

Those were the men in control in the national capital when Congress scuttled presidential plans for re-admission of the seceded states to the Union and substituted its plans for "reconstructing" them.

By the Reconstruction Acts of 1867, which were passed over President Johnson's veto, Congress declared that there were no legal civil governments in ten of the former Confederate states, Tennessee being excepted since it already had a radical Republican government and had ratified the Fourteenth Amendment. The South was divided into military districts with occupation troops under Grant, defying, in effect, constitutional provision making the president the commander in chief. Civil governments of the states were disbanded and military governments substituted.

The reign of the generals lasted in all ten states until the summer of 1868, and in several until 1870. Military commanders were given the right to arrest, as they saw fit, and try any accused before military tribunals, until new civil governments were duly created, pursuant to new constitutional conventions in which the delegates should be "elected by the male citizens of whatever race, color, or previous condition"—this, despite the Constitution which provided that qualification of electors is a right reserved to the states. Their determination that Southern Negroes should immediately be given the ballot was but another illustration of the hypocrisy of radical reformers in Congress. At the time, but six Northern states allowed the Negro to vote. However, for the revolutionaries, patent hypocrisy was no deterrent in the face of political possibilities the Negro voters would present. They had seen Northern elections lost to the Democrats, which would surely have been won had Negroes been permitted to vote. Those defeats had made them decide, Constitution or no Constitution, to avail themselves of all those potential Republican votes, despite the protest of one hesitating radical who tellingly observed that to argue that the freedman was ready for the ballot necessitated an admission that slavery was the positive good the planters claimed for it, since it must have done wonders for ignorant barbarians.

A start was made with the District of Columbia. A referendum on the proposal that District Negroes be given the ballot met with a two hundred to one adverse vote. But Congress passed the enfranchisement act anyway, an experiment which was so disastrous that in a few years, it would culminate in removing all local self-government from the District, disfranchizing all district residents. Far more tempting were the opportunities offered by giving the freedmen of the South the ballot.

With the organizing of the constitutional conventions of the seceded states, Washington conspirators pushed the revolution out into the Southern hinterland. No sooner had the conventions gathered than it became obvious that infection in Washington had spread to every Southern capital in a more virulent form, putrefying wherever it struck.

In preparation for the conventions, military authorities had seen to it that all the Negroes were registered and had done what they could to prevent from registration those whites who were not legally disfranchised. In consequence, when the time came to vote, a majority of those eligible to vote were ignorant blacks, not one in twenty of whom could read or write. Most of them had no conception of what was meant when they were told that they were being given the ballot. Many, when they went to register, thought that they were being listed for free distributions of something tangible. Some brought buckets and baskets in which to bring home the ballots they had been told they were being given. Twice as many blacks as whites, in proportion to their numbers, had been registered. It was suddenly apparent, as the conspirators had foreseen, that, through that numerical majority without political opinions except those of their mentors, the South was being delivered into carpetbagger hands, to be dealt with to their venal and vindictive hearts' content. It would be necessary only to insulate those minions of the revolution from the influence of their former masters and that could be easily done by flattery and commingling on the one hand and inculcating hatred and suspicion of their erstwhile masters on the other—a pattern which was to be faithfully followed for ten more awful years while real reconstruction awaited a more moderate day, when the force of the revolution would be spent.

Meanwhile, in the chaotic scene, a multitude of new forces had been appearing. In anticipation of the kill, a motley crew of adventurers, fortune seekers, politicians, and reformers had been flocking to the frontier the Yankee had created. The most notorious, the most unscrupulous, and also the cleverest of these were those who came intent on parlaying the contents of their carpetbags into fat fortunes. All through the frontier here and there, they found native Southerners of similar interests and equally devoid of scruples, men who would soon earn the infamous soubriquet of "scalawag." When the conventions gathered, it was soon apparent that those bodies from which property and intelligence had been excluded were little more than the

instruments of the newcomers and their scalawag confederates. Much
has been made of the large numbers of Negroes who were named to
the conventions. In truth, they were important only in that their
presence enhanced the power of the carpetbaggers and scalawags; for
it was impossible for the ignorant, mostly illiterate blacks, on their
own, to influence, to any extent, the technical deliberations incident
to drafting a fundamental charter, founded on a knowledge of Anglo-
Saxon jurisprudence, except insofar as they did the bidding of their
new white masters.

Generally, the constitutions which the conventions produced, being modeled on those of Northern states, were acceptable enough
and far more democratic than those they displaced; providing for universal manhood suffrage, free public schools, and homestead exemptions, although most of them also included vindictive provisions disfranchising specified classes of whites and one even forbade the use
of the words "Yankee" and "nigger," and three made Democrats,
white or black, ineligible to hold public office. Another prohibited
state aid for artificial limbs for former Confederates.

It was the conventions themselves that proclaimed the spread of
infection from Washington to every Southern capital. Never had
more rowdy and uncouth conventions been seen. Pistols, knives,
whiskey, and fist fights were ordinary adjuncts of the deliberative
procedure. Reason and justice gave way to power and pelf. Frequently,
the stealing started before deliberations, with fantastic amounts being paid for travel expenses based on false claims and the printing of
proclamations and proceedings in newly established radical newspapers, either owned by members of the conventions or willing to pay
acceptable commissions to carpetbaggers who were running the show.
However, these were but tokens of the morrow. The gates were now
open for ten years of good stealing, while radical revolutionaries in
Washington tried to make the South over into a profitable adjunct of
their interests and cure it of its deterring propensities.

The men who made up the Southern state governments, which,
after varying delays, were established pursuant to the constitutions
produced by those conventions, made them the most incredible creations in all Anglo-Saxon political history. Before considering them

and what they did to the South, let us return to Washington for a look at the progress of the revolution into the toils of which the South had been swept.

The rift between Congress and President Johnson had been widening with every passing day, as he stood steadfastly for the Constitution and refused to co-operate with the revolution in the North and a renewed invasion of the South. With the impatience characteristic of rebels generally, radical leaders determined not to await the election of 1868 to be rid of his vetoes and lack of co-operation with their schemes. On purely trumped-up charges and perjured testimony, Johnson was impeached. In his trial by the Senate, he was vindicated and the nation saved from its greatest disgrace by a single courageous vote. The President's impeachment was the price he had to pay for integrity in public office in a period when scruples were declassé. The long rough road he had traveled, from the humble cottage in North Carolina where he was born of an unknown father, to manhood in Tennessee, where he worked as a tailor's apprentice and was taught to read and write by the girl he later married, and on to Congress and the vice-presidency had been marked all along by battles for principles—for the Union, when both his native state and his adopted state voted for disunion, for the Constitution, when the radicals sought to trample it underfoot, and, finally, for the Union again, when the Congressional radicals declared that the Southern states were out of the Union and not entitled to the protection of its Constitution.

Foiled in their unscrupulous effort to seize the executive department by impeachment of the president, the rebels were forced to await the 1868 elections to find in Grant a more amenable tool, admirer as he was of great wealth without queasiness as to its sources, with a predilection for friendships with questionable characters, a soldier with more respect for order under the strong arm than under the less tangible mandates of the mere words of a Constitution.

With Grant in the White House and an intimidated Supreme Court ducking the fundamental issues of fundamental cases reaching it from the South, the radicals could now freely ride the crest. And the revolution rolled southward, sweeping the creations of time and man before it, leaving, in the name of reconstruction, little but destruction in its wake.

At the time Grant was riding alone to his inauguration, Johnson having refused "to witness the inauguration of a man whom he knew to be untruthful, faithless, and false," sordid drama was already unfolding in every Southern capital.

Samplings of what a Northern reporter declared to be "barbarism overwhelming civilization by physical force" will have to suffice and those without exactness as to chronology.

Louisiana, when Congressional reconstruction got under way, had already suffered years of humiliation under the iron yoke of the most vicious military governors. First, there had been Benjamin "Beast" Butler, who was eventually removed because of his brutalities, to be later rewarded with a Congressional seat and a high place in the radical leadership. Later, there had been a long period under the merciless whip of General Philip Sheridan, who gloated in his evil reputation. When the state emerged from military government to a semblance of civil government under the Congressional plan, dictatorial powers over the commonwealth had fallen into the hands of Henry Clay Warmouth, a twenty-six-year-old emigré from Illinois, who, according to repute, was accumulating a fortune at the rate of a hundred thousand a year on an eight thousand dollar salary. The Legislature, upon which much of his power rested, was a freakish travesty on a deliberative body. The House, presided over by another twenty-six-year-old adventurer, a carpetbagger from Maryland, was no more than a rowdy, ribald, and crude aggregation of ignorant whites and blacks who openly discussed, even on the floor, the prices of their votes between frequent trips to the state-supported bar below. In the Senate, presided over by a Negro lieutenant-governor, the scene was much the same. Despite drunkenness, disorder, and ignorance, these bodies were dealing in millions, ostensibly for the reconstruction of their crippled state, but, in fact, at least as much for the construction of fortunes for the whip holders and juicy pickings for their minions.

This parody on government was to continue for almost a decade, interrupted only by the internecine wars between the plunderers, as they fell out over the division of the booty. The annual cost of the

Legislature ran up to ten times its prewar cost, with the printing bill alone, to make adequate allowance for the pay-off, exceeding the entire prewar legislative costs by almost a half. But those were only the small swindles. The big grafts came through the appropriations for railroads, canals, and levees, which eventually increased the state debt almost fourfold for very little in return.

To insure themselves long tenure in the lush offices in which Federal bayonets had placed them, against other radical Republicans covetous of their perquisites of office, the Warmouth gang devised measures which, to say the least, were unusual in a country purporting to be a democracy. Newspapers under Warmouth's control were established at state expense. His henchmen in office were given absolute control over the election machinery, with the right to reject any voter for any reason and full control of the returning boards who declared the elections. Further to insulate from office all who might not be agreeable with the gang, the governor was given the right to refuse, at his discretion, to commission anyone who might be elected and the courts were deprived of all authority to interfere with any of these safety measures. To cap and seal his control, the Legislature granted him the right and the money to establish a sizable militia under his sole command.

Despite all these precautions, the mess was soon compounded by factional warfare. With President Grant's brother-in-law, the Custom House collector of unsavory reputation, as the power behind the movement and the Negro lieutenant-governor as its candidate for governor, the reign of the Warmouth crowd was challenged in the next Republican convention. During the chaos of the civil war which ensued, every device of power was employed. Patronage was used, Warmouth adding five hundred employees to the New Orleans payroll to offset Collector Casey's addition of an equal number to the Federal payroll. Hired bands of ruffians armed with bludgeons were brought into play. So also were Federal troops, the militia, bribery, expulsions from the party and, finally, appeals to the President himself who tipped the scales in favor of his brother-in-law.

Two years later, with the next election, there was chaos again as the thieves once more demonstrated the falsity of the maxim that there is honor among men of such stripe. This time the result was a paralyzing dual government which continued until Grant threw the weight of Federal military forces back of the more corrupt of the two. The distress which followed would be incredible if it were not history. An example of the brazenness of the plunderers—a railroad in which the State had invested $2,000,000 was sold to members of the gang for $50,000, while higher bids from outsiders were rejected. Taxes soared while property values plummeted to a small fraction of what they had been even in the distress of early postwar years. Auctioneers were overworked, offering thousands of plantations and farms for sale for taxes. In New Orleans alone, nearly 50,000 pieces of property went under the hammer in two years. And there were few who could buy, except the carpetbaggers and scalawags who had received so much of the money for which the taxes were levied. So they waxed richer through their bargain purchases and the strangle hold grew even tighter. That, in brief, was the state of affairs in Louisiana as its white populace, driven to grim desperation, awaited and planned for 1874 and another election.

As terrible as conditions were in Louisiana, those prevailing in South Carolina have made that state the classic example of the horrors of radical rule in the South under Congressional reconstruction. A look at the government that prevailed there in 1870 will serve to illustrate the conditions which continued for eight years. At that time, the central figure in the state's so-called "loyal" government was Robert K. Scott, an Ohio carpetbagger, an incident in whose career was the issuance of several hundred thousands of dollars in state railroad bonds while drunk and under the influence of a strumpet who received a cut from the booty. Among the other high officials was State Treasurer Niles G. Parker, a Massachusetts fugitive from justice. A power in the radical government was "Honest" John Patterson of Pennsylvania, who would go all the way to the United States Senate on his adeptness in graft, which was proved in the Legislature of that state, and later by his successful embezzlements during his service as a paymaster in the Union army. Another was Scalawag Thomas J. Robertson, who managed to retain his seat in the United States Senate through the direct purchase of the votes of Legislators at up to five hundred dollars each. But most notorious of all was the Speaker of the House, Franklin Moses, utterly depraved, but so successful at stealing that his talents were soon to win him the governorship.

The iron grip in which this little group held the suffering state rested upon a corrupt, subservient General Assembly, over which, by dint of fear and bribery, they exercised absolute control. The Negro majority in the state, registered and herded to the polls by the Union League, the Federal troops, and the swaggering mass of State militia, in which 90,000 Negroes had been enrolled and 20,000 armed, on the one hand, and the disfranchisement of many whites on the other had assured a heavy radical majority in both houses of the General Assembly. In the House, nine-tenths were radicals, three-fourths of whom paid no taxes whatsoever. Two-thirds were Negroes of whom eighty percent were illiterates signing by mark.

Their radical control covered every arm and every function of the state. While the juiciest plums always fell to the carpetbaggers and scalawags, there were always small pickings left for their black henchmen, dropped there to insure their unswerving loyalty. High officials boasted publicly of their cleverness in plundering. The public was lucky if more than a tenth of any appropriation finally reached its ostensible purpose. Although the Senate had but thirty-five attachés, pay warrants were regularly issued to three hundred and fifty. Enormous appropriations were made for the purchase of furniture for the State House, but only a tenth of it ever reached the State House, all the rest being delivered to homes of loyal legislators and other officials. Even lingerie for the mistresses of loyal radicals became a state expense, as was also a refreshment room which was established in the State House and which dispensed, on the average, a gallon of whiskey and forty-four cigars per member daily.

When a group of jealous radicals moved to impeach Governor Scott and Treasurer Parker, the impeachers were bought off with $48,000 drawn from the State's military fund. Even as radical rule began to be weakened from within by internal jealousies, the state's buoyant United States Senator, "Honest" John Patterson (dubbed "Honest" because of his unique reliability in paying the bribes he promised), was openly declaring that there still remained "five years good stealing in South Carolina."

Although higher positions and special opportunities for graft were reserved for the new masters, who in South Carolina were preponderantly white carpetbaggers with a sprinkling of scalawags, and a Negro carpetbagger was elected to the Supreme Court, lesser positions were freely distributed among the freedmen, regardless of their qualifications. There were two hundred trial justices in the State, practically all of them blacks, who could neither read nor write. Upon them devolved the duty of interpreting and applying laws they could not read and issuing writs, warrants, and orders which they could not write or even sign. Few of the fines and penalties collected in those courts were ever accounted for. A measure of the distress resulting from the justice by ignorance which prevailed is indicated in the frank wit of a Carolina scalawag who was commenting on the punishment he thought should be meted out to Mexico, with whom relations were strained at the time. To give Mexico her deserts, he suggested that, if he were president, he would "send down upon Mexico the army and the navy. I would direct them to kill and to burn and to slay; and when they had done their worst, I would send down upon the country the trial justices of South Carolina."

Although Louisiana and South Carolina suffered more than most of their sisters in misery under Congressional reconstruction, conditions were much the same in Mississippi and Arkansas, and only somewhat better in Alabama and Florida, and none of the seceded states entirely escaped its destruction and humiliation. In Mississippi, forty former slaves, only a few of whom could sign their names, were included among the State's lawmakers. A Negro carpetbagger from New York, while under indictment for embezzlement in that state, was elected head of the school system. In its elections, the usual pattern prevailed, with Negroes herded to the polls by the Union League's agents and Federal troops, most of whom were ex-slaves; of multiple registrations of Negroes under various names in adjacent counties, and even in the same county, to permit multiple voting; and the importation, on election day, of thousands of Negroes from adjoining states to cast their ballots. Mississippi, too, was torn by riots between warring radical factions. There, too, the government was steeped in corruption with bribery and graft on every hand, while taxes skyrocketed and property values plummeted and one-fifth of the state was sold for taxes.

Relatively, no state suffered more under carpetbagger rule than Arkansas. Although still sparsely settled and with a lower percentage of Negroes than many others, the combination of Federal armed force and the connivance of rascals succeeded in delivering it over to the radicals as effectively as those with far greater ratios of Negroes to whites. In proportion to its resources, no state provided more plunder for the carpetbaggers. In six years, $15,000,000 of state funds were squandered with nothing but ruin to show for it—other than the ostentatious new homes which radicals built for themselves in Little Rock. Public offices were brazenly sold, as were pardons for any criminal who could secure the price. Travelers reported that more champagne was consumed in the State House in Little Rock than anywhere else in America. The economic distress which resulted was so great that at one time, so many homes, farms, and businesses were advertised for sale for taxes that to list them in a country paper cost more than $12,000!

In Florida, the official printing bill of the radical government in 1869 exceeded the entire cost of the state government in 1860. A million acres of state lands were sold to a favored few at five cents an acre. In a single year, a half million dollars of taxes collected failed to reach the treasury. In Florida as in her sister states, millions in graft went into the plunderers' pockets, through the railroad enterprises of the radical government.

It was in Georgia that railroad swindles were boldest. Plans which included hundred percent profits for radical promoters were insufficient to satisfy their avarice and money was soon being paid for nonexistent railroad lines. Rufus Bullock, Georgia's carpetbagger governor, ranked with the worst in his exercise of dictatorial powers secured through the establishment of a subservient press at state expense, to which he fed twenty times the prewar cost of official printing, and in his control of the military, which he even called into the Legislature to expel by force the recalcitrant members of that body.

North Carolina, under a combination of scalawags and carpet-baggers, suffered comparable destruction. Virginia, Tennessee, and Texas experienced parlous years but, by dint of compromise, avoided the extremes visited on the other seceded states.

Through the good offices of the radical governments which they fostered in the South, of which but a skeletal description has been given, Congressional radicals and militant reformers largely gained, ostensibly at least, their objectives. They had answered the addicts of the "bloody shirt," the vindictive, and the blindly partisan, by visiting upon the conquered states a punishment that paled that which had been administered by force of arms. They had succeeded in altering the Constitution by adding more restraints on the states through addition of the Fourteenth Amendment, the "privileges and immunities" and "due process" amendment, as well as the one which deprived Confederate leaders of the right to hold office, and the Fifteenth Amendment giving the Negro the ballot. These additions had been effected through the unconstitutional puppet governments they had foisted on the conquered provinces at bayonet point. Even so, for radical leaders in Congress, that was not nearly enough.

The cotton tax was another instrument of vengeance which rested in the hands of Congress. Another was the national public works program. It is sufficient illustration of the extent to which Congress chose to use it simply to state the single fact that, in the reconstruction period, more Federal funds for public works were spent in the cities of New York and Boston, and twice as much in Massachusetts and New York, than in the entire South where the need was immeasurably greater. That Southern harbors should remain blocked by the wreckage of ships indefinitely that they might not compete with the ports in which the financiers of the revolutionists were interested was part of the plan. So also was the mounting tribute required of the South through higher and higher protective tariff rates imposed by the radicals, as required by those who backed them with the dollars which spoke with supreme authority.

Thus, while the planter class was being ground to shreds by the revolution, the capitalist class and business interests were marching to dominance in seven league boots. Along with their tribute-producing tariffs, they had, in the war period, restored the national banking system, against which the people, through Andrew Jackson, had revolted a generation earlier. Equally potent in strengthening the foundations of the revolution in the years to come was the Fourteenth Amendment, not because of its ostensible objectives in which only the racial equality zealots among the radicals were really interested, but rather because of the latent power of the Amendment in guaranteeing business a permanent umbrella under which it might always find protection from an unfriendly administration. It was the clever wording added to the Amendment in the drafting committee, by one who recognized the realities of the revolution, an astute railroad lawyer serving in Congress, which assured its use, in years to come, mainly as the bulwark of corporate immunities and relatively rarely for the protection of oppressed minorities. Corporations were to evoke the Amendment ten times as often as Negroes seeking protection.

The South 13
Becomes
a Conquered Province: 3

Although the radical government of the postwar years was successful in effecting, by extralegal means, great changes in the government of the Republic, the administration which accomplished those changes garnered less fame for its accomplishments in that respect than notoriety for some of its other attributes. Since it fathered, fostered, and supported the disreputable Southern state governments of the reconstruction era it would be surprising if there were not a paternal resemblance between the sire and the spawn it sent South to accomplish its objectives. History has recorded the truth of that resemblance.

The first glaring cracks in the integrity of the national administration appeared during the war, radiating out from the war office, under Secretary of War Simon Cameron, where profiteers and grafters were not only tolerated, but fed and coddled until checked, as scandal after scandal came to light. At the same time, there was a constant stench from the treasury as the unconscionable Jay Cooke was amassing his millions through special favor deals in sales of government bonds.

With the end of hostilities, the rottenness spread without restraint, until it became all but an orgy of corruption.

Almost every aspect of the corruption which prevailed in the carpetbagger governments in the South had its Washington counterpart. With more finesse than Georgia and Louisiana bayonet-point purges of uncooperative members, Congress, no less effectively, closed its doors against members or possible members who might be opposed to the revolution in progress. Contested elections were decided more on the party or political views of contestants than on the merits of the contest. Democrats duly elected from Southern and border states were rejected and sent home, simply because they were Democrats. Even Democrats elected from Northern states were in some cases refused seats on the flimsiest technicalities. The classic example of the propensity of the radical Congress to rid the government of all opposition to its revolutionary program was the impeachment of President Johnson on trumped-up charges and perjured testimony. The railroad swindles, which accompanied every carpetbagger government of the South, were matched in Washington by grants of empires in public lands to the promoters of the big roads, with full recognition that much of the money needed to sustain the radical power and forward the revolution in the interest of bigger, better, less restrained business, must needs come from those whom Congress was so handsomely subsidizing.

More exactly cut to the carpetbagger pattern was the Credit Mobilier scandal. Credit Mobilier was a corporation created by the promoters of the Union Pacific, so set up that all equity in the railroad and public munificence in the way of land grants were drained off into the promoters' hands, while the Union Pacific was left to its bondholders, mortgaged for its full value. To make certain of smooth rolling, blocks of Credit Mobilier stock, costing nothing but certain to produce rich returns, were distributed to a long list of men influential in the capital. The bribe recipients included Vice-President Colfax; Henry Wilson, later to become Vice-President; Secretary of Treasury Boutwell; and many members of both the Senate and House. When the scandal broke, consciences were already too dull to be much disturbed, and bribers and recipients alike were merely white-washed by the administration.

The Union Pacific scandal, together with many others no less savory, and all those which were fomented in the radical legislatures of the South, culminated in a crowning, but well-deserved, insult to American integrity—London bond houses closed their trading facilities to American railroad securities.

In Washington, as in Little Rock, "statesmen" lived high, entertained like millionaires, built ostentatious homes, and generally reveled in their new found riches.

While public offices not infrequently were as much for sale in Washington as in any of the Southern capitals, they were more discreetly disposed of, taking the form generally of continuing kickbacks to those whose power disposed of the office, usually under some protective guise. Akin to the selling of public offices was the common practice, among Congressional radicals, of selling appointments to West Point. Almost without exception, those who were exposed in such operations suffered no consequences. Amid all-pervading corruption, it ill behooved anyone to cast the first stone, or any stone for that matter.

The corruptions mentioned in preceding paragraphs are but token exhibits of the most degraded era in American history. Unfortunately for the South, it was her lot to fall into the hands of those who were wallowing in that degradation. On the other hand, perhaps a substantial measure of corruption flowed from the fact that a helpless and hated South had fortuitously been delivered into the radicals' hands, for it is a truism that those who remove from others the protection of the law inevitably remove themselves from the restraints of law. Be that as it may, the result was the same so far as the South was concerned. She suffered as no section of the nation has suffered before or since.

From the time of their ascendency during the war, the power of Congressional radicals had been built upon a combination of the forces of rampant business interests, of militant reformers, and the emotional appeal of the "bloody shirt." Until the panic of 1873 tarnished the lustre of business interests, their support of the revolution and the radicals, who were its instruments, mounted apace. However, even before 1872, there were signs of weakening ardor among the true reformers. The more perceptive of those ardent and generally sincere folk were gradually sensing the hypocrisy which was being practiced by the radicals. They had observed unrestricted Negro suffrage being forced on the South while most Northern states were still denying the ballot to their even better qualified blacks. They had seen the elimination of racial segregation forced on Southern whites while only a few Northern states, with relatively few Negroes within their bounds, had permitted its elimination at home. They had seen former slaves by the hundreds holding public offices in the South and lording it over helpless whites. They had seen them take seats on the floor of both houses of Congress, all at the command of the North where nobody had ever yet seen a Negro elected or appointed to public office. They had sensed the hypocrisy inherent in the furor over the appearance, at an official reception in Washington, of a mulatto girl in the company of an attaché of a foreign legation—a furor which required an official apology to quiet it.

They saw racial clashes which were occurring in the North being ignored, while similar outbreaks in the South were being widely proclaimed as Southern outrages and used as excuses for more severe treatment of Southern whites. They saw western railroads import Chinese labor and refuse to use Negro labor; but, when Southerners started a movement to employ Chinese during the period when the Negroes were roaming, refusing to work, and living by stealing, they had seen Congress pass fantastic immigration laws closing American citizenship to even cultured Chinese, while leaving it open to tribesmen from Africa. They saw all these things and some began to doubt the sincerity of the radical leaders. Among those were such old Abolitionists as Henry Ward Beecher and Charles Sumner, Horace Greeley, and even the editor of the *Nation*, which had campaigned so militantly against the white South. And there were those disillusioned reformers who went themselves to the South to see radical reform in action. Among those were Harriet Beecher Stowe who was embittered by the radicals' political enslavement of a people not yet fit to hold the ballot and Albert S. Pike, former Union general and old time

Abolitionist who, on visiting South Carolina and observing its suffering under Congressional reconstruction, returned to write *The Prostrate State*, an appeal for more understanding and justice for the South.

So long as the radicals felt no squeamishness in perfidy, they had ample resources to contend with the deflections of the reformers—at least, until they overworked those resources. Throughout most of their reign of degradation, events had amply proved that on the appearance of Democratic gains in the North or on any threat to the power of any of their puppet governments in the South, their power could be bolstered effectively by a sufficient waving of the "bloody shirt." Unreasoning emotions were most satisfactory antidotes to calm reasoning. The same remedy was effective in restoring the ardor of disillusioned reformers. Whenever, among the reformers, there were indications of deflection, new rebel outrages were proclaimed on the floors of Congress and pumped into a largely subservient press, to whip up a storm and clear the air of all cross currents. Over and over again the "bloody shirt" had proved its usefulness. It had thrown back each new sally of Democrats. Time and again it had sent military contingents southward to bolster the threatened power of puppet regimes there. The lack of current incidents to call forth the "bloody shirt" was never a deterrent. Any incident could be twisted into the appearance of an outrage and, if there were no incidents to twist, outrages could easily be invented as, in fact, they were many times.

However, people eventually tire of patterned performances. They lose the power to stir. Also they lose their credibility, especially when they appear too fortuitous or take on the appearance of a red herring. As the country moved toward the mid-seventies, there was growing skepticism abroad and noticeable waning in the power of the "bloody shirt" to revive the old virulent spirit of vengeance toward the South. As the corruption which pervaded the radical administration began to come to light, as exposé followed exposé, many began to doubt the truth of the mouthings of corruptionists on the depravity of Southern whites. There was a growing skepticism of radicals' charges that Negroes were being restored to slavery, that Negroes were being exterminated through mass murder movements, that twenty corpses of murdered Negroes had been found in a North Carolina pond, that torture of Negroes by the Ku Klux Klan was the Southerners' idea of amusement. Too many reporters sent to cover those outrages were sending back stories denying their occurrence. Kindlier voices, even words of sympathy for conquered provinces, were being heard without much rancor. Nevertheless, desperately seeking to bolster their waning power, the radicals continued frantically to wave the "bloody shirt" even into the campaign of 1876, displaying a demagoguery which put to shame the harangues of that brand which, in a few years, would lend a special notoriety to the Southern political scene, as a new generation of Southern political leaders began to fight fire with fire, imitating the methods the radicals had proved so highly effective in garnering unreasoning, emotional support. Listen to Senator Ingersoll summing up the "issues" of the campaign of '76:

Every State that seceded from the Union was a Democratic State. Every ordinance of secession that was drawn was drawn by a Democrat. Every man that endeavored to tear the old flag from the heaven it enriches was a Democrat . . . Every man that tried to destroy the Nation was a Democrat . . . The man that assassinated Abraham Lincoln was a Democrat . . . Every man that raised bloodhounds to pursue human beings was a Democrat. Every man that clutched from shrinking, shuddering, crouching mothers babes from their breasts and sold them into slavery was a Democrat . . . Every man that tried to spread smallpox and yellow fever in the North . . . was a Democrat. Soldiers, every scar you have on your heroic bodies was given you by a Democrat. Every scar, every arm that is missing, every limb that is gone is the souvenir of a Democrat . . . Shall the solid South, a unified South, unified by assassination and murder, a South solidified by the shotgun—shall the solid South with the aid of a divided North control this great and splendid country?

But, by then, the old unfailing effectiveness of such appeals was gone. It was too late for the radicals to hawk their outworn wares. For most Yankees, the war at long last was over. There were now more current issues and greater threats nearer home than any that could be imagined as emanating from the shattered and prostrate South. And these new, more absorbing threats were themselves the products of those who had been wont so long to wave the "bloody shirt." It was they who had steeped the government in corruption. Now, for the first time in almost two decades, emotion and prejudice had failed to deliver an election. The people had turned against Republicans and their studiedly selected inconsequential candidate, Rutherford B. Hayes.

The situation of the radical hierarchy was desperate and called for desperate measures. In the years preceding 1876, most of the Southern states, in one way or another, had escaped their shackles. Only Louisiana, Florida, and South Carolina remained in bondage and even those states had given the Democrat Tilden a majority and voted out their own carpetbagger regimes. But wasn't the election machinery still in the hands of the radicals in those states? Couldn't the official results of the election be changed? They would have to be changed in all three to give Hayes a victory. And to reverse all three election results long after election day would cause an unholy scandal. Nevertheless, undaunted, being long inured to scandal, high-placed radicals hurried South. A few days later came announcements that errors in the election had been corrected and the electoral votes of South Carolina, Florida, and Louisiana would go to Hayes. The election of Hayes was the radicals' last and greatest steal.

To accomplish this the radicals found it necessary to make concessions to the rising tide of independence in the South. Through it, South Carolina, Florida, and Louisiana purchased a full release from their already loosened bonds. Since, in the years preceding, all other former Confederate states had, in one manner or another, already secured their release, 1876 marked the South's final redemption from its long damnation. To complete the picture, we must return to where we left them under their radical governments and trace from there their several struggles to that end.

The South Becomes a Conquered Province: 4

14

ALTHOUGH, in 1870, conditions in much of the South had not yet reached their worst, some rays of light were beginning to pierce the gloom. Most significant were signs of an awakening conscience among people of the North. The *Nation*, which had long been one of the most severe critics of the South, was now saying of Southern whites that:

> they are "ex-rebels," but they are not thieves. They have owned slaves and revolted in defense of slavery; but they are influential, economical and trustworthy in the management of State affairs, and it was of the first importance not only to the Negro but to the whole Union, that, during the transitional or reconstructive period following the war, they should neither be driven into hostility to the local government nor prevented from giving it the benefit of their experience and ability. [But, continued the *Nation*, instead, enormities have been visited upon them] which the Czar would not venture upon Poland, or the British Empire toward the Sautals of the Indian jungle.

Taking heart from such indications of waning militancy, Southern leaders of the old ruling class were beginning to grope their way from the despondency into which defeat and ruin had cast them. Already, by bending to compromise and backing the least objectionable radical candidates in Tennessee, they had virtually regained control in that state. By the same process, in 1870, the power of radical Republicans was broken in Virginia.

By a slower and more painful process but through employing essentially similar tactics, North Carolina was launched on the road to redemption. There, riding the crest of resentment aroused by the brutal and high-handed conduct of a band of marauding militia which the radical governor had loosed on the state ostensibly to suppress activities of the Ku Klux Klan, the Democrats and their allies gained control of the lower house of the Assembly. Typical of the conduct of the radical governor's militia was the arrest, jailing incommunicado, and condemnation to death of a prominent editor, for daring to criticize the radical regime. For his part in those enormities, the governor was impeached and extreme radicalism ended.

It was in Georgia, however, that the conservatives first regained their ascendency without necessity of compromise or settlement for partial control. Bitter dissensions between radical factions there had brought Federal troops back into the halls of government to support the power of disreputable Governor Rufus Bullock. Resulting resentment and confusion and division of Republican votes allowed the Democrats to regain the reins in that state in 1870.

Back in Washington, the news of the loss of Virginia, Tennessee, North Carolina, and Georgia was profoundly shocking to the radical regime. A new determination was born to hold the remaining rebel states for the party, for plunder, and the revolution. The "bloody shirt" was frantically waved. The reins were tightened. Consequently, three more long years were to pass before there was another redemption.

But steadily, among the common folk in the North, a more kindly feeling toward the South was rising and, with each election, it reflected itself in Congress. In 1872, it had become possible to enact an amnesty law which removed the legal disabilities of all those who had supported the Confederacy, except for a few hundred of the more prominent and more notorious. With that enhancement of their voting strength and the psychological boost inherent in passage of the Amnesty Act, new efforts to regain control of their states were being formulated by the whites in those states remaining in radical hands. In the month that followed, Texas, Alabama, and Arkansas secured redemption from their plunderers.

In Arkansas and Texas, the radicals characteristically split into warring factions, permitting united conservatives to wrest control. The elections which ousted radicals in those states and in Alabama at the same time were the first in which the exploits and intimidations of the famous, but later infamous, Ku Klux Klan played any part of consequence, although anti-Klan propaganda had been used years before by North Carolina radicals as an excuse for strong-arm methods to keep themselves in power. From the long standing confusion in Alabama, the conservatives, by united effort, compromise, and retaliatory intimidations, had gradually wrested control from the least forceful of the radical regimes, completing their control in 1874.

Left in radical hands, after that date, were Louisiana, Mississippi, Florida, and South Carolina. Far greater obstacles confronted conservatives in those states. In all of them Negroes outnumbered whites. In all of them a well-organized and herded Negro majority, constantly supported by Federal troops and native militia, had given a firmer foundation to carpetbagger regimes than in their sister states. And in all of them, radical governments were so extremely radical and disreputable that compromise had been ruled out. In them, there were too few radicals moderate enough and decent enough for even the more liberal of the conservatives to be willing to support.

Mississippi was the first of those remaining states to work out her redemption. Again the Achilles heel of the radical regime was its external dissensions, growing out of rivalries for the spoils. In earlier elections, following the state's re-admission to the Union in 1870 under radical control, conservatives had twice tried to regain some voice in their government, by supporting the least objectionable of the factions, but, with the force of Federal authority opposing them, in each instance they had failed. In 1875, they succeeded in electing a majority of their candidates to the legislature. Thus armed, impeachment proceedings were immediately started against the carpetbagger, Governor Adelbert Ames, son-in-law of "Beast" Butler, forcing his resignation, and against the Negro lieutenant-governor, whereby he was removed from office and the state's redemption completed.

In the recovery of Mississippi's government, attention should be given the means by which a minority out of authority found it possible to unseat a majority entrenched in office and with vastly superior funds at its disposal, backed by a military array violently opposed to the challenging minority. The government was a composite of corruption and ignorance. Criminals or illiterates held most public offices. Taxes were skyrocketing, having risen fourteenfold in five years, while property values fell and distress was widespread among those who had property. In a single month, in 1875, a half million acres of Mississippi land and four-fifths of the properties in the town of Greenville went under the tax collector's hammer. In addition to a moving cause, counterrevolutionists were aided by a spreading disillusionment among the blacks. As the effects of flattery and promises with which the radicals had courted them began to fade, the more intelligent began to perceive that they were being used as tools and that the promises by which they had been seduced were empty. Disillusioned, some of the braver joined their former masters while many more simply lost interest in politics and avoided the polls. But most of all, whites relied upon their own superior ardor, intelligence, and experience.

Conservative clubs were organized in every county. They attended opposition political rallies en masse, heckled speakers, and accused them of their crimes before their followers. When the radicals countered those tactics by organizing and arming secret political clubs among Negroes, the whites quickly organized "rifle clubs" in every county, drilling and parading with great display of banners and pageantry. Under strictest orders to avoid violence lest it bring Federal intervention, this show of force nevertheless had great effect on the Negro masses. Briefly, those were the tactics employed by the white minority to accomplish a political miracle and recover control of their state.

Although, as has been noted, there were many factors involved in that miracle, pageantry and intimidation certainly played an important role. In Mississippi, they had taken the form of an open display of prowess, as was also to be the case later in South Carolina. But even in those states, and in all other crucial elections in the South, a more or less important role was played by the secret intimidation tactics of the Ku Klux Klan, although, unquestionably, the extent of its influence has been, since then, enormously exaggerated by romanticists and by propaganda the radicals spread for political purposes.

Founded in Tennessee in 1865 by a group of bored young men, the Klan began as a social club with no thought of political potentialities. Sometime later, those potentialities were discovered by sheer accident, when club members, riding in their ghostly regalia, noted with amusement the terror with which they were regarded by Negroes they chanced to meet. After that discovery, the movement quickly spread over the South. Although its main objective was to discourage, by intimidation, the political activities of radical Negroes, some groups went beyond that and engaged in all manner of violence, holding secret trials and administering punishment as they saw fit. To those excesses were added many others perpetrated by bands of hoodlums in Klan regalia and even some committed by the radicals themselves, designed to discredit the Klan and stimulate action against it.

Before the end of 1868, the Klan's reputation had suffered so severely that many of its prominent members resigned, and General Bedford Forrest, its Grand Wizard, formally disbanded it. But still some Klan-like activities persisted. Even as late as 1871, Klan activities, or violence imputed to the Klan, were the justification for moving Federal troops into a large part of South Carolina and suspending the *habeas corpus* there. However, with each election after 1870, the Klan played a lesser role. Mississippi had proved that more honest, open, and safer tactics could be just as effective and were more respectable and more becoming to gentlemen.

Meanwhile, in Louisiana only the empty framework of democracy remained. Its substance was gone completely. To bolster their strength, radicals had registered thousands of Negroes from adjacent states, importing them to vote on election days. They had also added thousands of fictitious names to facilitate multiple voting. A Northern traveler reported seeing a court adjourn for want of a jury, when only three authentic names could be found on the jury list. Nevertheless, the whites staged a determined effort in the election of legislators in 1874 and were convinced that they had won, but the election was contested. The election board was completely in radical hands. In desperation, Democrats formed the White League, its members openly arming themselves against the militia. Anarchy and chaos followed, bringing yet another intervention by Grant.

The hated Sheridan was returned to the scene, where he soon shocked not only Louisianians but the whole country by a request for authority to declare the whites bandits and to deal with them accordingly. When the legislature finally assembled, the Democrats, catching the radicals napping, succeeded in electing one of their members as speaker. Whereupon, troops with fixed bayonets invaded the House chamber, removed the speaker from his chair, replaced him with a radical and removed enough Democrats from the hall to insure against any further such occurrence. The whole nation was shocked by that travesty on democratic government. A Congressional committee hastened to New Orleans where a compromise was worked out, leaving the carpetbagger government in power with Democrats dominating the legislature. The stalemate thereby created continued until the fateful election of 1876.

To the election that year, conservatives and radicals alike dedicated themselves as if it were a life or death affair, which it virtually was. When ballots were counted, they showed a majority of several thousand for the Democrats. But word arrived from radical powers in Washington of absolute necessity for a Republican majority. The election board had not announced official results. Party bigwigs descended on New Orleans and took over direction of the manipulations. After feverish negotiations behind closed doors, an absurdly inconsistent compromise worked out by a partisan Congressional committee gave Louisiana's electoral votes to the Republican, Hayes. To make their steal more palatable, they made an under the table agreement to remove Federal military support of the radicals and let the Democrats assume power. But in the bargain they saved their darling, corrupt carpetbagger, W. P. Kellogg, for whom they reserved a seat in the United States Senate. Locally, at least, Louisiana was at last redeemed.

The story of Florida's redemption from carpetbagger control is briefly told. A division of radical spoil-seekers into rival camps had persisted throughout the Reconstruction period. The rift between them had become so wide that, in the 1876 election, conservatives were able to march into office through that rift.

Of all struggles to loose the radical hold from state governments that in South Carolina was the most colorful and dramatic. There the old order, symbolically at least, was pitted squarely against the radicals and lines were drawn for a "straight out," uncompromising battle. With General Wade Hampton, personification of the old planter aristocracy, carrying the banner as candidate for governor, the campaign of '76 was launched under the fiery leadership of an aggressive back countryman of the farmer class.

To the whites of the state Hampton was more than a man; he was a symbol and a rallying point. Reared in a sumptuous plantation home and well-educated, famous for physical prowess and for matchless skill as equestrian and sportsman, he was also possessed of a magnetic personality and courtly manners. As a young man, he had dutifully served in the state Senate and built a wide reputation for his success as a large-scale cotton planter and ideal master of hundreds of slaves in both South Carolina and Mississippi. The war had brought him wider fame as a dashing cavalry officer—and tragedy, too, in the loss of one son and another grievously wounded, the destruction of his great plantation home, and the loss of his fortune. Perfectly, he represented the glamour of the prewar South, its valor in war, and its fortitude in adversity.

Drawing heavily on the methods which had been successfully used in Mississippi in the previous year, conservatives made careful plans. Those plans called for intimidation without violence or direct threats of violence. They called for confronting and discrediting radical leaders in the presence of their constituents and much showmanship, all organized with military efficiency.

Throughout the scorching summer of '76, almost every white man of voting age, at enormous cost in the neglect of his farm and business, was dedicating himself to the all out struggle. Along dusty Carolina roads bands of them in flaming red shirts were riding—riding to every town, village, and crossroad to whip up enthusiasm for the cause. They were riding to every Democratic rally within reach, to make the countryside ring with cheers and rebel yells and plant an impression in the enemy mind that their numbers were unbeatable. With telling effectiveness, they were riding to every Republican gathering to heckle speakers and confront them with the crimes and corruption of their party, and to demand a division of time for their own speakers. Most of the radicals were cowed by an encircling mass of red shirts and meekly accepted their verbal lashings, thereby losing face before their simple followers.

It soon became apparent to the radicals that their only hope lay in checking the aggressive tactics of Red Shirts and that the only possible way of checking them was through Federal bayonets and martial law. To secure military intervention they needed at least some token violence upon which outrage propaganda might be hung, but the Red Shirts were dedicated to the avoidance of all efforts to incite them to use the arms they carried. However, before the summer was over, luck played into the hands of the radicals in the form of two incidents. The first was the Ellenton riots, growing out of an attempt by officers to arrest a Negro for an attack on a white farmer's wife and child. When the officers were fired upon a posse of neighborhood whites joined in the manhunt. Soon there was plenty of shooting and several were killed. Despite the fact that the incident had nothing to do with politics and the Red Shirts were not involved, Grant promptly branded the native whites as lawless bands "who ride up and down by day and night in arms, murdering . . . peaceable citizens." A few days later, a group of unarmed whites were attacked by a band of armed Negroes. Casualties of the ensuing fight were five whites and one Negro. Nevertheless, in an appeal to Grant for martial law the radicals called it a Negro massacre and they got the martial law they sought.

Even so, when election day came and votes were counted, Hampton was the winner by a thousand-vote margin and the Democrats had won a majority in the House. These results were immediately challenged by the radicals, who charged fraud in some precincts, and the dispute was referred to the radical-dominated Board of Canvassers, who threw out the votes of two counties which had returned large Democratic majorities. Democrats appealed to the Supreme Court, composed of two carpetbaggers, one white and one Negro, and a scalawag. Surprisingly, the Court reversed the action of the Board of Canvassers, leaving the radicals with no appeal, except beyond the law, to the President and his troops.

On receiving their appeal, Grant again backed his old friends by ordering troops to seize the State House and hold it against the Hampton party. Whereupon Hampton and the Democratic majority of the House withdrew and proceeded to organize a new government. For the next few months, the state was in the bewildering position of having two governors and two competing lower houses. The functions of government were paralyzed.

That was the state of affairs when negotiators, seeking the state's electoral votes for Hayes, arrived on the scene. Spokesmen for Hampton promised Hayes the electoral votes he needed for his election; spokesmen for Hayes promised the removal of Federal troops from the state. Accordingly, one of the first acts of the new President when he took office in the spring was the removal of Federal troops from the State House. Without bayonets to back them, the radicals knew full well that their long orgy was done and the government was surrendered to men who had ridden so tirelessly toward that hour in history.

Only then, after almost two decades of blood, sweat, and tears, were all the eleven former Confederate states back in the Union they had sought to leave. Meanwhile, the government to which they were returning had become something very different from that which they had left. It was now something alien to the Southern *ethos*, a creation with which they were out of step. The government they had left had been designed in the interest of a rural society of farmers and small landowners. That to which they returned had been redesigned by the revolution which had precipitated their withdrawal. It had been redesigned in the interests of commerce, industry, and an urban society. Freed, in their absence, from the deterring influence of the South, protective tariffs had been multiplied, a national banking system controlled by the financial interests of the East had been established, and the government had arrogated to itself, through a liberal construction of the Constitution, undreamed of regulatory powers. In the Fourteenth Amendment a bill of rights for financial interests had been added to the Constitution.

Beyond those changes were others of even greater portent to returning states. The Jeffersonian republic which they had left had been studiously designed by individualists, who created it to permit and preserve a maximum of diversity between the states which composed the Union. Neither the government which had supplanted it nor the interests it was designed to enhance could function smoothly in the face of the wide diversity and variety of conditions contemplated by its predecessor. A high degree of uniformity had become essential; business functions best under such conditions.

To a large degree it was that compelling force toward uniformity which, in the early years of mid-century revolution, had driven the North to adopt the aggressive attitude toward the conservative South which precipitated the war between the sections. It was that compelling force toward uniformity, amplified to meet the day, which had impelled Congress to launch its ruthless effort to remake the South, to require it to fit into the pattern of a changed society and a changed government. But despite the economic and political helplessness of the conquered South, when an attempt was made to fit it into its Procrustean bed, the Negro and the Southern bent of mind foiled those efforts to a large degree. The war, and the counterforce which the efforts of Congress bred, enhanced and solidified the Southern state of mind even as the Negro was proving his dependence on that state of mind and his inadequacy to fit the place the radicals had reserved for him. When the North finally tired of its efforts, the South was still the South—a region apart and little changed in its basic *ethos.*

However, although the South's prevailing state of mind emerged from the ordeal of war and Reconstruction little changed, great changes had been wrought, especially in relation to the North and the changed nation the South was rejoining. Poverty, austere and all-pervading, had become the section's hallmark. The problem of the Negro, released from restraints of slavery and carrying his Reconstruction burden of enhanced hate, had become vastly greater, coloring every facet of Southern society, economics, and politics. Probably the most significant change which had been visited upon the South was its dethronement from its former exalted place in the nation and in the nation's leadership. Now by circumstances bound to an alien economy and an alien government with which they were out of step and out of sympathy, Southern voices would no longer be heard as the voices of the nation's leaders. The Jeffersonian republic had been their government and they had led it brilliantly. Now, under an alien government in an alien economy, theirs would be but the voices of protest, protesting the leadership that insisted on carrying them with the nation in new directions toward which they were ever reluctant to follow.

The South

Becomes

a Conquered Province: 5

15

TANGIBLE DESTRUCTION suffered by the South in the war was stupendous. Other economic distresses it brought were perhaps equally great. But the plundering, the years of lost production, the years of stymied progress, and the general chaos of Reconstruction probably exceeded all losses of the war years. However, it was the intangible destruction wrought by the period, ironically called Reconstruction, which rendered it immeasurably more damaging to the South than the war itself. It was the lasting damage to the mind, spirit, and culture of the South that made it so devastating. Reconstruction broke the South's spirit, planted hampering prejudices and frustrating hates, and paralyzed its will to move forward with the nation and the world.

Naturally, hate accorded the Yankee enemy by Southerners mounted throughout the war. But among many, a good measure of respect for the Yankee had persisted. Reconstruction killed every vestige of that respect. Identifying the Yankees generally with their radical representatives in Congress, it was impossible for anyone, and especially Southerners accustomed to affairs of honor between friends or respected foes, to maintain any respect for a people apparently devoid of magnanimity toward a vanquished foe and studiedly determined to perpetrate vengeance on a defeated enemy. The depths of that disgrace in Southerners' eyes was increased by the firm conviction, which proved to be largely true, that that vengeance was cold-blooded, perpetrated for political and economic profit. Also, the crass hypocrisy of the radicals, in forcing the South to accept its freedmen as full citizens, while denying their own better-qualified Negroes the same status, and enforcing Negro officeholders upon the South, while denying their own Negroes all public offices, was generally associated with Northerners and was enormously resented. Nothing is more devastating to respect than hypocrisy.

Finally, although Southerners had long regarded Yankees as a money-mad race, they had not thought of them as venal rascals. Reconstruction, however, with its display of corruption among their representatives in Washington and doings of their carpetbagger representatives in every Southern capital, went a long way toward convincing most Southerners that Yankeedom was a place without honor or integrity where money was involved. When Southerners, already driven by an indiscriminate hate, noted all those things, there were few among them of sufficiently discriminating judgment not to regard them as the usual attributes of any Yankee.

Deep-seated hates and suspicions are more damaging to their harborers than to their objects. For the South, its hatred, contempt, and suspicion of everything tainted with Northern associations became, to a degree, literally a consuming passion. Whatever came out of the North, whether it was universal free education, woman's suffrage, commercial innovations, or mass production in manufacturing, had to make its way in the South against a strong current of prejudice. Since the doors of America mostly opened out from the commercial East, there were even few foreign innovations which failed to pick up a Northern taint on their passage to the South from their portals of entry. That stiff-necked resistance to all "Northernizing" influences greatly enhanced the section's innate conservatism and very materially slowed its progress. This was no briefly passing influence. It is still a vital, though diminishing, influence in the thinking of most Southerners to this day.

When native whites determined to expel radical usurpers from their states, they found it necessary, in some instances, and expedient, in most instances, to fight fire with fire. The radicals' herding of their pawns, intimidations, bribes, and election frauds were fought by corresponding counter tactics by conservatives. That descent from the high political standards that had prevailed in the South until then was pregnant with lasting consequences. Throughout the long history of planter-dominated bodies politic of the South, its public offices, even down to such minor posts as justices of peace and county commissioners, had been fed largely from the planter class, the most intelligent and best educated of the region. Among the members of that class, there had been a long standing sense of obligation to public service, as a duty incidental to their status rather than as a means to personal power, profit, or ambition. Until destroyed by Federal force, this tradition had given the South political institutions of a quality seldom found elsewhere. When the counterattack was launched against the radicals, many of the old governing class found themselves unable to resort to fighting fire with fire. Others, of lesser scruples and frequently of lesser qualities, took their places in authority. Never again would Southerners approach public office with the sense of high responsibility, nor politics with the freedom from demagoguery, which their planter forebears had exhibited during the two centuries of their ascendancy.

The blatant and flamboyant demagoguery which was to color and disgrace the Southern political scene in decades to follow was also no less a product of Congressional Reconstruction than the burning of Atlanta and Columbia was a result of the war. When radicals waved the "bloody shirt" for political purposes, Southerners replied in kind. If extravagant demagoguery could deliver to radicals the solid support of ignorant blacks, it could, and very soon would, deliver to conservatives the solid support of ignorant masses of whites. Thus a lesson was taught which was not soon forgotten and it was one that would not lose its effectiveness so long as ignorance and prejudice, black or white, was prevalent.

When the North forced Black Reconstruction on the South, it forced the racial issue on the South, hammered it to white heat, utterly failed to solve it, succeeding only in making it vastly more imponderable, then dumped it in the lap of the South and returned its attention to the enjoyment of Northern prosperity.

When the problem was turned back to Southern whites, the race issue had been so crudely forced that there was no longer any hope that recent freedmen might assume the position in society that had been enjoyed by freedmen in the old South. The problem was turned back to Southern whites only after the radicals had staged a disastrous demonstration of what might be expected if Negroes were given the right to participate in government. Of the Yankee's noble experiment in forcing the racial issue, only that disastrous object lesson remained to live on and on in Southern memories and thereby render the problem of full and freely given civil rights for Negroes vastly more difficult of solution even to this day. It was hopeless then to convince Southern whites that perhaps all, and certainly most, of the qualities that had made the Negro so untrustworthy and incompetent in government had nothing to do with his being a Negro but were rather the result of lack of education, experience, cultural background, and identity with democratic traditions. Nor did it help materially that there were whites, native scalawags as well as Yankee carpetbaggers, who were equally disgraceful as public officials. Most Southern whites had long been accustomed to think of Negroes as beings of a basically inferior race. The radicals had set out to demonstrate that this attitude was wrong and had ended by seeming to prove it right. It was as simple as that. And even today, with the educational and cultural picture greatly changed for the better, many Southerners consider all arguments for Negro participation in government as sufficiently answered by a reminder of life and times under Black Reconstruction.

When the North assumed responsibility for forcing the racial issue on the South and for its experiment in governing the South through the Negro, she, at the time, assumed responsibility for the disastrous failure of her experiment and for making the South's solution of her racial problems immeasurably more difficult. By any standard, morally the North still bears that responsibility as much as white Southerners today bear responsibility for the results of slavery.

It is a rankling grievance among Southerners, especially among those who know a little history, that the North persists in ignoring that responsibility.

Of all those who were grievously wronged by the Black Reconstruction program which was forced on the South by radical revolutionaries, the Negro himself suffered the greatest wrong. It magnified the race issue and firmly saddled it on the South in a hard, crystallized form. Southerners of all opinions were driven together into a solid block of anti-Negro sentiment. Haunting fears of horrors of Negro rule, illustrated by Santo Domingo, Haiti, and the contemporary chaos in Jamaica, became vastly more real after concrete examples of it had been witnessed on American soil. When Black Reconstruction was overthrown, the Negro was confronted by a solid determination among the whites that thereafter he must be kept out of the machinery of government. Events had silenced the voices of many Southerners who, at the close of the war, had visualized the Negro's gradual admission into full participation in government.

In yet another respect, Black Reconstruction had dealt a cruel blow to the Negro. Gone now was much of the old warm affection that had generally prevailed between blacks and their white masters and acquaintances. Now, shorn of that warm affection, the Negro was abandoned, left on the doorstep of the Southern white where his future state would turn heavily on the state of a heart that had been hardened.

Finally, the Negro had been cruelly dealt with through Black Reconstruction by the frauds which had been perpetrated upon him. Under the guise of full freedom he had, for a decade, suffered the substitution of political slavery, substitution of unscrupulous, self-seeking political masters for the generally more kindly masters of an earlier day. His new masters had given him nothing of value. They had used him only for their own advantage. In place of food, land, and a responsible place in society which he wanted, they had given him the ballot which he could neither eat nor wear and did not want. They had tempted him and led him by promises of "forty acres and a mule" which they had no intention of really giving him. No one seriously proposed that lands be purchased from ruined planters and be given or even sold to the freedmen to help them on their way. Instead, blacks were bribed by mere promises of confiscation and distribution, those promises being only the empty talk of demagogues, never really seriously considered.

Although Negroes were the most cruelly dealt with by Reconstruction, it was the poor whites who suffered most from it. Although prior to the war and Reconstruction, as the dregs of an aristocratic society, the poor whites had not enjoyed much in the way of worldly goods, they had enjoyed an ego-warming claim to superiority of race and a certain freedom of motion which the Negro could not claim. Reconstruction attacked and threatened their single claim to superiority and, at the same time, it gave the Negro an even greater freedom of motion, for, although the poor whites continued to suffer most of the economic handicaps of the Negro, they had no Freedmen's Bureau or missionary groups active in their behalf. Beyond that, they suffered, simply because they were white, most of the acts of vengeance meted out by the radicals indiscriminately against all whites—disfranchisement, insults, and a one-sided justice. Consequently, as their condition deteriorated, they became the very core of resistance and resentment of Northern reforms. As their idleness and discouragement mounted, so did their drunkenness and brawling. They, like the planters, cast their eyes backward to earlier, better days and away from a future too discouraging to contemplate.

Direct competition with freedmen further lowered their economic standards, down to that of the freedman himself. And that competition continually fed the poor whites' hatred for the blacks. A heritage was created for their posterity which continues to come to light in the mid-twentieth century, in Klan memberships, race baitings, and the Little Rock mobs.

In 1877, an astute New England editor editorialized:

> . . . if we keep on treating Southerners as our political inferiors, scoffing at them as whipped and unrepentant rebels who richly deserve all the punishment that fate has meted out, and calling

them hypocrites whenever they profess any wish for the future glory and prosperity of the reunited nation—if we do this much longer, there is a dismal probability that we shall make of "the South" a "main question" that will vex American politics through all coming time.

What the editor did not realize when he penned those words of wisdom was that what he warned of was then already a *fait accompli*, that the wind had been sown and, inexorably, as the future unfolded, the whirlwind would have to be reaped.

More specifically, that editor did not realize the extent of the great bonding influence of the all-pervading hate and suspicion in the South for Yankees and Yankee ways, nor the bonding force of being on the defensive. He did not realize that already, through war's destruction and Reconstruction's strangulation, the South had been reduced to a stagnant economic frontier, dependent almost wholly on agriculture, an almost incurably conservative environment. He did not realize that already the race issue had been pushed to such a point that the whites of all classes were welded together into a unit, in the face of that single ever-present issue. Nor did he realize that the ordeal of Reconstruction had already persisted so long, that old enmities between Whigs and Democrats had been forgotten in the face of its enormities, and the politically solid South had been created.

The North had sought to change the South through force of arms and had failed. It had then sought to change it by strait-jacketing it with Reconstruction and had failed again. It had succeeded only in ruining it and greatly delaying the changing process it had sought to force on the region. It remained for the South itself, through the slow processes of time, to change itself and gradually rejoin the changed nation it had been forced to leave.

The South   16
Becomes
a State of Mind

A MANNER OF SPEAKING, an accent, a quality of voice, common in a large measure to all Southerners regardless of race, creed, or color are the most widely possessed and most obvious characteristics of Southerners. Less superficial and of vastly greater import are other characteristics of white Southerners, which, for a long and significant period in the evolution of the South, were almost as universal as the special quality of Southern speech. Chief among those are two interrelated Southern propensities: a fierce sectional pride, so deeply ingrained that it persists irrespective of contemporary conditions; and an unreasoning touchiness, a sensitivity to criticism regardless of its justification. These Southern bents of mind still bulk large in the South's difficulties in meeting challenges of the twentieth century, but there was a time when they bid fair to turn the South indefinitely into a state of social, economic, and intellectual stagnation.

During the seventy-two ante-bellum years between the inauguration of Washington and that of Lincoln, Southern men had filled the presidency for almost fifty. Southern chief justices had presided over

the Supreme Court for all but twelve years and almost two-thirds of
the justices had been selected from the South. Almost half of all the
members of the several cabinets, more than half of the speakers of the
House of Representatives, and more than half of the diplomats representing the nation in capitals of the major powers had been Southerners.

In these facts and in the part Southerners had played in establishing the nation, Southerners took great and justifiable pride. Ignoring
its inequitable distribution, they took great pride, too, in the wealth
they had garnered from Southern soil, as shown by the relatively high
per capita wealth of Southern states. In 1860, Louisiana and South
Carolina were second and third, respectively, while Mississippi was
fifth among states in per capita wealth. In spite of illiteracy and poverty of learning among the masses, there was pride, too, in the South's
relatively high proportion of the well-educated and cultured. And
despite their failure to achieve democracy in the modern sense, despite frank avowal of a political aristocracy, Southerners had conducted their governmental affairs, in the ante-bellum era, on a higher
plane and with more integrity than had (or has since been) observed
on the American scene. Upon these things the pride of Southerners
had long been well-fed—so well-fed, in fact, that "proud" became the
most common adjective used to describe not only the Southern
planter and statesman but also the ordinary Confederate soldier and
small time yeoman farmer.

In pride-searing contrast were stark realities of the post-bellum
South. Gone now was political power and glory. In the whole half-
century following Lincoln's inauguration, only he, who had long before moved from the South, and Johnson, who had turned his back
on his section in its greatest crisis, had carried a Southern accent to
the White House, and the latter had suffered impeachment because
of his sympathy for his native section and its basic tenets of government. No other Southerners had even been nominated or seriously
considered as possible nominees of either of the major parties, either
for president or vice-president. Only a tenth of the cabinet officers,
less than a fourth of the justices of the Supreme Court, a sixth of the
speakers of the House of Representatives, and a tenth of the diplo-

matic representatives to major powers had been drawn from the South.

Gone also were the pomp and pride of wealth that had marked the South's ante-bellum governing class. The great majority of formerly great planters had lost their plantations in those years. Their ladies had retired from their parlors to their kitchens. Planters themselves were commonly found operating country stores, holding minor political positions, or fighting an uphill battle against poverty through greatly curtailed farming operations, while many a famed Confederate general was gaining his livelihood as a ticket agent for a railroad or as justice of the peace at a crossroad.

By 1880, Louisiana had slid from second in per capita wealth, South Carolina from third, and Mississippi from fifth to near the bottom in the Union. The average per capita wealth of the South, $376, was about a third that of the remainder of the country, and no Southern state was nearly so wealthy as the poorest non-Southern state. Despite the section's bountiful resources, grim poverty was on every hand.

A no less humiliating slide had occurred in culture and education. The exigencies of war and poverty of the postwar years had effectively foreclosed a whole generation, even scions of the prewar privileged class, from all but the most rudimentary sort of education. Even as late as 1880, only a little more than half the population of the South over ten years of age could read and write. In some states, considerably more than half were illiterate. The war had closed many of the South's under supply of schools and colleges. Although Black Reconstruction had served greatly to reduce Negro illiteracy through the many schools that were established for freedmen, there was no comparable activity for alleviation of the almost as appalling illiteracy among poor whites. Reconstruction had proved even more damaging than the war to the section's colleges and academies.

No one has ever seriously questioned the dedication and integrity of men of the ante-bellum South in the field of public service. Among them, demagoguery and depravity were all but unknown. The aristocratic code of the dominant class had effectively seen to that. That pride-inspiring historical tradition, counterpoised against the trickery, frauds, and demagoguery which appeared on every hand in the post-bellum political scene, constituted the most pride-dispelling contrast of all. However much such noxious expedients were justified by arguments that one must fight fire with fire or that survival depended on such methods and ends justified the means, they still inspired pride in few and shame in many hearts.

To have one's store of pride is a basic human need; whether it be of one's origin, capacity for corn liquor, collard patch, or achievements of worth. When white Southerners in post-Reconstruction years looked about them, they saw little in which they could take pride; a region looked down upon by its dominant fellow countrymen, bleak poverty and ignorance on every hand, demagoguery and power politics in the halls of government, and an all-pervading discouragement on every hand, a discouragement which cast a gray gloom over any outlook for the future. But, in the past, the sky was yet still bright with a shining glory. Although it was but afterglow of the glorious sunset of a magnificent day which was done, it was still something with which Southerners could identify themselves to relieve the terrible gloom of their contemporary lot.

Southerners soon tended to enshrine the past—the only bright element in the whole post-bellum firmament—to magnify its magnificence and render it devotion and fealty with a solidarity that had never been accorded the social, economic, and political institutions of the old South even at the height of its so-called glory. Placing the entire blame for their downfall on a ruthless and jealous North, scions of the old aristocracy fed their pride on the former glory and glamour of their origins, ignoring the short duration of their aristocratic heritage. Lesser folk, frequently with greater ardor, embraced the mode and busied themselves with establishing genealogical ties with the old ruling class, which could usually be done by virtue of the simple mathematical progression by which the numbers of anyone's ancestors are multiplied, seizing upon those ancestors and connections which were fruitful for pride and ignoring blood derived from the inconsequential multitude. Even poor whites joined the ersatz feast and nibbled at the heavenly cheese of a glorious past, as they harked back to a day when they were not degraded by direct competition with the blacks, to a day when they could at least regard their white skins with heart-warming pride as their badge of superiority over the masses of enslaved blacks.

That tendency of Southerners to look back to glory was not something suddenly born. It had come into being before the war, during those years of frustration when Southern prosperity began to lag markedly behind that of the North, when control of the nation's destiny was wrested from Southern hands, and when Southern institutions were under severe attack from outside. Even then, there were many who dwelt on the region's past glories, and the reaction had come in a strong tendency to ignore contemporary challenges and buttress against them by freezing society ever more rigidly into its pristine mold. The bitter internal dissensions which characterized the Confederacy and loss of control by the old aristocracy augmented the ranks of those who found the past their most comforting refuge. Defeat in the great battle itself, despite its gallant defense, the wreckage it left in its wake, and destruction of the section's whole social fabric impelled many more to seek solace and pride in retrospect. Although for most, the discouragements were already too great and the path ahead too strewn with obstacles to be undertaken, there were still some resilient enough to undertake it with good heart. But even from the ranks of those of stronger fiber, many were turned back to the well-occupied refuge of their weaker brethren by the frustrations and disappointments of the Reconstruction years.

Once the glorified and purified conceptions of the old South as a golden age without shadows and the Confederacy as all dash, gallantry, and sacrifice were embraced, they were enshrined in Southerners' hearts. In effect, Southerners had made a religion of the old South and the Confederacy, replete with unchallengeable tenets, ritual, hallowed saints, and sacred shrines. Any criticism, even any factual derogation of those enshrined concepts came to be regarded as blasphemy. Even such gentle and constructive critics as Walter Hines Page, despite his obvious lifelong devotion to his native section, were widely regarded as blasphemers and apostates and all but driven from the fold. Resulting blind sectional loyalty became something the like of which elsewhere has never been displayed on American soil.

If the South had had its way and become a separate nation, that sectional fervor would have been described as fierce patriotism and widely commended. Instead, it has been marked as blind sectionalism, provincialism of the narrowest sort. Beyond the seas, history has afforded similar examples of the enshrinement of a glorious past. It has marked, unhappily, oft conquered and persecuted Poland. Nearer home, and with closer historical parallels, it has marked the Scots and their poor backward land which supplied the South with so much of its tortured blood for yet more torture in a sunnier clime. As with the American South, Scottish history harks back to a glamorous past, conquest after a valiant defense against insuperable odds, long years of poverty and isolation from currents which were sweeping England forward, persistent sectional prejudices leaving scars which mark it today; scars which take the form of a flamboyant tendency to enshrine its past, a tendency to cling to its old customs and ways, and a stubborn resistance to change.

It is unusual for civil struggles to evoke in the vanquished the attributes which the American civil struggle gave to the South. But western history does not afford many examples of civil strife with a mutual geographical exclusiveness between the contenders as in the United States. Had the contestants of the 1860's been spread throughout the country, schisms would have quickly healed once the conflict was over. The ultimate cause of differences that yet mark the South hark back to the geography that made it different, that invited a peculiar social system, that segregated the vanquished and insulated them from all internal healing influences.

Once the past was enshrined to the exclusion of the future, old leaders of prewar and Confederate days were called forth to lead again. But they, too, being of the past-anointed, were generally unable to lead forward. They, like their constituents, preferred retrograde movements designed simply to hold as much as possible of the enshrined past. They made their fiery addresses, waved the "bloody shirt," and paeanized the lost cause at unveilings of stereotyped Confederate monuments which soon graced every courthouse square. Every year, at thousands of cemeteries and hundreds of battlefields, when Confederate Memorial Day or Decoration Day rolled around, they were the featured speakers. With emotion-charged oratory, they fanned flames that lighted the past with a high romantic glow. Meanwhile, all but ignored, swift currents of the nineteenth-century Western world flowed past and the South slowly revolved in its self-contained eddy.

For a long time, the great bulk of the South, its leadership and the vast majority of its people, crouched defensively with eyes looking backward, its politics dedicated to little else but the retention of such vestiges of the past as could be fitted into the new framework which the revolution had decreed. The economy languished, education dried on the vine, universities closed their eyes and ears and often even their doors, and all stimuli toward anything forward looking passed unheeded.

This paralyzing state of mind had gradually taken hold of a whole people through a succession of accretions of the ranks of those overwhelmed by disaster and discouragement. It was to wane even more slowly, for the post-bellum nineteenth century supplied the region with no inspiring encouragements or emotion-gripping distractions.

It remained for earth-shaking events of the twentieth century to effect any great erosion of that state of mind, a process yet but partly done. In the South, voices of the past continue to speak with an authority outsiders find difficult to understand.

The South Becomes the New South: 1

17

S EVERAL YEARS after the last of the Southern states had been wrested from carpetbagger domination, Whitelaw Reid, editor of the New York *Tribune*, who, as a reporter, had observed the South immediately after the war as a region ready to set out in new directions, if given the proper direction by her conquerors, now took another look at the region. "Fifteen years have gone over the South," he now wrote, "and she still sits crushed, wretched, busy displaying and bemoaning her wounds."

She continued to bemoan her wounds, for they remained gaping and unhealed. The heart of Charleston, destroyed in the war, was still a mass of rubble. There, and in most Southern ports, docks had fallen into decay as trade languished. Travelers reported similar signs of grim poverty, dilapidation, and stagnation in small towns of the region. Roads and railroads alike were barely passable. The "big houses" of the plantations, if still standing, were often deserted and falling into ruin. There was but a semblance of a public school system, and conditions were even worse in higher education. Some colleges which had closed during the years of tribulation had not reopened, while others were barely hanging on to life. Walter Hines Page painted a graphic picture of some of those of which he had first-hand knowledge at that time. He tells of Trinity, now Duke University, with an annual gross income of $3,000, seeking to maintain and educate a student body of one hundred and twenty. Its president divided his time between teaching, administering his institution, plowing his fields, serving as smithy in the local blacksmith shop, and operating a saw mill—all that the college might survive those austere years.

Exhausted by unremitting tensions of prewar years, the strain of its great war effort, its struggle to regain control of its local governments, and paralyzed by political necessities of its altered society and its poverty, the South was subject to a numbing torpor. Few indulged in hopes beyond the morrow and fewer still dared to act on those hopes. For the first time in its long history, there was a shortage of superior leadership in the section. Too many who might have been its leaders at this time had been war casualties. The education and training of most of those who had survived had been foreclosed by the war and its aftermath. The leaders who were now coming to the forefront were a diverse lot stemming from backgrounds of wide disparity. Their aims and objects reflected their diversity and the dreams they espoused for the salvation of their people were equally varied. Regardless of the direction of their aim, those who were able to raise themselves above the pervading apathy of exhaustion and to espouse with vitality a hopeful direction perforce became new leaders. By the early 1880's, these men of hope were energetically bending their efforts to start the stalled economic, political, and social wheels rolling again, each in the direction where he thought he saw the semblance of a dawn of a better day.

The three decades of activity in new directions, of conflict and contrast, of pride and disgrace, which were ushered in by those espousers of hope came to be known as the era of the new South, a misleading title connoting an unwarranted assumption of entity and an exaggerated degree of change. Actually, the only common denominator inherent in that era of contrast was the spirit of hope. And that hopefulness was about the only thing new in the new South.

At the time of the Hayes deal, men in authority in most of the former Confederate states had been drawn from the old ruling class. Most of them were conservative, former Whigs or men of Whiggish sentiments rendered even more conservative by the reaction against radicalism, to whom the leveling democratic principles of Jefferson and Jackson were abhorrent, although they never ceased to give lip service to the former, even as Southern conservatives have been wont to do ever since with little comprehension of the directions in which Jeffersonian principles, actually applied, would lead them. Fundamentally, the political allegiances of these men, who have been unjustly dubbed "Bourbons" in support of the assumption that they could learn nothing new, were far more agreeable to the conservative, business-dominated Republicanism of Hayes than to the universal democracy principles of the urban-dominated Democratic party into which they had been compelled by circumstance. It had been that conflict of principles that had made possible the delivery of requisite Republican electoral votes for Hayes. Being men of property, albeit now without plenty, it is understandable that their vision of the South's salvation lay in an alliance with dominant business interests of the North, notwithstanding the necessity of crossing party lines to effect it. The interests, which had financed and directed the revolution which had torn the country asunder, were now quite thoroughly entrenched, regardless of party ascendancy. No longer essential to their purposes was the political support of the social reform elements of their party or the overworked diversions of a chaotic South. Even most of the reformers themselves had wearied of frustrated efforts to remake the social fabric of the stubborn section. At the same time, quite suddenly, vast undeveloped resources of the South had become the brightest prospect on the horizon of Northern business interests.

The Bourbons were equally aware of the potential wealth inherent in unexploited forests and the rich mineral deposits of their domain, as well as in the rehabilitation and expansion of its banking, communication, and transportation facilities. Confronted with a paucity of industrial and technical skill among their people and an even greater lack of capital available for investment on the one hand, and on the other, a possible alliance with Northern political and business interests amply supplied with capital avidly seeking lucrative investments and ready and willing to abandon social reform and political meddling in Southern affairs in return for a more hospitable industrial climate in the region, Southern leaders believed they saw opportunities to place their stagnant economy on the high road to a prosperity comparable to that which had made the North rich and powerful. Apparently, here were all the essential ingredients which, if brought together, could bring economic and possibly even political salvation. With little hesitation, they seized upon every opportunity to bring those ingredients together without foreseeing either the extent to which the South's resources would be exploited or the colonial type of Southern economy which would flow from their expedient.

When Bourbons and other redeemers of the South welded their alliance with money interests of the North, the second important internally conflicting marriage of interests in the postwar South had been consummated. The first of these historically pregnant mésalliances had been the marriage, in outward form, between white Jacksonian Democrats and conservative aristocrats under the common roof of the Democratic party. This second incongruous mésalliance found the erstwhile Southern dominant class in working wedlock with the very class which had directed the revolution that had destroyed the Southern way of life. It was with the forces of business dominance that had been their nemesis that they now joined hands to seek resuscitation of the Southern economy.

Carpetbagger regimes had already taken the first steps toward wedding Northern capital to Southern opportunities. However, except for the delivery of control of most of the South's railroads into Northern hands through their machinations with railroad bonds and subsidies and the enactment of laws granting liberal tax concessions to new industries, little had been actually accomplished. Capital was repelled by chaotic conditions which prevailed and the notorious unreliability of governments of the Reconstruction era. Now with relatively stable governments reestablished under the control of conservative men of tried integrity, the industrial climate had become hospitable enough for even the most wary capital; and Chauncey Depew, altering the advice of an earlier spokesman of business interests, was proclaiming his advice to the fortune seekers of the North;

"Go South, young man," for "the South is the Bonanza of the future. We have developed all the great and sudden opportunities for wealth —or most of them—in the Northwestern States and on the Pacific Slope," while in the South there are "vast forests untouched, with enormous veins of coal and iron" awaiting exploitation.

Before observing results of the open armed reception in the South of those who heeded such advice, we should, for a moment, take a look at another facet of the agricultural South's sudden alteration in its aspirations, permitting it now to welcome a way of life it had traditionally despised. This part of the story involved neither Yankees nor Yankee capital. It was built around the inspiration of a small group of able Southerners, few of whom were of the planter-aristocracy. Their prophet was William Gregg, a successful Charleston jeweler, who, more than a decade before secession, was campaigning, by both precept and example, for the salvation of the South from its stultifying cash crop economy through increased industrialization. To prove the practicality of his arguments, he built the South's first large-scale cotton mill in central South Carolina. When success crowned his venture, using his mill as an object lesson, he launched an aggressive campaign to convince the South that its future lay not with Calhoun's abjuration of manufactures, nor in the aristocrats' disdain of all pursuits save the professions and agriculture, but rather in a more balanced economy including a strong system of manufacturing enterprises. Another motive which drove him to seek factories was the desperate condition of poor whites, whose salvation he envisioned flowing from mill wages. However, few Southern leaders heeded Gregg's advice, hardened as they then were into a defensive loyalty to their traditional way of life which was then under mounting attack from other quarters. Discouraged, he concluded that "the hand of enterprise is not among us."

Years rolled on and the South continued to eschew its industrial opportunities. Even the war and the frantic rush to makeshift industry which it stimulated, and the defeat, so clearly attributable to the South's industrial deficiencies, failed to convert the section's leadership to Gregg's sound theses. Postwar leaders in the movement for internal industrial development were men less trammeled by the traditions of the past. They were mostly men of middle-class origins and almost all of them were editors.

If Gregg was the prophet of the new South, his Paul was Henry Grady, dynamic editor of the Atlanta *Constitution*, through the columns of which he eloquently proclaimed the new gospel. It was he, more than any other, who attracted nationwide attention to the South's changing attitude toward industry and spread abroad the term "new South" to emphasize the change.

No less imbued with the spirit, and only a little less articulate in proclaiming it, were Henry Watterson of the Louisville *Courier-Journal*, English-born and educated Francis W. Dawson of the Charleston *News and Courier*, and the young Virginian, Richard H. Edmonds of the *Manufacturers' Record*.

Closer to the field of action, eloquent with precept, and persuasive with successful example was plantation-born, Northern-educated, Calhoun-kinsman, Daniel A. Tompkins, who carried the gospel of the "new departure" to towns and villages all across the Carolina Piedmont. Even as those in authority were spreading the welcome mat for Yankees bearing capital in search of latent resources, these men and their disciples were already inspiring in the Southern Piedmont the erection of cotton textile mills which were destined to become the symbol of the new South.

Once under way their campaign took on all the fervor of a religious crusade. Capital for the enterprises was raised locally in dimes as well as dollars. Spurred into being by the plausible sounding, if unsound slogan, "bring the cotton mills to the cotton fields" (unsound because it ignored the necessity of sending North for finishing the coarse "grey goods" which was the product of most of the early mills, at even higher freight rates than for raw cotton), in the eighties and nineties, cotton mills were erected in the Southeast wherever a little capital, an aggregation of job-hungry poor whites, and water power could be found together. In those years some two hundred and forty of them were established, bringing textile mill employment to nearly 100,000 needy Southerners.

The significance of these mills far transcended the capital involved and the numbers employed in them. At the close of the century they, and those already in existence in the South, represented less than a quarter of the nation's cotton manufacturing capacity. It was their relative success which was of such great importance in the South's development. Despite the fact that that success was largely attributable to new machinery and incredibly low wages paid operatives, the mere demonstration that they could prosper while their Northern competitors languished worked wonders for Southern morale. The simple proof which they furnished, that by risking a little capital in new directions, tightening their belts, and getting to work, Southerners could outdo the Yankee in his special field of prowess did much to inspire like adventures in other fields. Most notable of those was the processing of the product of the section's second great plantation crop —tobacco.

The same two critical decades that witnessed the rise of the Southern textile industry saw the evolvement of the tobacco industry, from its handicraft status as a tobacco farm adjunct to a major industry, employing mass production methods. Without significant competition from other sections, the tobacco industry became the most exclusively Southern of any major industry in the country. Its raw material, its capital, its mass production inventions, most notable of which was the cigarette machine, and the leadership of the Dukes, the Reynolds, and other scions of the yeoman farms of the Carolina hills were all exclusively Southern.

As important as was injection into the South's agricultural economy of the wages and profits of these new industrial enterprises, and those of woodworking and other lesser industries which arose during the same period, there was more significance in their social impact on the region. Raw towns like Durham and Winston were quickly transformed into cities supported by tobacco industries. Every cotton mill brought with it its village or town, peopled by men whose identity with the farm was receding to mere memory. Urban living was beginning to develop a measure of urban thinking—the South's most telling lack throughout its history. Traditional farm wrought independence was being transformed into a dependence upon others, upon those who ran the mills, upon their customers, and each other. At last a South that had rejected all efforts of outsiders to mold it to their liking was beginning, through its own volition, to fit a more modern mold.

Thus, by seizing the torch which Gregg had lighted and carrying it on into a receptive period, Grady, Dawson, Watterson, Edmonds, and Tompkins inspired the new South to action. First the term "new South" had been a rallying cry, a call to work, a call to look forward and not backward. Later, it became a new and vital state of mind. Finally, that state of mind, by its tangible results, became a period in the history of the South—and the nation.

All the while, into the increasingly receptive atmosphere created by those evangelists of a new day, representatives of Northern business, with capital resources far beyond the reach of Southern economy, were busying themselves with acquiring, developing, or securing control of most of the non-agricultural resources of the region in order to feed the North's pyramiding industrial complex with raw and semi-processed materials essential to its own expanding operations.

The prime essential for creation of a colonial type of economy is control by the dominant region of transportation facilities of the exploited land. Southerners had never owned any appreciable share of the shipping which served their ports. It had first been British and then Yankee. The South, which through the years produced most of the country's export tonnage, was already accustomed to inevitable diversion from its economy of the shipping costs of most of its staples.

On the other hand, prior to the war, most of its railroad facilities had been under the control of its own people. But, during Reconstruction, confiscations, bankruptcies, and the machinations of carpetbaggers had transferred the ownership of the great majority of them into Northern hands. With the return of stable governments, Northern interests invested heavily in Southern railroad ventures, far more than doubling the section's railroad mileage in the 1880's alone. In the years that followed, by means of numerous consolidations, effective control of the main arteries of North-South traffic was in the hands of a small group of New York financiers and railroad magnates. True, there were Southerners among them but, with few exceptions, they were but front men and subalterns, generally recruited from the old aristocracy, partly, at least, for their political influence with the Bourbons. Typifying them was able Patrick Calhoun, grandson of John C. Calhoun, general attorney for the powerful Richmond Terminal Company. As his grandfather had symbolized the old South, he symbolized the status of his class in its new South alliance with Northern business interests.

There is also a symbolic story in the railroad history of the day. So strong were the winds of the new departure, aided and abetted by the authoritative voice of Northern money power, that the puritanical, evangelical South was persuaded to stage a wholesale desecration of a Sabbath in May, 1886. On that memorable day, thousands of Southern workmen bent brawn and sinew to the task of moving, a few inches to the east, one rail along 13,000 miles of trackage, and shortening the axles of thousands of pieces of rolling stock to match the Northern, the "standard" gauge, that goods might thereafter freely flow, untrammeled by gauge differences, from the tributary region to the dominant.

At the close of the war, cotton fields occupied the site where Birmingham now stands. Chattanooga was a sleepy village beautifully located on a great bend of the Tennessee River where two railroads met. Roanoke, then Big Lick, was an even smaller village isolated in the hills of southwest Virginia. The Confederacy had died largely from a lack of the potential products of the earth around those places—the iron and steel which Southerners had failed to produce from the ores, coal, and limestones of the Southern highlands. Chattanooga was launched on its industrial way by former Federal troops who had campaigned in the area of Lookout Mountain and Missionary Ridge, only to become so attracted by it and its possibilities that a veritable army of them returned to make it their home and, in a brief span, despoil much of its natural beauty with smoke, grime, furnaces, and factories. Almost as suddenly, Northern capital, attracted by the latent resources of its environs, changed the village of Big Lick into the industrial city of Roanoke.

The story of the Birmingham area was extreme. There, with an industrial potential unmatched elsewhere in the country, owing to its unique propinquity to rich deposits of coal, iron ore, and limestone, speculations and developments on an imperial scale were launched soon after the close of hostilities. Under the aegis of British and Northern development companies and the Yankee-owned Louisville and Nashville Railroad which had acquired a half million acres of mineral-rich territory, mines were opened, railroads built, furnaces and rolling mills erected, while cities and towns sprang into being as if by magic amid waves of unrestrained speculation. Production mounted so rapidly that, by 1888, the mineral tonnage hauled by the L. and N. alone exceeded the average weight of the entire cotton crop of the South.

But already the very success of the Birmingham area had aroused forces which were destined to clip its wings. When, in depression years of the middle eighties, Southern iron appeared in the Northern markets, underpricing its Pennsylvania competitors, there was consternation among Northern steel tycoons. The threat immediately inspired planning among them to secure a more restraining control over Southern iron producers to insure that, in the future, Birmingham's natural advantages should not continue to threaten the profit margin of Northern producers. It had already been decided that, willy-nilly, Southern iron regions would have to be forced into colonial status and kept in their proper place.

One of the richest and most easily exploited resources of the South was its magnificent forests. Most of the land not suited to tobacco, cotton, and sugar cane—the swamps, the pine flats, the sand hills, and the mountains—were still covered with majestic virgin forests. Coincidence of the exhaustion of Northeastern and Great Lakes timber supplies and the demands of a rapidly developing postwar North had focused the attention of Northern lumbermen southward during the Reconstruction period. Taking advantage of the economic distress of the day, lumber barons, would-be lumber barons, and speculators acquired vast timber stands at incredibly low prices from land-poor planters or at tax sales. Through carpetbagger corruption, vast areas of public lands likewise passed into their hands. The cooperativeness of the Bourbons, who succeeded the carpetbaggers, combined with empty state treasuries to further facilitate the transfer of extensive forest areas to lumber syndicates or speculators, who in turn made them available to exploitation.

Thus, in the next thirty years, did Northern capital, Southern labor, and Southern timber combine to create the era of large-scale lumber mills, intent upon cutting and marketing what remained of Southern forests—cutting and getting out when the job was done, a forest exploitation that was perhaps the most wasteful and destructive in the history of the nation. Raw mill towns which sprang into being at the sites of large-scale operations were transformed just as precipitately into somber ghost towns when available timber was cut. Fires swept the cut-over areas and the land joined the abandoned workers in mutual destitution.

Those which have been mentioned were only the major fields which attracted the intrusion of Northern wealth and Northern control. There were many others. Within a few years after the war, half the great sugar plantations along the Mississippi and the sugar mills which received their harvests were under Northern control. Northern life and casualty insurance companies and Northern financial institutions moved into the void created by the destruction of Southern concerns which had once functioned in those fields, effectively preempting them to the practical exclusion of Southerners.

Thereby, as Northern money interests seized the opportunities for wealth offered by the frontier, created by the war waged by their political protagonists, initial moves were made leading to the conversion of a conquered province into a servient land with a colonial economy, in which its resources, human and material, might be effectively controlled by and exploited for the enhancement of the wealth of its dominant conqueror-neighbor.

Freshened by hope, the air of the new South had breathed a measure of vitality into the region and had brought in its train dramatic developments in commerce and industry during the final decades of the century. But for the masses of the South, both black and white, who continued to seek their livelihood by tilling the soil, there was still little hope and little vitality. For them, those decades were simply long years of increasing hardship, long years of unrelieved purgatory. Even with the added efforts of greater numbers, it had taken two decades simply to bring their harvests back to prewar levels. But even as production rose, prices received for their crops fell, although the cost of production continued to rise, for tired soils required more and more fertilizers. The farmers' unrelieved distress continued year after year. A prominent Northern radical familiar with the South, writing in 1887, observed that "apart from the New South, by which I mean the country around the region of the rapidly developing iron industries . . . , the same wretched poverty prevails among the Southern people now, twenty-two years after the war."

Consequently, for the eighty percent of Southerners who gained their livelihood from the soil, the hope of the day met the unrelieved hopelessness of realities of the day and was cancelled out. They, like their fathers before them, were hopelessly enmeshed in the rigid colonial pattern of cash crop farming. A picture of the Southern farmer's plight, attributed to Henry Grady, depicts his complete involvement in the economy which kept him enslaved:

> [He] gets up at the alarm of a Connecticut clock. Puts his Chicago suspenders on a pair of Detroit overalls. Washes his face with Cincinnati soap in a Philadelphia wash pan. Sits down to a Grand Rapids table and eats Indiana hominy fried in St. Joseph lard, bacon from Kansas City, and biscuits made of flour from Tennessee all cooked on a St. Louis stove. Drinks a cup of coffee from Brazil or a cup of tea from China. Goes to a lot fenced with Pittsburgh woven wire. Puts a St. Louis bridle on a Missouri mule, rides to the field in a Kentucky wagon. Hitches up to a Syracuse plow. Works all day on a farm covered by an Ohio mortgage. Comes home at night and reads a chapter of the Bible printed in Chicago. Says a prayer written in Jerusalem. Crawls into a Grand Rapids bed and covers himself with a blanket from New Jersey, only to be kept awake by the howling of his hound dog—the only home raised product on the farm.

The average size of farms in the cotton states fell from three hundred and forty-seven acres to one hundred and fifty-six acres between 1860 and 1880. Within fifteen years after the close of the war more than two-thirds of the cotton plantations of the Mississippi valley passed from the hands of those who had owned them. The postwar South was definitely not moving toward the Jeffersonian ideal of a society of small independent farmers. Actually the trend was in the opposite direction. What was reflected was simply a change in the farm labor system. Instead of working in gangs, as they had under slavery, soil tillers were now working in family units. Instead of their maintenance being a first claim on proceeds of the harvest, to whatever extent was necessary, they now worked for a definite predetermined share of the crops on assigned fields which were, in effect, their work detail. In theory, the sharecrop system represented a long step upward from slavery, but, in practice, the sharecropper's dependence upon his landlord was almost as binding as under the old system, except that now he was bound by economic rather than enacted laws. And the bondsmen under the new system were not confined to the blacks. Within a very few years, to replace the hordes of Negroes who had drifted away from farm work and into the towns, hundreds of thousands of poor whites had sought to relieve their squalid existences by securing better lands to till under the sharecrop system. Eventually, millions of Southern whites found themselves in hopeless economic bondage under it.

Outsiders have long been wont to look disapprovingly down uptilted noses at the South's sharecrop system, regarding it as a Mephistophelean plot of heartless landowners to exploit their fellow men for their own enrichment. It would be equally just to carry that disapproval on back to those responsible for the ruin, which called the system into being as an expedient for mutual survival in a moneyless society. The landowner had generally a few mules and his land and little else except, more often than not, a heavy mortgage upon which interest payments at ten to twenty percent had to be met at every harvest season—in money. And money could be gotten only from something which could be sold to the North or abroad—where, in that day, the sources of all money lay.

In the cabins on his place lived Negro families, an average of six per plantation unit. Their only tangible economic assets were their hands and brawn. Their skill seldom went beyond a rudimentary familiarity with planting, tending, and harvesting the traditional plantation crops of the place. Confronted with the mutual necessity for survival—that the land be made to produce—there was little room for social or economic experimentation or theorizing. Let each contribute the essentials he possessed: the landowner his fields, cabins, and mules; the laborer his labor, that they both might survive. There remained only the problem of how they were to eat and be clothed until crops were harvested and sold. That was the facet of the problem which made their simple arrangement iniquitous.

The problem of how to live during the months between planting and harvest time was met in various ways, none of which was entirely satisfactory to both owner and cropper. If the owner had not exhausted his source of credit, he usually opened a plantation commissary and stocked it with the essentials for simple existence, which he doled out to his croppers, charging the retail price and interest against their share of the crop, with the practical result that, usually, the cropper had consumed his share even before it was harvested, the deficiency being charged over to another year. The chances were that the owner was also in the same plight. To obtain his necessities and stock the commissary, he usually found it necessary to pledge his part of the prospective crop to a factor, banker, or supply house. It was all risky business, lending money on crops ungrown, and his interest rate reflected the risk involved; often he also failed to "pay out" at the season's end. If the landowner lacked the necessary credit or the plantation unit was too small to justify a commissary, both he and the croppers were forced into the toils of the lien merchant in town, who, secured by a pledge of the sharecrop agreement, made advances of livestock, tools, fertilizers, clothes, and provisions against the crop to be grown.

As farm tenancy, usually with rent paid in the staple commodity rather than dollars, began to supplant sharecropping, the lien merchants, secured by a mortgage on the tenant's crop, similarly supplied his needs. The lien merchant's margin of profit and interest charges constituted a terrible drain on the farmer's profits, but his interest charges and costs were also high and risks great. While many grew rich and turned bankers or town-dwelling planters for the social prestige thereby secured, many others went down in bankruptcy when hard years came.

But the heaviest price paid by the South for its expedient for survival lay in slavery to a system which it fastened on the region. And this new slavery was no respecter of race or condition, cropper or landowner. It chained its minions inexorably to a single cash crop—a crop which could be readily turned into cash when the time came for accounts to be toted up. Through no other crop than the storable and marketable staples of the region could the system operate. Neither landlord nor lien merchant could use unlimited quantities of cabbages, beans, potatoes, or apples. Almost always it had to be landvoracious, inedible cotton or tobacco.

The farms that resulted were a far cry from the independent, selfsufficient farms of pioneer days and an equally far cry from their Northern counterparts. They tended to enslave the farmer to production of a single article for market. If he was helpless, so also was his landlord. He, too, could produce only the crop against which the banker or lien merchant would advance credit—always cotton or tobacco. No other crops were acceptable media of exchange. Soil mining was part of the law of the system. As crop rotation calls for other crops and the system had no use for other crops, soils deteriorated at a fearful rate. More and more fertilizer was required, fertilizer which had to be bought through the lien merchant. And the wheel of destruction took another turn and distress and poverty mounted.

With the production of staple crops thus artificially stimulated by the system, regardless of the laws of supply and demand, greatly increased endeavor and greatly increased yields went for worse than naught. They brought only greater distress, as prices and net returns fell faster than production increased. The price of the lien systems, which incidentally fitted nicely into the colonial economy being fashioned for the South, was inevitably reflected in crop statistics.

By way of illustration, the price of cotton fell from fifteen cents a pound in 1873 to less than eight cents in 1890, which was less than the cost of production on even the better plantations, to a disastrous six cents in the closing years of the century. Of the estimated wealth of the nation, in 1880, of fifty billion dollars, the whole South, with all its rich resources, represented but a little over five and a half billions, and its per capita income of $376 was only a third of that prevailing outside the region. Even after its burst of industrial development had had an opportunity to show itself, in 1900 Southerners' per capita wealth was still only a little more than a third of that enjoyed by those living in other sections—figures which continued to point with blame at cash crop agriculture, fettered to the region by the lien system.

All the while, chains of thralldom to the system were padlocked in place by the toll levied on the South's economy by protective tariffs, which the successful revolution of business interests had made possible on the withdrawal of Southern states from the Union. All the South's great staple crops except sugar were, to a large extent, grown for export, and prices received were determined by demand in a free-trade world. But most of the things Southern farmers had to buy reflected in their prices the fifty percent tariff which prevailed all during the era. The net effect on the agricultural South's economy was the same as if a fifty percent tax had been levied on all its purchases of manufactured articles and the proceeds distributed by way of subsidy to manufacturers in the North.

Faced by the never ending frustrations of those conditions, in a desperate hope that they might relieve their plight through mass action, more than 200,000 Southern farmers joined in the Grange movement of the seventies. In addition to planning a system of cooperative buying and selling, the Grangers clamored for government regulation of railroads, fertilizer inspection laws, and the establishment of agricultural schools. But the Southern Grangers hesitated to commit their organization to direct political action for fear of dividing the ranks of the whites just when the last of the seceded states were being recovered from the radicals. With the same fear in mind, Bourbons granted many of their legislative demands, while the movement died on the altar of white unity. However, it had planted in the mind of Southern farmers the idea that relief from distress might be obtained through government intercession—an abandonment of their traditional opposition to economic and social legislation.

The Grange prepared the field for the Farmers' Alliance which gave the South the most rigorous shaking in its post-Reconstruction history. Fifteen years after its organization in Texas, it had spread all

THE SOUTH BECOMES THE NEW SOUTH: 1 217

over the South, boasted a membership of more than a million and a half, and had become a powerful political and sociological force in every Southern state. Although it drew the color line to a degree, its Negro affiliate enlisted more than a million colored members in the common cause of agrarian relief. When, in the latter years of the 1880's, the Alliance turned militantly political and radically sociological, consternation swept the ranks of the Bourbon oligarchy which, since Reconstruction, had dominated the political life of the South. The internal political storms which arose from the sea of unrest created by the Alliance provided the region with the only winds of vitality that marked the otherwise unbroken strain of political mediocrity in the South of the post-Reconstruction era.

Those who think of the South as a walled bastion of conservatism are familiar neither with its history nor with the latent radicalism which persists among the yeoman farmers. The rise of the Farmers' Alliance and its association with Populism was the outward manifestation of a continuing internal conflict, and it illustrated the workings of forces which have since kept that radicalism in latent status. The platforms and legislative enactments which appeared in the South in the wake of the Alliance movement must surely give pause to those who entertain preconceived notions of its "incurable conservatism."

The widely touted Wisconsin primary had long been part of the political machinery of most Southern states before Wisconsin "invented" it. The proddings of the Grangers and Alliance men had early secured "trust busting" and utility regulation legislation as powerful as any in the nation. Unfair practice laws to curb utilities, mine inspection laws, pure food and drug laws, anti-lobbying acts, and even initiative, referendum, and recall acts were soon found on Southern statute books. With progressive, rather than radical, innovations in the field of municipal government, the South proved that its traditional political genius was not entirely moribund. In the interest of greater efficiency, hurricane-ravaged Galveston invented the commission form of government. A few years later, Staunton, Virginia and Sumter, South Carolina devised and established city manager governments.

The innovations were, however, far less radical than the Alliance program. Since the actual enactment into laws of any part of its program involved compromises with conservatives, these laws reflect only a watered-down version of Alliance demands which had increased the Grangers' clamor for railroad regulation to a call for government ownership, sought legislation abolishing the national banking system and prohibiting all grants of public lands except to bona fide settlers. Its monetary program was both ingenious and radical. Its "Sub-Treasury Plan," which had a strong logical appeal, called for the issuance of currency against storable commodities placed in government warehouses.

Even more frightening to politicians of the old school and their business-minded allies of the new industrial South were other tendencies of this agrarian revolt. When the Alliance broadened its membership to embrace industrial and commercial laborers as well as farm workers and moved on to make a working combination of forces with organized labor, which was then enjoying an unprecedented growth in the region, bitter political warfare flared in every Southern jurisdiction. Riding the crest of the enthusiasm engendered by the revolt of the masses, which the Alliance movement fostered in 1890, the agrarians gained control of the legislature in South Carolina and elected "Pitchfork" Ben Tillman governor; gained control of the Florida and Alabama legislatures, and secured substantial representation in others; elected the governor in Texas, and many Congressmen. All this was done within the framework of the Democratic party, despite the incongruous inclusion of more than a million Negroes in the Alliance which had now, in effect, become a wing of the white man's party.

At this juncture, Populism rolled in from the West with a program closely paralleling that of the Alliance, but bearing also the seeds of disaster for the Alliance as a political force. With objectives so nearly identical, the Populist movement drew off most of the political strength which the Alliance had exerted through the Democratic framework, but in doing so, it posed a threat to white supremacy which not only doomed the movement to failure from the start but also tolled the death knell for the whole agrarian revolt, with all its progressive vitality. With reckless disregard for the politics of expediency, Populists added demands for yet more reforms. They called for abolition of the convict lease system which in some states had become revolting beyond description. It had been brought over from Reconstruction days when it had been established to care for the sudden influx of Negro convicts who, in slavery days when transgressions were paid for by corporal punishment, had required no prison facilities. The system was conducive to wide abuse, and wide abuse resulted. Conditions among prisoners was frequently shocking; friends of the Bourbon administrations, several of whom were powerful new industrial tycoons, waxed rich under favorable contracts for their lease and free labor suffered from competition in the labor market and their use as strike breakers. To their advocacy of the abolishment of the system, the Populists added even more opposition-stirring proposals. They called for severe measures to eliminate lynch law and to protect the Negro's political rights.

Those proposals provided militant advocates of white supremacy with all the emotional appeal necessary for defeat, especially just at that time when the Lodge "Force Bill" proposing Federal supervision of Southern elections was threatening passage in Congress. That, and the death of Leonidas L. Polk, inspiring leader of the Farmers' Alliance, insured a disastrous defeat for the Populists in 1892, carrying with it many Alliance men who had been tainted by association with the Populists. The South had reaffirmed its fundamental political law which had been evolved in its struggle for redemption from the radical Republicanism of Reconstruction, which law decrees that, however widely divergent the issues between its white voters, wherever Negroes reside in substantial numbers, those issues must be fought out behind the protective wall of party solidarity.

The defeat of Populism did not mean the end of agrarianism in the South. Perhaps even a majority continued sympathetic to much of the Populists' program. Trammeled thereafter by the necessity of sharing a Procrustean bed with their conservative fellow whites, those who had balked at leaving the protective canopy of Democratic party and those who had been brash enough to try it have continued to carry, in the fundamental genes of the hybrid Democratic party of the South, a not inconsequential measure of agrarian radicalism which, from time to time, persists in cropping out to the amazement of those who think the South is ideologically solid. And certainly the conditions which called for the agrarian revolt had not measurably improved. The cotton crop of 1894 exceeded any previous crop by two million bales but brought $50,000,000 less than the crops of a dozen years before. Among the tobacco farmers there was even greater distress.

The economic distress which chronically plagued the farmer and seemed perversely only to grow worse in response to greater effort and the distant inchoate ogres, "money power," "Wall Street," and the trusts whom the Agrarian and Populist leaders blamed for the farmer's distress, offered rich opportunities for demagogues, and no sooner had the movements gotten under way, than such opportunists were on hand to grasp them. Prototype, and most successful of them all, was harsh, sharp-tongued Ben Tillman who, after a turn as a Bourbon-slaying governor of South Carolina, was sent on to the Senate, pledged impartially to destroy the Republican "money interests" ensconced in Wall Street and to stick his pitchfork into the fat ribs of Democrat Grover Cleveland, sitting on his money-supported throne in the White House. Before long, imitators would be searching even farther afield for imaginary culprits or perfect scapegoats who could not bite back, such as Tom Watson of Georgia found in the Pope, against whom he campaigned vigorously.

But the most perennial of all scapegoats was the Negro who, although near at hand, yet fitted the formula both by virtue of his relegation to the side lines, where he could not strike back, and by the latent fear he traditionally has aroused in many whites wherever he is present in numbers. Men like James K. Vardaman rose to power by whipping that fear into vote-producing emotions. To get the full vote potential of all the prejudices and suspicion harbored by their constituents, most rabble rousers of the day gave at least second billing to the "race issue," which was no issue at all, but only a continuing state of affairs during the years of the ascendancy of the demagogues.

Also, among the demagogues were clowns like Jeff Davis of Arkansas, colorful entertainers like James H. ("Cyclone") Davis and H. S. P. ("Stump") Ashby of Texas, and disgusting hypocrites with a gift for rabble-rousing like Theodore G. Bilbo of Mississippi and Cole L. Blease of South Carolina. They and their numerous imitators, lesser lights of the same ilk, comprise a pride-dispelling list; far too long, even after allowance is made for those such as Tillman who turned more sincere or more conservative after thoroughly securing their power, and even after due allowance for the fact that some who are called demagogues are simply progressives out of place or out of time.

That the production of a fantastic array of demagogues should have so long persisted as recurring phenomena on the Southern scene is, of course, partly accounted for by the grinding poverty of people to whom they appealed and the low level of education, which was largely the result of that poverty and the rural isolation in which they lived and the hunger of the lonely and isolated for the stirring entertainment which such figures provided without fee. The demagogues provided psychological cathartics for the miserable masses from whom they drew their support. There was vicarious release in their extravagant diatribes that made more tolerable the frustrations of existences which were the lot of most of their faithful followers.

In truth, for all the free entertainment they provided and despite the free shows they staged, Southern demagogues in the composite carried a heavy price tag upon which Southerners have been paying installments during all the years of their day. Not the least part of the toll they exacted was the part they played in violence, which prevailed in the years of their suasion. Their inflammatory speeches, their diatribes of hate could not but contribute to the record of violence of an already violent region, where frontier violence persisted with frontier conditions. Lynchings rose as sharply as did the number and influence of the demagogues, to an appalling rate at the turn of the century. When the rude, the ignorant, and the chronically frustrated heard unrestrained preachings of hate and flamboyant threats of violence from the lips of their high-placed idols, there is little wonder that they found in them ample balm for their dull consciences, especially those in isolated hinterlands where there was a minimum of conditioning to the restraints of law.

Although the great majority of the victims of frontier "justice" were Negroes, by no means all were. In the years since 1882, lynchings of whites in Arkansas far exceeded the toll of rip-roaring frontier California, and Virginia, with a quarter-millennium of civilization behind her, lynched as many whites as the frontier state of Iowa.

Not alone in its shocking lynching record did the new South distinguish itself without glory. Relatively dignified meetings on the field of honor to settle personal differences gave way to shooting on sight to settle a score and gun "toting" became all but universal. Shocking statistics reveal the results. Old South Carolina, which should have long since outgrown frontier ways, in 1890 reported nearly three times as many homicides as all New England, with four times South Carolina's population, including large numbers of unassimilated immigrants. These figures cannot be explained away by her large Negro population, for the white homicide rate was then comparable with the Negro rate; and, although some race violence existed, Negroes almost always confined their violence to other blacks, and whites generally showed a parallel racial discrimination in their killings. Even after making allowance for a violence record among Negroes running generally five to ten times the average rate for whites, the South's record was shocking by comparison with any other section. Unquestionably, the atmosphere of militancy, hate, and defiance of law, which the demagogues fostered and thrived upon, contributed mightily to that disgraceful distinction, especially in respect to the increase in Negro lynchings.

Demagogues also played a sorry role in promoting election frauds which marked the era. The Machiavellianism, which the redeemers had employed against election manipulations of the carpetbaggers, had tended to disappear as the Bourbons secured a paternalistic sway over Negro voters. But in the frenetic days of the Agrarian Revolt, of Populism, and the emergence of the demagogues, election frauds became commonplace. Once they gained power, new leaders secured control of the election machinery and thereafter manipulated elections to suit their designs. Despite the fact that no party but the Democratic was involved, almost two-thirds of all the elections contested on the ground of fraud or irregularities during the final quarter of the nineteenth century took place in the South.

But beyond question, the greatest toll exacted from the South by

demagogues was in the realm of race relations. So long as slavery sub-
sisted there was no hatred but only a latent fear of Negroes among
those whites of the planter class. On the contrary, the controlling sentiment was a paternalistic affection, a sentiment which, the war would
prove, was generally reciprocated by Negroes. Although the Negroes'
conduct during Reconstruction had shaken that relationship, the
harvest of hatred which that era produced was mostly for their carpetbagger and scalawag mentors. When redemption was effected and the
old order to a large extent resumed control of seceded states, the general tenor of restored governments toward their black constituency
was an adoption of the paternalistic, planter-slave affection. Wade
Hampton had not hesitated to propose enfranchisement of qualified
Negroes even before constitutional amendments began to provide for
it. And later, in his campaign for governor against the carpetbagger
forces, Hampton had openly solicited the Negro vote, despite the
scornful disapproval of his back country lieutenants.

On the other hand, the far more numerous poor whites and small
farmers of the hinterland entertained no such sentiments. Their
heritage was devoid of the warm personal master-slave relationships
which most planters had known. Instead, theirs was a heritage which
was a composite of fear of the unfamiliar and different, resentment of
the low standard competition of the blacks, and a pride of race exaggerated by the lack of much else in which to take pride. The total
of these was a great, indiscriminate hate, enhanced and justified in
their minds by the events of Reconstruction. It was from those classes,
or from others intimately associated with them, that the challengers
of the Bourbons had risen. An awareness of the sentiments of those
elements, and their numerical preponderance, clearly marked for the
demagogues their way to power. It was simply a matter of fanning
existing fears and hates to a sufficient pitch to arouse those classes
from their political apathy and get them to the polls. With the magic
formula tried and proved against the Bourbons, it became standard
procedure of the demagogues, militating always against the development of a fair and respectable bi-racial society.

As soon as those representatives of the folk of the recreated fron-
tiers inflamed their way to positions of authority, they began to pay

their indebtedness to hate and prejudice. The old order had been satisfied with Negro franchise restrictions with some relationship to merit, even though, in imposing those restrictions, the ballot was also denied many whites. But now all semblance of legal impartiality was thrown overboard. Involved registration laws, susceptible to flagrant partiality in their administration, became part of the plan to close the political arena to blacks. The requirement of receipts showing payment of poll taxes took further toll of the potential Negro electorate, as did also the list of disqualifying crimes which was carefully designed to include common Negro transgressions. Thus, through the curious workings of inflamed emotions did the wider democracy born of the Agrarian Revolt and Populism, both of which had been biracial movements, finally emerge as a wider democracy for whites only.

However, closing the political arena to Negro participation should not be regarded as simply a capricious exertion of prejudice. Candor requires the observation that there was a desperate need for raising the standard of the Southern electorate of the period. In the elections of 1892 and 1894, when the whites divided, the blind and herded votes of masses of the Negroes had been almost as scandalously employed by the Bourbons and redeemers to defeat Populist and back country candidates as they had been by the radicals of the Reconstruction era. Had the disfranchising measures been impartially administered, to exclude also those whites who were no better qualified to exercise the ballot than most of the Negroes, they would have been justified, for the sorry state of Southern politics in the eighties and nineties fairly shouted for reform.

Actually, disfranchising measures were but one aspect of the picture of an era when the majority of Southerners abandoned all attempts to find a constructive and just solution of the region's stupendous race problem, just as the radicals had abandoned the problem a dozen years before. What was now sought was a way to avoid the problem and defer its solution. Into the prevailing atmosphere of discouragement and confusion surrounding the race problem came the Negrophobists, in the train of those who had risen to power on their fears and hates, with a pat recipe for indefinitely avoiding the necessity for solving the problem. They would avoid for the present and indefinitely defer the problem by erecting a rigid caste system based indiscriminately on race.

Post-Reconstruction rulers, drawn as they were from the old planter class and military leaders of the Confederacy, had shown little inclination to establish any caste system. In fact, many of them had openly averred their preference for decent blacks over the mudsill whites so common in the land. Only in providing for separate public schools for the races and prohibiting interracial marriages had they indicated any disposition to even a semblance of caste. That, and the separate churches which Negroes chose of their own volition, comprised the only segregation of consequence in the Bourbon period. Now, discredited and toppled from power by the "red-necks" and "wool hats," their moderate efforts to meet the problem came abruptly to a close and the gates of hate were opened wide.

Although for twenty-five years after 1865, Southerners had moved forward from the nadir, into which they had been cast, without feeling the necessity to impose by law more than a minimum of segregation, now, as the demagogues sought to satisfy the hates they had inflamed, beginning in the latter 1880's, came a flood of legislation; "Jim Crow" laws, designed to provide a complete legal framework for the caste system through which they hoped indefinitely to defer knotty essentials of the ponderous race problem. During the next fifteen years, a fantastic volume of segregation laws appeared on the statute books of every Southern state. Beginning with laws requiring segregation of the races on railroad cars and in stations, the mixing ban was soon expanded to require separate facilities in jails, public buildings, public toilets, and those of business establishments. Common use by the races of hotels and restaurants and unsegregated employment in factories were soon proscribed. After the Supreme Court upheld the constitutionality of these laws in 1897, yet more areas of possible social contact were covered. Cities and towns commonly provided for separate use of parks and playgrounds and some even undertook to separate residential areas for the races. The height of absurdity was reached in Atlanta where, by custom, separate elevators were provided for Negroes. Eventually, in many parts of the South only streets and stores remained to common use.

In the same period, through the unwritten laws of custom, almost as immutable as the "Jim Crow" laws themselves, many aspects of the South's economic life were likewise segregated. There were "nigger jobs" and white man's jobs, for which all interracial competition was eliminated. Textile mill jobs were for whites only, whereas only Negroes could qualify as Pullman porters. In between were industries in which certain jobs were reserved for whites and others, usually the more unpleasant and those requiring the greater physical strength were for Negroes only. Thus did law and custom combine to complete the rigid fabric of the caste system which came into being.

Protagonists of the system contended that its workings militated for improved race relations; that by marking out by clear lines of demarcation in most of the areas of group contact and by minimizing the areas of competition, the possibilities of friction and conflict between the races were reduced to a minimum. In support of their thesis they could point to the marked decrease in Negro lynchings which followed the establishment of the system, although a comparable drop in white victims indicated other explanations for the decline.

Critics of the caste system, of whom there were remarkably few, even from the North, where the ardor for elevation of the Negro to full participation in society had spent its drive and died of frustration, generally deferred their onslaughts against its workings for forty years, while the system hardened and became an accepted way of American life wherever there were people of color in substantial numbers. Senator Hiram Johnson, who delighted in flourishing his liberality and taking verbal pokes at the "reactionary" South, saw no inconsistency between his progressive views and his support of legislation tending to establish a similar caste system to perpetuate white supremacy against Orientals in California. And even as the Southern system was being constructed, law by law, it was being adopted as the American system by being employed to take care of race problems presenting themselves in territories newly acquired as a result of the Spanish-American War.

The South

Becomes

the New South: 2

18

THOSE NEGROES WHO SOUGHT ESCAPE from the restraints of rigid stratification in the South by migrating North found no more welcome in that direction than had been accorded the 30,000 from Mississippi and Louisiana who had been sent back from an inhospitable Kansas soon after the Civil War. Northern trade unions were usually no more open to them than most unions in the South. Most of them, in both sections, strictly drew the color line. Those Negroes who tried to break through the color line even in the North frequently met with violent opposition. In a single year in Northern cities, there were at least fifty strikes in protest against the employment of Negroes.

For the Negro himself, despite the caste system which had been imposed on him, the era of the new South was one of steady advancement. In fact, contradictory as it may seem, the caste system itself in many respects contributed greatly to his advancement. The Negro districts which it tended to create gave support for merchants and service establishments insulated, to a considerable degree, from direct competition with white establishments better equipped with capital and with better trained personnel. To some, such as undertakers and restaurateurs, custom provided complete protection from white competition. Although, regardless of the caste system, whites continued to monopolize the professions requiring long training, the pulpits of Negro churches were a Negro monopoly, and thousands of Negro teachers found dignified employment in Negro schools. They would have been eliminated by better trained whites except for their monopoly on those positions.

By the "Year of Jubilee," the fiftieth anniversary of emancipation, Southern Negroes could look back on their progress upward from their status as penniless bondsmen, but a step removed from barbarians of the African jungles, progress represented by these figures; 128,557 farms owned by Negroes; 38,000 places of business; 550,000 homes owned; and ownership of most of the $700,000,000 in wealth attributed the Negroes of the nation. Their illiteracy rate had plummeted from close to a hundred percent to about thirty percent. They had colleges, admittedly with low standards but also with low costs, which were producing leaders for their race. Their greatest leader, Booker T. Washington, had placed the stamp of acceptance, if not of approval, on the system in urging his people to "put down your buckets where you are" and earn the deserts of full participation before demanding it.

On the other side of the ledger, there was a marked deterioration in fundamental race relations during the period, attributable largely to the continuous fanning by the demagogues of race hatreds in support and justification of the caste system. Some of these demagogues occupied high places throughout the era.

In spite of distractions incidental to the turmoil of the Agrarian Revolt and the dynamic, abortive revolution of the Populists, in spite of marked retrogression in the sphere of race relations and the Rip Van Winkleness apparent in so many poverty-ridden Southern towns and hamlets, in spite of the continued slavery of most Southerners to the traditional single cash crop economy of their forefathers and the appearances of political isolation behind the protective wall of a single party, the true mark of the new South was "progress." Those others were mostly surface marks, giant eddies beneath which the deep current flowed steadily in the direction of progress. They indicated the persisting individualism and vital diversity which recurring ordeals had failed to iron out, continuing in constant ferment behind the solid front which expediency had raised in the face of adversity. They were the indicia of internal divergencies that persisted in reflecting themselves in the extreme variety of Southern leaders; divergencies that precluded (and yet preclude) the discovery of a clear way into the future which might promise any solution of the section's formidable social, economic, and political problems. Even so, the hallmark of the new South was "progress."

In the first decade of the new century, amazing progress was made in the realm of public health. Few people had suspected the extent to which chronic ill health had hampered the South through the years, how greatly it had contributed to the picture which commonly came to mind at the mention of Southern poor whites; a picture of forlorn folk, lantern-jawed, cadaverous and sallow, bewhiskered and barefooted, utterly listless and incredibly lazy. Now came the revelation that the causes of that caricature of the lower income Southerner lay, not in any innate deficiency in his moral or physical being, but rather in the endemic diseases of the region, aided and abetted by poverty. The work of the Virginian, Walter Reed, with American troops in Cuba had pointed the way to lift the debilitating curse of chronic malaria from the South. Within the next few years, researchers found the source and control methods against hookworm, malaria's twin in sapping Southern vitality. Discovery that the elimination of pellagra, which constantly incapacitated tens of thousands, was simply a matter of improving the customary diet of the very poor, showed the way to eliminate a third insidious deterrent to Southern progress.

Soon after those discoveries were revealed, influential Walter Hines Page, intimate of the rich and powerful and gadfly of the philanthropists as far as the South was concerned, induced John D. Rockefeller to spark a public health movement in the South, through a campaign against hookworm. Stimulated by the success of that undertaking, Southern states launched their own campaigns against malaria and pellagra. The results were miraculous; an incalculably great deterrent to progress had been lifted from the region.

The greatest fundamental progress of the new South was in education. Throughout its history, the South had persisted in a peculiar indifference to that basic key to its salvation, the education of its people—and not just those for whom leadership seemed probable. In the ante-bellum South, only token steps had been taken toward anything approaching universal education by the establishment of the merest skeleton of a public school system. Ironically, it remained for the uncouth governments of carpetbaggers to add a measure of substance to that all but empty framework. But during the tightened-belt administrations of the redeemers, the schools, along with all other public services, had been all but starved out of existence in the desperate effort to rebuild the ruined credit of states with little more than dry tax wells from which to draw. Even after representatives of the masses had climbed into the saddle, the resistance to taxes on a desperately poor economy continued too great to permit anything approaching adequate support for the pitiful school systems of the region. In 1900, no Southern state was providing even as much as half the national average per pupil in appropriations for its school children and in several, the funds available were only about a sixth of the national average. When the relatively large proportion not in attendance is taken into account, the disproportion in school expenditures per child was much more glaring than those comparisons indicate. About half the Southern children of school age were not even getting the daily "five cents worth of education per child" which was being made available in the typical Southern school system. The average public school teacher in the South was being paid $159 per year to teach in the crowded classroom of a school building with a value of $276.

Those deficiencies showed in the section's illiteracy statistics of the year; almost two million whites over ten years of age who could not read and more than two and a half million illiterate Negroes. The problem presented by those statistics was compounded by the South's vital statistics and by its economy. Southerners, in 1900, had twice as many children per adult, and their incomes were so meagre that, in order to provide as much per child for education as the North, their tax rates would have to have been five times as great—a patent impossibility in view of prevailing poverty. The South was thereby confronted with a truly difficult dilemma—unless better education was provided, Southern income must inevitably remain too low to provide the education which was the essential key to the section's economic salvation. It remained for a crusade to arouse the South to face that dilemma and take action to resolve it.

Again, as in the forward surge in public health, the key figure was the South's devoted and talented emigré, Walter Hines Page. Before 1900, he had recognized the urgency of the problem and in a series of addresses which received wide acclaim, he pointed up the problems and pointed out the steps to be taken toward their solution. He dramatically described the masses of poor Southerners who, for want of education and opportunity, were being by-passed by progress as "contemporary ancestors" and personified them as the "Forgotten Man," both of which phrases were to become clichés and the latter, with a new and wider connotation, was destined to become a presidential campaign piece in a later day. For the "Forgotten Man," he made his appeal, "Since both the politician and the preacher have failed to lift his life after a century of unobstructed opportunities, it is time for wiser statesmanship and a more certain means of grace."

Again Page interested his friends, who directed the great philanthropies and secured their support. Through that support and the cooperation of a group of able, forward-looking, and enthusiastic Southern educators, a veritable crusade for education was launched in the South. State by state, through meetings often resembling the religious revivals to which the region had long since proved itself peculiarly susceptible, a broad and powerful demand for more and better education was fomented. The effectiveness of the new fervor was soon reflected in statistics. In the first dozen years of the new century, expenditures for public schools in the Southern states more than tripled, a forward stride even more impressive in terms of the sacrifice involved. To reach even that inadequate level, some Southern states were finding it necessary to devote more than half of all public revenues to their schools alone. Results, too, revealed the progress. School terms were substantially extended. Compulsory at-

tendance laws were adopted. And, most telling of all, the Southern illiteracy rate dropped almost half in little more than a decade.

However, the most significant of all developments in the era of the
new South occurred in the economy during the years between the
turn of the century and the beginning of World War I. During those
years, accelerated economic developments perfected the transformation of the conquered province into an exploited colonial economy,
subservient to a dominant and dominating North. That development
was most apparent in the iron and steel industry. With the unique
advantage its geology had given the South by laying down in close
proximity essential raw materials for the production of iron and steel,
the shining hope of the industrial new South was its iron industry.
Although its development had been mostly financed and directed by
the Northern-controlled Louisville and Nashville Railroad and other
Northern interests, the industry held great promise for the uplift of
the South. Its advance from early beginnings had been phenomenal.
By 1898, Birmingham was the nation's largest shipping point for pig
iron and one of the largest in the world. The Tennessee Coal, Iron,
and Railroad Company had absorbed most of the companies operating in the area and had become the industrial giant of the South.
However, Northern steel tycoons, with enormous stakes in the Pittsburgh area, viewed the success of their Southern competitor with
mounting concern. Early in 1904, their concern gave way to alarm
when Northern railroads controlled by the Harriman interests placed
a record-breaking 150,000 ton rail order with the Tennessee company.
That order became the signal for action.

Before the year was out, through the offices of banker J. P. Morgan,
the United States Steel Corporation had secured control of its Southern challenger. The effectiveness of the move was almost immediately
reflected in the Birmingham area's production statistics. Southern
growth was stopped in its tracks, as its Northern competitors resumed
their forward strides. By 1913, the South's share of the national output
of iron, which had risen so spectacularly, dropped even more spectacularly. This calculated result, so pleasing to its Northern captors,
had been accomplished through bold manipulations whereby the
Southern product was priced out of the market. There was first the

"Pittsburgh Plus" system, by which Southern steel, although much less costly to produce, was given the price tag of Pittsburgh steel plus the cost of freight from Pittsburgh, regardless of the proximity of the customer to Birmingham whence his order was delivered. Later, the "Birmingham Differential" was inaugurated, putting a three dollar per ton extra charge on Birmingham steel, although the Southern product cost less than seventy-five percent as much to produce. Thus, in the iron and steel industry did the pattern of economic colonialism for the South take shape and the South's brightest dream of industrial prowess withered away.

When Banker Morgan was playing Disraeli for the Pennsylvania iron imperialists, he was fresh from acting, on his own account, the part of a Bismarck with numerous railroad kingdoms and principalities of the South. A dozen years earlier, he had secured control of and reorganized the old Richmond and West Point Terminal Company which served the most populous sections of the older Southern states. Through a rapid series of mergers and manipulations, in a short time he was virtual dictator of a 7,500 mile railroad colossus, the Southern Railway, with lines extending across almost every Southern state east of the Mississippi and reaching into almost every mining and manufacturing area of the South. Within ten years, he acquired control of the Atlantic Coast Line, which had already absorbed the Plant System extending into the agricultural regions of Florida, and secured control of the giant of the trans-Appalachian regions, the Louisville and Nashville. Then by a series of consolidations, he organized the Seaboard Air Line running through the middle of the eastern tier of Southern states. By 1906, every main route across the South east of the Mississippi was subject to Morgan control. Although that in itself spelled monopoly on an imperial scale, it was the way the monopoly was exercised that contributed so greatly to the South's colonial status.

A system of rates was established which averaged more than fifty percent higher per ton-mile than those prevailing in the "official" (Northeastern) section. Rates on Southern iron, "at the request of the Pennsylvania iron men," were especially discriminatory. Those discriminatory rates in themselves were revealing enough of the intent of the dominant men of the dominant region; but when higher rates were set for manufactured goods moving north than for raw materials moving north and lower rates prescribed for manufactured goods moving south, their intent became as glaringly obvious as was "Pittsburgh Plus." Every possible road block was being erected against Southern industry while encouragement, at the same time, was being given the low pay, extractive industries of the South through which its raw material wealth might be secured and exploited by the Northern industrial complex. In effect, yet another tariff falling heavily on the South had been imposed, with the Potomac and Ohio rivers as the trade barrier line—except that the proceeds of these new imposts went, not to the coffers of the government, but into the pockets of the holders of the scandalously watered stocks of Morgan's railroad empire.

The industrial new South had dared Northern competition in only two major fields, the iron industry and textile manufacturing. Challenged Northern interests had found it easy to squelch the South's competition in the iron industry, but its textile challenge presented a much more difficult problem. Concentration of the bulk of the South's iron production in one company and that of the North in only a few giants made possible concerted action for the capture of the South's iron industry. On the other hand, in both North and South, the textile industry was composed of hundreds of independent plants, some large, some small, but none giants. And most of the South's textile mills were Southern-owned and were the pride and joy of the whole new South. They were generally highly profitable, although by no means always. Beyond that, they were symbolic and jealously guarded. Consequently, although by 1900 New England textile mills were feeling Southern competition even more heavily than had the iron industry, seizing Southern competition was out of the question.

Feeding on its own success, the evangelistic fervor of the movement to bring cotton mills to the cotton fields had outlasted the century. Led by the old arch-rivals of the political arena, South Carolina and Massachusetts, which added zest to the contest, the battle for dominance in the industry had mounted through the years, with the South showing a steady gain. By 1904, the South passed New England in production. By 1914, she was producing more textiles than the rest of the country combined. On both sides in the long drawn out battle for dominance, the casualties had run high—casualties in human misery. There was tragedy, at least temporary, in the thousands left jobless in New England towns as mill after mill closed its doors in the face of Southern competition.

In the South, there was unceasing stark tragedy in able-bodied men, heads of families, working seventy-two hours or more a week at three cents an hour, the average rate in 1900. Even greater tragedy marked the lives of tens of thousands of children for whom all carefree days of youth, and all education, were foreclosed for the sake of the desperately needed ten cents a day for a twelve hour day. But in that day in the South, there was even greater tragedy in the hills beyond the squalid mill villages where many more people, far worse off, waited hungrily for the comparative wealth represented by such wages and the paternalistic philanthropies with which most mills sugared their wage rates.

There is no gainsaying that success of the textile industry in the South was primarily the result of the desperate poverty of Southern masses, who were grateful for wages far below those necessary to attract labor anywhere else. New England textile men might and did bitterly criticize Southern wage rates and excoriate the use of child labor, but there was little else they could do—except move their own mills south and employ some of those remaining hundreds of thousands waiting hungrily for jobs which offered the relative prosperity of fifty cents a day. And hundreds of them did just that, or built new mills in the South to gain the further advantage of more modern machinery. In that way, the colonial pattern began to show itself in the South's textile industry, too.

Many Southern mills had been organized by men possessed of more enthusiasm than business acumen. Many others, sadly undercapitalized, were heavily mortgaged to Northern machinery manufacturers. A recession in business, a common occurrence in the textile business, was often sufficient to ripen those undertakings for plucking by textile magnates of the East. And many were soon plucked. Thus, year by year, the North's stake in the Southern textile industry grew steadily toward a dominance only somewhat less complete than that enjoyed in other Southern industries. In the inner workings of the industry also, the colonial pattern was commonly observed. Often, the partly finished "grey goods," the manufacture of which involved the cheapest labor in the industry, were shipped north for the higher paid process of finishing. Management, supervision, marketing, and other "white collar" functions were usually reserved for Northern owners or Northern agencies, to the end that, before the end of the new South era, a large part of the profits of the Southern textile industry were accruing to the North's benefit, leaving only the tobacco industry dominantly Southern in its operations, management, and ownership. And even in the tobacco industry, principal officials and owners showed an almost invariable tendency to move northward to the traditional habitat of the tycoons who controlled the colonial South.

Except for the South's coal fields and iron veins, the great bulk of the section's mineral wealth lay hidden beneath its soil, concealed from exploitation, until the first few years after the turn of the century brought the discovery of oil fields, sulphur deposits, aluminum ores, and extensive new phosphate areas, to take their places in the expanding colonial economy of the region. The richest of these was the oil of western Southern states.

The economic consequences of the discovery of gold in Sutter's millrace a half-century earlier was suddenly dwarfed, early in 1901, when an experimental drilling at Spindletop, near Beaumont, Texas, produced an 80,000 barrel a day gusher. At the time, Eastern wells which were supplying the nation's oil needs were averaging two barrels a day. Spindletop, and the discovery soon afterward of numerous other rich pools, set in motion a regional boom the like of which the world had never seen. Along with tens of thousands who set out for the region of the new bonanza were swarms of agents, representing Rockefeller's Standard Oil Company, the Mellons' newly formed Gulf Company, and John Gates' hastily organized Texas Company. There on the scene and back in the Eastern capitals of finance, arrangements were soon made for division of the rich new oil domain into separate areas of influence. Among them, they quickly established an iron control over practically every drop of Texas oil by means of their mutually co-operative control of all the pipelines for its transportation, and refineries for processing the crude product.

With those essential facilities under their control, it was a simple matter to dictate the price which any producer might receive, or, if the company desired it, acquire the producers' holdings at its own price. In exerting their persuasion by price dictation, the companies forced some producers to accept as little as a cent a barrel for their oil or let it run down the creek, which alternative many of the stiffer-necked chose for a helpless while. Through such tactics, independent producers were forced to sell out their oil holdings on such terms as the companies chose to specify—while the exploiters' dividends reflected the magnificent success of the exploitation by rising to phenomenal rates. Almost overnight, Texas oil, all but geographically, had become a Yankee asset.

Sulphur, along with oil and iron, is a prime requisite of a modern industrial economy. Along the Gulf Coast of Louisiana and Texas, hundreds of feet below the surface, lie almost all the sulphur deposits of the nation, and the richest in the world. As soon as the Texas oil discoveries rendered the necessary fuel available, a newly discovered process for bringing sulphur to the surface was applied by Northern-owned Union Sulphur Company. It was soon producing eighty percent of the world supply of that chemical essential to both industry and agriculture. But it was also diverting from the South what might well have been a key to a unique industrial development. Instead, the raw sulphur was almost all consigned elsewhere for processing in the chemical plants of faraway places. Union's monopoly permitted the company fabulous profits, running its annual earnings up to as high as $3400 per share for its absentee owners, a substantial portion of which was, ironically enough, drained from the flat pockets of Southern farmers, the major fertilizer consumers of the country.

The Mellons' Aluminum Company of America took over the bauxite deposits of Tennessee and Arkansas, the nation's entire domestic source of aluminum. It was practically the same story with every resource of the resource-rich but, ever contradictory, poverty-ridden South.

Even so, all the developments spelled a sort of progress. However automatic the extractive means, some wages had to be paid to extractive workers. The wages of miners, oil derrick operators, pipe line and railroad workers stayed in the South, temporarily at least, until spent for purchase of products of the North, many made with Southern materials. What with oil derricks marching across the prairies, the glare of new iron furnaces, and aluminum smelters lighting the countryside, and new textile mills being rushed to completion, the air was full of the appearance of progress. Inevitably, Southerners of the day, few of whom were versed in economics, regarded it all as wonderful progress. And, certainly, by comparison with what they had known, they were quite right. So with each new development, regardless of its exploitative aspects, their enthusiasm for the new South mounted and there was an optimism abroad in the land out of proportion to the realities.

Only a bit of the enthusiasm of the era, a bit of its new hope, percolated out into the isolation which all but walled the farmers off from events of the day. There had been a bright glimmer of hope in the work of Seaman A. Knapp, a teaching genius, who, under philanthropic sponsorship, had started the demonstration farm movement, through which farmers were shown in their own fields or those of their neighbors how they might double their yields by employing improved practices.

But the shining hope for a measure of prosperity based on growing two bales where one had grown before was soon dashed against the stout walls of the colonial economy which held him prisoner, walls from within the protection of which he must of necessity acquire most of the necessities of existence, while the product he produced was fed into a world market, unprotected by walls, where the prices were based on the subsistence-level labor of China or Egypt and were always subject to the unrestrained free action of laws of supply and demand.

Even as the era of the new South ended, ultimate discouragement of the idea of prosperity through increased production under such economic bondage was being meted out to the Southern cotton farmer. In 1914, despite terrible inroads of the boll weevil, a crop of sixteen million bales, three times that of 1880, tumbled the price to a record low of five and a half cents a pound, just a little over half the cost of production.

However, beyond the great realms of the inedible crops, cotton and tobacco, some of the new South progress did reach out and touch farming. Protected by tariffs and mechanized and now under Northern tutelage, sugar growing boomed to new heights, as did also Louisiana rice growing even as its culture died in its earlier Carolina province. Truck farming and fruit growing for the populous East made a significant and hopeful start toward a new farm prosperity in selective areas. All the states had established agricultural colleges, and they were busy with new ideas that would transform agriculture into an industry wherein the labor of one, with sufficient capital and training, might equal the production of ten or even twenty. And therein lay at least a new and even brighter hope for another day.

Regarded as a whole, despite the drag of colonial involvement on its farmers and the degree of exploitation in most of its industries, the economic picture of the new South is one of definite progress. In 1880, the average wealth of Southerners was only forty-two percent of the national average. By 1913, that percentage had climbed to more than fifty. Although, so far as Southerners themselves were concerned, that statistical improvement is falsely exaggerated by the inclusion of Northern-owned railroads and industries, one must also consider the fact that during the same period the wealth of other sections, against which the South's progress is measured, also greatly increased. At least the South was no longer falling behind in economic progress. And that in itself was great progress, highly hopeful progress, considering its long history of relative retrogression.

In other categories, the new South presents a bewildering picture of progress and retrogression. The encouragement indicated in a ten percent increase in urbanization and a like decrease in its farm unbalance was largely offset by the steady and fearfully costly migration to other sections of many of its more ambitious youths, a migration great enough to earn for the South the reputation of being the "seed bed of the nation."

Again on the credit side was the firm establishment of a public school system, inadequate but hopeful, and the restoration of its system of higher education, although admittedly second-class and under-supported, as indicated by the fact that Harvard's income exceeded that of a total of sixty-six colleges in seven Southern states.

There was also a big debit charge in the field of intellectual achievement. Never before in the history of the South had the forces of ignorance, bigotry, and demagoguery taken such high places in the section's affairs.

On the credit side, the Negro had shown remarkable progress in adapting himself to a useful place in society—but, partly owing to that progress itself, relations between the races fell to their nadir. There was a marked movement toward a broader democracy—but a simultaneous narrowing to exclude the Negro, to the end that it was democracy for whites only which resulted and that frequently sustained by political corruptions all but unknown to the old South. Restored frontier conditions produced a new vitality, receptive to change and progress, but also conducive to an appalling tendency to violence, typical of the frontier of an earlier day.

There are those who despise the new South because it jars with their idyllic conception of the old South. They despise it for all its tawdry aspects, its demagoguery and violence, for its brashness and radical tendencies. They like to forget that the obscure middle-class whites and illiterate poor whites, whose era it was, were also part of the old South, a far more numerous part than the planters with whom those of nostalgic bent always associate themselves. Those are the same persons to whom miserable Negro shacks and mud-daubed cabins of the whites are picturesque and romantic, rather than objects of shame and pity. Ignoring efforts upward from the new frontier represented by long hours, starvation wages, and child labor which marked the period, they put themselves in the position of resenting a half a loaf for those who had had no loaf at all—only corn meal. For those critics to be consistent, they should also look down their noses at the frontiersmen and the low standards under which they lived in the hope of building a better society on what they had at hand.

Viewed in the realistic light of the frontier that existed in the South of 1880, the twentieth-century new South was a magnificent harvest, garnered from seeds of hope planted thirty years earlier, amid the hopeless desolation of land and spirit, by Henry Grady and his fellow apostles of the new South.

It was fitting that the era of the new South should end on a note of high hope. On March 4, 1913, Woodrow Wilson, Southern-born, Southern-educated scion of Southern hill country Presbyterians, was driven to the White House, after taking his oath of office as president, elected to that office by the largest electoral majority ever before accorded a candidate. There was likewise a heavy Southern accent in the cabinet he had summoned to Washington to take office with him and it had been a Southern Chief Justice of the Supreme Court who had administered the oath of office to the new President. At last, after a half-century of practical ostracism, Southern voices had returned to the classic halls of government in our national capital.

The South   **19**
Embraces
Change: 1

I<small>N</small> 1914, <small>THE STAGE WAS SET</small> for earth-shaking changes that were soon to be felt in the South.

When America was finally swept into the vortex of the world conflict which had started with the shots of a fanatic in faraway Serbia, men of the South were more responsive to the call to arms than those of other sections of the country. Whether this was because of the military traditions of the South, or a poverty that made even army pay of that day attractive, or the South's traditional warm affection for England or simply a desire to escape the boredom of the farms and small towns from which they came, the fact remains that Southerners joined the ranks in numbers far exceeding the region's quota. Soon, hundreds of thousands of Southern boys were having the first look of their lives at the world beyond the ingrown isolation of the rural South. When the Selective Service Act began to function, they were joined in the outside world by tens of thousands of colored boys, who, although they were in work battalions under white officers, were also getting a look at a world outside where there was no color caste.

For the first time in a century, Southerners in numbers hobnobbed with Yankees and found, to their amazement, that they were not very different from the boys back home. They had seen New York and they had seen Paris; and what they had seen had effectively loosed the hold of the hopeless little farm back home, the dusty village, the general store. What for a half-century had been a steady attrition from the "seed bed of the nation" of its most valuable resource now took on more the appearance of an exodus as the more ambitious, the better trained, and more restless young people (median age of migrants: twenty-four years) left their farm homes for towns, whence most moved on to more promising fields offered by the booming North and West. Most of those migrants were white, as had been those involved in the out-migration during the era of the new South. It was not until the dire distress caused by the boll weevil threatened their survival that northward migration of Negroes took on major proportions.

Meanwhile, back on those farms and back in those depressing little market places on which their young people were turning their backs, folks were tasting the first prosperity, and it of a brand that even bordered on luxury, that they had ever known—the first substantial flow of real money in three generations. Shining new automobiles appeared among battered wagons on the streets, as a new cotton madness spread across the region. High prices and good crops, combined with the flow of money from army training camps, most of which were located in the "sunny South," combined to create a short-lived boom.

But it was not for long. The postwar crash of '21 struck the South and quickly cast it back into its old time doldrums, as the price of cotton dropped. Before the South could struggle to its feet again, an insect appeared to compound its miseries. In 1924, the boll weevil crossed the Mississippi and entered the humid portion of the cotton belt, where its destructiveness was far greater than in the dry West, which it had plagued for years since entering the country from Mexico. Behind his forward march east and north, the weevil left a trail of ruin and destitution. In a single year, as he marched through Georgia, 300,000 Negroes trekked north to avoid starvation. Country banks closed their doors even faster than they had been opened during short-lived prosperity.

Outside the realm of cotton, conditions were less hopeless. Southward movement of the textile industry, which had begun with the century, continued unabated. By 1920, the South's chronic labor surplus, its low wage scales, its aversion to organized labor, its low taxes with exemptions for new industries, and its ample power supply had already attracted almost half the nation's textile industry. The war had stimulated the establishment of new chemical industries. The region's coal and oil production had greatly increased. The South's share of the nation's manufacturing had risen from twelve to fourteen percent. Great strides had also been made, partly with local capital, in the development of hydro-electric power.

The twenties also saw the rise and crash of the Florida boom. Throughout its long history, the South had shown itself to be particularly subject to the madness of booms and inevitable shocks of deflation. But what happened in Florida in the twenties dwarfed all previous land booms in American history. By comparison, the Mississippi Bubble was puny. Sparked by its rediscovery by the war-rich East, Florida sand, under a semi-tropical sun, soon simulated gold. Millions of people and hundreds of millions of dollars were sucked into the fantastic boom. The contagious madness presently spawned satellite booms along the Gulf shore; and, even in the mountains of North Carolina, neat white stakes, stenciled with lot numbers, marched through narrow defiles and up the precipitous slopes of millions of inaccessible acres.

Then the big bubble burst, and literally millions who had counted themselves rich one month woke from delusions to find themselves bankrupt. Over-extended towns, cities, and counties were likewise engulfed by ruin.

For more than four decades, the South had been making uninterrupted progress along the arduous uphill road from ruin. But now, under the succession of bone-jarring blows of the twenties, the deflation of the cotton land boom, mounting world surpluses plummeting the prices of its world trade commodities, a series of disastrous tropical hurricanes, the boll weevil, and the debacle of the Florida boom and its lesser imitators, the South was down on its back a full two years before Wall Street's Black Thursday. Consequently, when the rest of the country began to reel under the impact of the Great Depression, the South had already been depressed for more than two years. Banks with closed doors, desperate job seekers, and wholesale farm foreclosures were already commonplace. That earlier start down the road to depression, the long-standing paucity of fat on the economic bones of the South, its chronic labor surplus, and its heavy preponderance of particularly susceptible extractive industries all conspired to make the Great Depression far more devastating in the South than in any other section.

The relative intensity of the South's distress soon invited a resurgence of those who would drastically remold the South, economically and socially. A widely publicized study called the South the "nation's economic problem No. 1." Consequently, the section soon became the special province of planners of the New Deal. A disproportionate share of the relief and public works programs were directed southward, as were also farm relief and crop control programs. The South became a special field of endeavor for experimenters in socialism—planned communities, government subsidized demonstration farms, cooperatives for purchasing and marketing, urban community rehabilitation plans, and programs for the conversion of sharecroppers and tenant farmers to owners, all capped by the bold experiment in rural rehabilitation and public power represented by the Tennessee Valley Authority.

Some of these tradition defying experiments worked, but most of them, having been planned and executed by men with little understanding of Southern history, fell flat. Fatuous attempts to rescue the cotton farmer by restricting the domestic production of a crop, the price of which was determined by world production, served only to curb the potential income of the farmer and set in motion new waves of migration from the farms to towns and northward. Aside from stimulating migration and accomplishing some redistribution southward of a little of the national wealth, the only fruit of all those social and economic experiments of the New Deal years was the enhancement of the internal social and economic conflicts of the South.

Most of the New Deal programs were anti-individualistic experiments. Even as they were being instituted and accepted in desperation, they were bitterly criticized and unmercifully ridiculed. Although the utterly have-nots refused to look these gift horses in the mouth, most other Southerners soon developed a hearty distaste for the whole New Deal, symbolized as it was in their minds by an array of unrealistic socialistic planners. That disaffection was widespread and real. There was great concern over what these experiments and programs might do to the South's social system. There was fear that relief payments based on Northern rates of pay might both "spoil" the Negro and cost the South its competitive advantage of "cheap" labor in its efforts to attract industry. Consequently, blind to the fundamental principle that prosperity must be based on purchasing power of the masses, Southern leaders demanded and secured lower relief rates for their section. Nevertheless, lacking any visible alternative and bound by its single party system, Southern support of the New Deal at the ballot box deluded many an observer into the impression that the South liked the medicine prescribed for it by New Deal doctors. Only gradually did its disaffection become apparent through the airing of sentiments of rebel Democrats in the halls of Congress.

As the depression wore on, the stricken textile industry, by adopting the "stretch-out" system, putting more work on each operative, and through a terrible price in wage cutting managed to struggle to its feet. Those measures enabled it so to undercut Northern competition that most of the remaining New England textile mills had to choose between liquidating or moving south. Drastic survival measures invoked by the Southern textile industry brought a militant eruption of labor unionism and a series of violence-ridden strikes. However, they were premature and abortive, doomed to failure from the start. Southern textile workers had nothing to fall back on in a strike and Southern market places stood, as always, in uncompromising opposition to "Yankee, communistic" unions. When the mills won out and chastened workers returned to their jobs, much of their remaining New England competition, facing its unhappy alternatives, chose to move south, adding impetus to the section's slow recovery.

To that impetus, at the same time, was added that of a new and more economically significant industry. On the heels of the discovery by a Southern chemist, Charles H. Herty, of a practical method whereby paper could be made from resinous southern pines, the kraft paper industry sought out sites for pulp and paper mills in the land of the quick-growing pine, in what has been described as the greatest rush of an established industry into a new area, in the entire history of industry. Once again it was an industry of the extractive sort which had found its place in the South, but it was one which reached out into almost every woodland patch in the land, supplying a new and vital source of income to the poorest in the land-poor region.

By dint of the revival and expansion of the textile industry, the stimulus provided by the new paper industry, and the draining off through migration of some of its excess labor supply, as the depression merged into the economy of a new world conflict, the South was back on its long trail upward toward the still far distant goal of economic parity with the other sections of the nation.

Superficially, at least, the story of World War II and the South was much the same as that of the earlier world conflict, only on a much greater scale. Again, Southerners displayed relatively more war ardor than those of other sections and Southerners voluntarily joined up in greater numbers. Again the South was the principal training ground for the armed forces. The war greatly stimulated industrial expansion in the region, as elsewhere. Although industrial expansion incidental to the war did not increase the South's share of the nation's industry, those that were established as war industries in the region provided a greater measure of industrial diversity. Shipyards, synthetic rubber plants, airplane manufacturing, metal working establishments, the gigantic atomic installations at Oak Ridge, and a wide variety of chemical industries became permanent postwar contributors to a more balanced economy.

However, the most significant effects of the war, from the standpoint of the South's sectionalism, were less patent. Under the stimulus of high wartime wages in labor-hungry industries of the North, Midwest, and Pacific area; the migrations, mostly of Negroes, from the rural South, in places took on the aspects of an exodus. The extent of that migration from Southern farms to Northern cities can be judged from the first postwar census, which revealed that by 1950, the five largest Negro cities in the country were all north of the Potomac and Ohio Rivers.

Most white Southerners were deeply concerned by wartime developments which indicated that the country was moving toward the abandonment of the Southern way in race relations which, at the turn of the century, had also become the American way. Disturbing forebodings for the South's folkways in race relations were indicated in successive moves toward racial integration in the armed forces. On the civilian front there were similar implications in the executive Fair Employment Practices directive and the inclusion of non-discrimination clauses in all government contracts, although the enforcement of these provisions nowhere approximated their objectives. Beyond these pressures for change, there were pregnant implications inherent in the fact that almost a million Negroes had been inducted into the armed forces and over half of them had been sent overseas in a war which, at least partly, was being fought as a result of racial discrimination. And Southern servicemen of all classes were being deeply indoctrinated, by the war, with world concepts. Their families, too, as they studied maps and followed the news learned that colored people, at least yellow ones, were matching the abilities of white Americans—all to the detriment of provincial views and folkways.

These changes were contributing to a greater focusing of attention on the South's traditional social patterns, especially its legally buttressed caste system, and an inevitable re-examination of those ways in the minds of thinking Southerners, a questioning of their validity and justice, more frequently openly expressed, put new strains on the ever uneasy conscience of the South. A defensive and sensitive touchiness, humanly enough, took hold of a South beginning to be torn again by a directional dilemma.

Four years of war and severely restricted production of consumer goods had built up a backlog of consumer demand far exceeding the productive capacity of the nation's existing industrial installations. Technological advances during the war had opened numerous new opportunities for the manufacture of products unknown before the war. The South's perennial labor surplus, its bountiful and varied natural resources, of which unpolluted water in vast quantities had become one of the most essential; these and other luring attributes on the one hand, and the discouragements of labor strife in the old industrial regions, the paucity of good water, and a new and studied aim toward decentralization of industry, on the other, strongly focused attention on the South.

The consequences of that attention was the most dramatic transformation, of a rural-agricultural society into an urban-industrial society, in the nation's history. References to the South as the "nation's economic problem No. 1" were now only historical. Suddenly, all the talk was of the South as the "nation's economic opportunity No. 1." The weird shapes of oil refineries and petrochemical establishments appeared along the bayous, synthetic fiber plants rose in the middle of riverside cotton fields, and the smoke-belching stacks of pulp mills became the dominant landmarks of sleepy Southern harbors; while low, clean-lined, usually stackless lesser industries dotted the countryside. The latter were of a far wider variety than the region had ever seen—plants for the production of apparel, hardware, electrical appliances, furniture, insect repellants, and agricultural chemicals, and a multitude of other products. In the textile field, the woolen and hosiery industries began repeating the history of cotton textiles with a wholesale southward trek. In the long standing rivalry between New England states and old states of the Southeast, the former, by 1957, had been finally overtaken in the total value added by manufacturing processes. In Florida and along the lower Mississippi, transformations approached the sensational. As if to give a fitting symbol, in a sparsely populated area in South Carolina the Atomic Energy Commission located its Savannah River Plant, the greatest construction project ever undertaken by man.

Lower wage rates continued in some instances to be a factor in the southward movement of industry, but it was one of diminishing importance. Gone were the starvation wages of cotton mills of the new South. Although a differential persisted between Northern and Southern wage rates, year by year it grew narrower, inexorably approaching complete extinction.

Southerners looked upon these developments and they appeared good in their eyes. But during the same postwar years, there were other developments, also indicating a uniformly maturing nation, and, likewise, products of the machine age, developments which Southerners found far less acceptable aspects of the machine age, not so much on account of immediate effects but because of their frightening long-term implications. In a series of decisions, the United States Supreme Court had opened the white Democratic primaries to Negro voters, thereby destroying the main instrument through which the region's caste system had been built and maintained; opened the graduate departments of many Southern universities to Negro students; outlawed racial segregation on public conveyances; and finally, carrying its reinterpretation of the Constitution to its final degree, the Court had declared the legal maintenance of separate but equal public school facilities for the races to be inherently discriminatory and illegal.

With these decisions, a deep uneasiness welled up in the South, an uneasiness which soon developed into a state of unrelieved and all-pervading tension, reaching out and coloring almost every aspect of Southern society. A new invasion of the South, this time with words and writs, but no less determined than that of 1861 to rid the country of Southernism and its folkways, had been launched.

The events of the years, between the inauguration of Woodrow Wilson and the latter fifties, wrought enormous changes in the South, largely concealed even from Southerners themselves by the distractions of cataclysmic events of those years—the two greatest wars in history, a "police action" in Korea, a continuing "cold war" with Communism from which there is no relaxing, and a depression which shook the foundations of democratic government and the free enterprise system. As those events were transforming the world, the South too, in its way, was experiencing equally drastic changes.

The South's resistance to changes involving the Negro have created the impression of an unchanging region. On the contrary, its history reveals changes more drastic and more precipitate than those experienced by any other section. In its early days essentially an aristocracy, after 1776 the South embraced democracy. The Civil War and its aftermath forced changes unparalleled elsewhere. In the 1880's, it experienced a sweeping, if partially ephemeral, change to radicalism. In the era of the new South it had, at least in its aspirations, embraced industrialism. Now in the era of the changing South there were significant changes in everything. Of all the peoples of the Western World who have lived through the past half-century of accelerating change, Americans have been the most affected, for here the creation of so-called modern civilization has proceeded farther than in any other nation. And of all the sections of the country, the changes this half-century has wrought in the South have been vastly greater than those experienced by any other area.

In early years of this century, less than one Southerner in six lived in even a small town. Illiteracy was rife. Public schools were few and poor, and compulsory education was far in the future. Paved roads and streets were practically nonexistent and electric lights and indoor plumbing were luxuries enjoyed by only the relatively rich—and they were few in the poverty-ridden section. Living more like the children of ancient Greece or Rome than our children today, Southern boys of all classes grew to manhood barefooted except in coldest weather. Their recreation, untouched by its modern synthesization through organization, was whatever they could devise on their own—a vastly different world from that of the organization-ridden, television and movie entertained, ever "bewheeled" youngsters of today. And for adults too, the contrast of life then and today was almost as great. Then, in the South as in ancient Greece or Rome, the whole social structure rested on a work force which was a class apart, in many areas a numerical majority of the people, which remained all but *de facto* slaves, a class nowise considered citizens other than in theory, a class living at the barest subsistence level, uncouth and untaught.

Older Southerners, looking about them at the current scene and then casting their mind's eye back to the scenes of their childhood, see there a land that is strange and alien by today's standards, a way of life that has all but gone with the wind.

To get a meaningful picture of the changes that were taking place in the South during those years of distraction, to get a clear view of the forest despite the trees, calls for a detailed and comparative examination of the principal facets of the South's economy and its social constituency during its twentieth-century era of change. Since economic laws commonly speak with more authority in free societies than do the studiously enacted laws of parliaments, so that a region's economy is always the most powerful molder of its society, the changing economy of the changing South is of prime importance and deserves first consideration.

Prior to World War I, the South's share of the nation's industry was only twelve percent, although it then had about thirty percent of the nation's population. By 1956, its share of the country's industrial production had increased fifty percent, giving it eighteen percent of the national total, although its share of the total population had fallen seven percent in the interim. The increase in manufacturing wages, between 1929 and 1950 in the South, was 294 percent as against 204 percent in the rest of the country. During that period, while the proportion of Southerners employed by industry was rising to eighteen percent, the proportion so engaged in the North, as distinguished from the West, fell to twenty-eight percent, showing about the same percentage fall as Southerners showed increase. Those figures become even more impressive when consideration is given the fact that the South's population includes a much higher percentage of children to workers, and much more impressive when consideration is given the fact that they are calculated against a North and West rapidly advancing all the time.

In other words, while still far behind in a fast race, the South was closing the gap resulting from the leader's head start and closing it at a truly amazing rate. Assuming only that trends in progress will continue, and they have been accelerating year by year, statisticians are calculating a day, within a decade or two, when the South will be as industrial as the remainder of the nation. That acceleration is reflected in recent employment figures which show that since World War II industrial employment in the South increased two and a third times as fast as in the country as a whole.

Even as Southern industry was surging ahead, the production of oil fields and mines of the South rose at a phenomenal rate. By 1956, more than half of the nation's mineral production was coming out of the South, in marked contrast to the all but negligible Southern production early in the century. Two-thirds of the country's oil and all such essentials as sulphur, bauxite, and phosphates are now part of the broadening economic base of the section, although the area still benefits relatively little from these riches, for the colonial pattern under which they were first exploited continues largely unchanged. Texas is still "New York's richest foreign possession."

As important as industry is in a balanced modern economy, there are better criteria for measuring the progress of a society toward the highest standards of the day. This is particularly true of the South where so much of its industry remains "colonial" and so much of it is of the low pay, extractive type. More cogent criteria of progress are inherent in the types of employment within an economy. A close, direct relationship obtains between the standard of living enjoyed by a society and the ratio of its population engaged in service enterprises. Similarly, a high ratio of laborers and domestic servants and a low ratio of women employed in business and manufacturing are ordinarily indicia of a low standard of living.

Statistical studies covering the past two decades reveal striking changes in the South in these indicia. In practically every respect, the distribution of the South's labor and personal service forces is moving rapidly toward greater resemblance to non-Southern states, just as with industrial employment. For example, in the latest census period, the South increased its undersupply of craftsmen more than three times as fast as the rate outside the South. Much the same happened in professional and clerical categories. In 1910, the South had but half the national proportion of its people engaged in trade and service, but by 1950, it had about the same proportion as other sections. And, tardily following the national trend, Southern women flocked to offices, service establishments, and factories. At the same time, the South's overproportion of domestic servants and unskilled laborers dropped sharply in comparison with the labor force outside the South.

These categories are but examples. Practically without exception in every comparative statistical analysis of the South and the non-South, if a number, index, or percentage for the South is lower than the national average, it shows a far more rapid rise than the corresponding figure for the nation. If the figure for the South was higher than the figure for the nation, it shows a movement down toward the national figure, or, with much the same result, the national figure is seen to be moving upward faster than that for the South.

As sensational as were changes in the South in the industrial aspects of its changing economy, it was in agriculture that the most radical and varied changes occurred. In the first decade of the century, five out of six Southerners were farm folk. As late as 1940, a third of Southern workers were engaged in farming. But in the ensuing decade, a third of those found other employment, as did another twenty-five percent in the period between 1950 and 1956, leaving only about one worker in six on the section's farms.

During those years of agricultural change, world competition, the boll weevil, and government crop restrictions had conspired not only to topple King Cotton from his throne but almost to choke the breath of life from him. In the eastern realm, his passing was ephemerally memorialized by rows of empty Negro cabins; some falling to ruin, others serving as makeshift barns for the crops that had taken over his realm. In Georgia, where he first mounted his throne, farmers were receiving more than twice as much from the sale of broilers as for their cotton crop. In South Carolina, his second province, tobacco had outstripped him in importance. There also, the production of a single synthetic fiber plant exceeded the value of the entire state's cotton crop. Synthetic fiber production, mostly in Southern localities, was now rivaling the poundage of the entire national production of cotton and already greatly surpassed it in market value. It was a chastened potentate fleeing westward, out of the South to which he had in his day brought such incalculable misery, to New Mexico, Arizona, and California where cotton culture is largely freed from the vagaries of weather and the boll weevil and where mechanization is practical. Except sentimentally, his passing was little mourned. A more diversified, less soil destroying, and more prosperous form of agriculture took over his abandoned provinces. In Georgia, signs at the entrances to a formerly great cotton county proudly proclaim it as a county "that's gone to grass"—where sleek cattle embellish grass-covered hills once devoted to cotton. A statue to the boll weevil in an Alabama town gives due and grateful recognition to that insect for new found agricultural freedom from the old enslaving tyrant.

Despite the loss of four out of five of its farm workers and drastic reductions in acreage cultivated, Southern farms, which traditionally supplied about half the nation's farm production, continued to produce almost the same proportion of the greatly stepped-up agricultural output of the country. Utilization of modern machinery, conversion to crops less demanding of hand labor than cotton, relegation of cotton growing to those areas where even its production could be largely mechanized, and the consolidation of farms into larger units all contributed to the changed picture.

The South continued to find it possible to produce four-fifths of the country's rice and cotton, practically all its tobacco, nine-tenths of its sweet potatoes, all of its sugar cane, a quarter of its poultry, a third of its fruits and nuts, most of its vegetable oils, almost a third of its vegetables, and more than a third of its beef cattle.

This partial enumeration of mid-century crops of the South suggests how far the agricultural South has moved away from the woes of its cotton, tobacco, and sugar cane economy. Many of its present crops are recent innovations. The agricultural South is even now the scene of accelerating changes. In fact, farming is rapidly taking on all the attributes of business. Capital requirements for land and machinery, including the booming movement to irrigation, are mounting steadily. No longer is it possible for anyone who hasn't anything else to do to turn to farming with any real hope of success. An experienced Southern agriculturalist advises anyone against going into farming unless he has at least $50,000 starting capital available.

Despite its dramatic alteration, agricultural changes taking place in the South are yet far from complete. At mid-century, three-fifths of the farmers of the region were still tenants, comprising two-thirds of all farm tenants in the country. And the South still remains heavily burdened by the heritage of King Cotton's long misrule. Millions continue hopelessly bound to the only agriculture they know—small scale cash cropping, blindly devoted to cotton growing. Three-fifths of the nation's eroded lands blot the countryside of the South as symbolic reminders of his tragic reign. Southern farmers still have far the lowest per capita income of any in the country.

But even into these darker quarters, the light of hopeful changes are falling. The number of farm tenants in the South has been falling at an accelerating rate. Their numbers dropped by half in forty years, but they dropped by twenty-five percent in the first four years of the current decade. Eroded areas are now in process of being returned to profitable production, mostly through planting in pines. Indications of a better day for the Southern farmer lie in statistics which show that, decade by decade, his income is rising at a faster rate than that of farmers generally.

Although agriculture remains an important element in the total economy of the South, its twentieth century economic developments along other lines have been so many-faceted and so sweeping that the region is no longer even heavily dependent upon the vagaries of weather or the price fluctuations of staples. But seven percent of the gross income of the South, in 1956, was derived from agriculture. Only in its persistent habit of thinking of itself as agricultural does the South remain agricultural.

Another product of Southern soil, its timber resources, closely inter-related with its agriculture, especially since it has become a crop to be harvested rather than a resource to be exploited, has also been subject to twentieth-century changes fully as revolutionary, if not as varied, as those which appear in the region's agriculture. Back in the austere days of the new South, when timber barons moved in and slew the remaining primeval forests of the South with little or no consideration for the future, Southern forests supplied something over half the nation's timber needs. Today, even in competition with great forests of the Northwest, about forty percent of the country's lumber needs are supplied by Southern forests; in addition, they are furnishing about half the raw materials for the nation's paper mills.

The forests of the South are growing faster now than they are being cut, giving the industry a future there which is not enjoyed in rival Western regions where the cut regularly exceeds the growth.

The great changes that made resurrection of the South's timber industry possible have been concentrated in the past quarter-century. In the twenties, realization drifted into the South that its forest lands were potential self-replenishing mines of green gold. Inspired by that realization, a forestry crusade swept the region from end to end. Within a few years, every state had undertaken a fire protection program, established nurseries for the growing of billions of tree seedlings to replant understocked areas, and provided for free technical guidance to encourage good timberland management. In several states, proceeds from forest products were soon rivaling those from agriculture. It was as if a rich and entirely new source of wealth had been discovered, and most of that income was now going into Southern pockets. When the timber barons of the new South moved out, most of their great holdings, then considered little better than worthless, had passed into Southern ownership. Moreover, now much more of those forest products are being further fabricated in the South, into paper, plywood, furniture, and specialized, treated timbers.

In the course of a mere half-century, agriculture, which had comprised almost the sole economic base of the old South, had been relegated to a minor place in the South's economy, being now far surpassed by both manufacturing and mineral recovery and being rivaled by timber production, the income from resorts and tourist expenditures, and the payrolls of military and civilian employees of the Federal government. Of all those, only the production of farms and forests were of consequence before the first decade of the twentieth century. The combined effect of these sweeping changes in the South's economy is indicated in these figures: In the first quarter of the century its wealth increased fourfold and, since then, per capita income in the South has risen more than 250 percent as against a national increase of 170 percent. That improvement was reflecting itself in better living. For example, in the first ten years after World War II, the consumption of electric power in the South increased sixty-seven percent faster than in the country as a whole, telephone installations showed the phenomenal increase of 135 percent in eight years and the dollar value of new construction increased more than three and a half times as fast as in the nation as a whole. But, being percentage increases, those figures, by implication, point up the poverty of the South in those earlier years, for, despite sharp increases, Southerners still have less than two-thirds the average income of people of other sections.

Such vast changes in the Southern economy inevitably wrought corresponding changes in other aspects of the South. Unquestionably their greatest effect, the one most loaded with future significance, has been exerted upon the population pattern of the region, both racial and geographical.

The South 20
Embraces
Change: 2

WITH AMAZING RAPIDITY, the rural South had, by 1955, become an urban South with a vast array of diverse interests. The influx of industry, a changing and mechanized agriculture, and increased wealth offering more opportunities in service vocations, all precipitated phenomenal growth in the region's urban population. Between 1910 and 1950, Southern towns and cities grew 130 percent while those of the country as a whole increased but forty percent. As impressive as those figures are, they show but part of the actual urbanization of the South. Most of the developments that were transforming the South occurred after the automobile came into common use, obviating necessity for a worker to live near his work. Consequently, approximately two-thirds of those still officially counted as rural dwellers are employed in town or in an industry associated with a town and are fast becoming oriented away from the farm and toward the town. Perhaps a majority of those non-farm rural dwellers are already sociologically part of the town.

Despite this powerful influence retarding their officially recognized growths, Southern cities have shown a growth more rapid during the past twenty years than that experienced by the great urban centers of the country during their rise. Of all the cities of the South, only three failed to exceed the average growth of non-Southern cities in the last census period. Twenty-seven of the forty-five cities of the nation that grew more than a third during that decade were in the South, and all but two of those not in the South are in the West. Moreover, recent special censuses indicate that the phenomenal growth rates of Southern cities, as revealed in the 1950 census, are still accelerating.

The growth of Southern cities in recent decades reveals one facet of a transcending and continuing change taking place in the South—a population on the move in both intra- and intersectional migrations. About half of all Southern families were involved in these migrations, which took on massive proportions after the close of World War I. The largest movement was of those moving to town from the farms. In addition to young people who had glimpsed the world outside, those most involved were the poorer farmers, farm tenants, and share-croppers who were finding a livelihood too hard to come by in the face of the recurring disasters which beset farming in the South in those years and ever-increasing crop restrictions. Negro rural dwellers were possessed by a particularly strong urge to move to town. There, in their own sections and under the exigencies of urban living came a measure of relief from rural rigidity of the caste system, the city being a more impersonal society.

For every farm dweller who moved to a Southern town or city one also left for a different section of the country. About ten million Southerners have left the South for other sections during twentieth-century years, most of them being drawn from Southern farm population which lost four million people in the 1940's alone. By 1950, some 7,500,000 Southerners were living outside the South. Partly offsetting that loss were 3,500,000 who had moved into the South from other sections.

The loss of four million people in that exchange represents one of the prime factors which have been operating to keep the South relatively poor. Until the last twenty years, when Negroes came to dominate intersectional migration from the South, most of those who left were the cream of the section's youth. Those who left averaged a year more schooling than those who stayed behind. Their average age was twenty-four. The South had borne the expense of rearing and educating them and had received nothing of economic value in return. Conservatively estimated, the South's economic loss from this unfavorable balance of population trade has amounted to more than fifty billion dollars in this century alone—a terrific drain on the economy of a poor section, especially in the austere years when much of that loss occurred.

The intersectional population exchange has had, and is continuing to have, a great effect on the South's racial constituency. Except for the intervention of this wholesale population exchange of the twentieth century, the proportion of Negroes to whites would have mounted rapidly to an overwhelming Negro majority unless interrupted by a major alteration in the birth rate differential between the races. Although the Negro birth rate has long been about half again as great as that of whites, the greater death rate among Negroes through the years had kept them from increasing as fast. However, when the public health program of the latter years of the new South era began sharply to reduce the Negro death rate, there was nothing to prevent the South's Negro population from submerging the whites beneath overwhelming numbers. It was only Negro migration that forestalled that prospect. Although during pre-World War II years, northward migration was an indiscriminate one of both whites and Negroes, the countermigration southward was exclusively of whites. And, beginning about 1939, the migration from the South was predominantly Negro. Consequently, in recent decades, the Negro population of the section has shown little increase, but in the North, and more recently in the West, it has risen at a phenomenal rate.

In 1940, seventy-seven percent of Negroes in the United States lived in the Southern states. By 1950, only sixty-three percent remained there. It is likely that already more than half the American Negroes are living in states outside the South, for there is no indication that their tendency to migrate from the South is lessening. Indeed, there is reason to believe that it may be accelerating. This was indicated in New York's interim census of 1957. There, in the years since 1950, while the city as a whole lost population, its non-white population jumped by forty-one percent, a numerical increase (320,221) greater than that which occurred in the entire previous decade. During the first fifteen years after the war boom began in 1939, it had been the ready availability of well-paid jobs in the North, especially in its great cities, that had stimulated Negro exodus from the South. In recent years, their northward movement has been sustained by increasingly drastic government crop restrictions which curtailed the permitted acreages of major Southern crops to such an extent that the position of the small farmer became untenable, by the continued mechanization of farming, and by the often chimerical prospect of living in a section free from racial discrimination.

If these forces continue to operate for two more decades as tellingly as they have in the past two, there will be little difference between the racial composition of the South and the remainder of the nation; the highest ratios of Negroes to whites will prevail in New York and Illinois instead of in Mississippi and South Carolina.

Of all changes in the changing South, none was more momentous than that in public education. The educational crusade of early years of the century had doubled public school revenues by 1910. But that was the merest beginning. By 1930, school appropriations had been upped again from $28,000,000 to $415,000,000, and the value of school properties had increased a hundredfold. Still, Southern schools lagged behind those of other sections. The handicaps under which the South labored, in its efforts to measure up to the educational achievements of other sections, were great. In 1930, each 1,000 adult males in the South had responsibility for the education of 1,300 children as against 800 in the North and only 600 in the West, and Southerners had only a little over half as much income as those others to perform their greater responsibility. Moreover, the South's ruralness and its dual school systems posed further difficulties and added to the expense. Although, by then, the South was contributing a larger portion of its income to education than any other section, it still trailed in the educational procession.

The return of a small measure of prosperity as the Depression waned, rising urbanization, advent of the school bus permitting the consolidation of one and two-teacher country schools, and the mounting shame of sorry facilities commonly provided for the Negroes, all conspired to spark a new enthusiasm directed toward bringing the South's school systems up to the national norm. The flowering of that renewed determination came during the years following the second World War. The South's school building program in that period was relatively the greatest undertaken in any section. New school buildings of latest design, those for whites undistinguishable from those for Negroes, suddenly became as characteristic of the Southern scene as tradition would have pillared mansions and magnolias.

Higher education likewise came in for its share of the enthusiasm. By the middle fifties, colleges and universities of the South were comparable in relation to the population, and in their ratio of students to professors, to those of other sections. They were attracting more outsiders as students than those of any other section. Only in their income, which was still sadly deficient (which prevented them from holding outstanding professors) and in their relatively weak graduate departments did they remain markedly deficient.

All in all, the South was moving at an extraordinary rate toward the educational par of the nation, just as it was in practically every other economic and social aspect. In public health, birth rates, death rates, and crime trends the same tendency was observable as has been pointed out in those facets of Southern life which have been mentioned.

When, early in the century, philanthropies launched attacks on hookworm and malaria and demonstrated that the scourge of those diseases could be substantially eliminated, they also set in motion a public health program that worked miracles in ridding the South of its appalling death and incapacitation rate from preventable diseases. The very measures employed to conquer malaria also brought to an end the intermittent but devastating forays of "yellow jack." From those victories, a stimulated public health movement moved on to a successful attack on typhoid fever and encouraging progress was made in campaigns on venereal disease.

Official death rates give dramatic proof of accomplishments. From far the highest in the nation, the death rate of Southerners fell steadily toward the national average and then on to a figure substantially below the national death rate, at mid-century. That lower-than-average death rate indicated that the improved public health program embraced the South's Negro population as well as the whites. Census figures which gave Negroes a life expectancy of sixteen years less than whites in 1915 gave only seven years less in 1956. Infant mortality, which had been especially high in the Negro population, dropped from more than twenty percent above the national average in 1940 to barely above that average fifteen years later.

Birth rates of the sections showed the same marked tendency to move toward uniformity. Between 1910 and 1940, the Southern birth rate, which had always been much higher than that of the rest of the country, fell almost twice as fast as it did in other sections. After 1940, the Southern rate, which was still twenty percent greater, continued to decline, while that of the non-South rose sharply. The sectional differential almost disappeared.

Even criminal records of the section, despite their wide disparity of pattern, display the same tendency to move toward similarity. Between 1940 and 1950, the South's crime index fell from 142 to 118, while that of the rest of the country rose from 64 to 66. The South's greatest improvement was in the category of violent crimes, which, from early frontier days to the present, has been one of its special claims to notoriety with rates in the past running from five to ten times those for other sections. By 1956, the Southern violent crime rate had fallen to only about three times the rate outside the South. Without doubt, that decline is partly a reflection of decline in the relative number of Negroes, who display propensity to crimes of violence, but it cannot account for most of it, for Southern whites, too, have always shown a greater disposition to violence than whites of other sections.

A more reasonable explanation lies in a mounting inurement to the restraints of law through a greater degree of urbanization and education. In other crime categories in which the South was traditionally better behaved than the rest of the country, such as robbery and larceny, the Southern crime rate rose to approximate the national rate —yet another instance of the all-pervading tendency to identity with the nation as a whole.

What of the crime which is most closely associated in the popular mind with the South? Under the euphemism of "frontier justice," except when it took place in the South, lynching was a fairly common folkway of most of frontier America, continuing so long as the frontier persisted. When frontier conditions passed with the maturing of the frontier, so did "frontier justice." Only in the South did frontier conditions persist into the day of lives in being, and only in the South did "frontier justice" persist as a phenomenon of conditions which had historically countenanced it. Lynching was almost invariably a rural crime, and lynchers were almost equally invariably of the most ignorant and benighted classes. Under the combined influence of education, urbanization, diminishing isolation, and stern disapproval of the better elements, lynching, by 1948, had become but a besmirching historical record and a nightmare memory of the frontier that had passed so slowly. As against the fifty-two lynchings of 1915, there were but eleven between 1948 and 1955, and none since. A maturing South, of its own volition through its own internal forces, had rid itself of its greatest disgrace.

The impact of most of twentieth-century changes in the South affected whites and Negroes alike. Although many new industries, by choice or in compliance with custom, offered direct job opportunities overwhelmingly to whites, even in these instances Negroes garnered secondary opportunities along with the community in general. In most other respects, the changes of the changing South were non-discriminatory. Where the need for change was greater among Negroes, resulting changes, so far as Negroes were concerned, were likewise greater. That was true of the rising income. The per capita income of Southern Negroes showed far greater percentage advances than it did for whites. The same was true of infant mortality and longevity. It was also true in education. On the other hand, the Negro's crime rate failed to improve. It even tended to counteract the improving over-all Southern crime record. Disturbingly, the Negro's criminal tendencies appeared to rise with the lessening of political and social oppression, and this despite sharply improved educational opportunities and a greatly enhanced economic position.

A similar alarming tendency to breach the rules of society appears in the Negro family integrity. While illegitimacy declines among

Southern whites it is rising sharply among Southern Negroes. For example, the latest figures available in South Carolina show that now a fourth of all Negro births there are admitted illegitimates, a bastardy incidence more than thirteen times as great as among whites.

Of some of the changes, the Negro was the special recipient. The elimination of terror of the lynch mob was one of those. There were others in several changes, some voluntary, others forced by courts, which all but freely opened Southern ballot boxes to Negro voters. With little justification in fact, liberals have long regarded Southern poll tax laws as iniquitous devices for disfranchising Negroes, whereas, in fact, they probably disfranchised far more whites than Negroes and they never applied to women or the elderly. Repeal of poll taxes appeared to produce no notable upsurge in Negro voting. Nevertheless, during the past two decades all Southern states but five eliminated the requirement of poll tax receipts as a prerequisite for voting and all but one of those retaining it had far more exceptions than inclusions. Other developments, such as court orders opening white primaries to Negro participation, education, and an energetic Negro leadership did arouse Negroes from long political apathy. Only a little over 150,000 Southern Negroes voted in 1940. By 1948, 750,000 were registered. In the next four years, the latter figure was multiplied more than threefold. Presently, there are an estimated two and a half million qualified Negro electors in the South. The Negro has suddenly become a potentially potent factor in Southern politics.

Mention of the Negro's political potential suggests a look at the Southern political scene in the years of the changing South. Of all significant facets of the South, it was the one which gave least evidence of change. There was good reason for that. When Reconstruction governments were set up by the radicals, they were carefully designed to give maximum power to the freedmen concentrated in plantation districts. When the redeemers took over from the carpetbaggers and the power to direct the freedmen's votes passed into their hands, they had no inclination to change the pattern and their governments congealed in their rural molds. With those rural frameworks unaltered, the population shifts of the South took place.

Although Black Belt areas were depopulated, their political power remained. Cities grew phenomenally, but the political power of counties in which they were located did not grow commensurately. Today, it is not unusual to find Southern rural counties with ten times the proportionate legislative representation of some urban counties. Consequently, Southern legislatures bear a heavily rural stamp and they are more responsive to the conservative folkways of their rural minority than to the more liberal city ways of their urban majority.

The political South is far more conservative than are Southerners themselves. That is why twentieth-century Southern politicians have so completely failed to provide vital leadership for a drastically changing South. Yet more discouraging is the realization that political changes commensurate with other changes on the Southern scene will neither be soon nor easily come by. Rural legislative majorities will naturally resist so long as they can, all moves for constitutional revision or amendment which will topple them from power.

Politicians of the changing South continued to reflect the diversities and internal conflicts of the South. Around one pole were able, respected, and staunchly conservative men of the Jack Garner, Harry Byrd, Walter George school, men who served the nation well in supplying the braking power needed to keep the New Deal juggernaut from running wild and wrecking the American system through its radical momentum. At the other pole were ever and always poor reproductions of Tillman and Watson, rabble rousers full of sound and fury, thriving on hate and effectually preventing the South from calmly considering its grave problems and moving forward toward their solution. From among those warmed-over servings-up from the day of demagoguery, ignorance, and prejudice, only Huey Long attained the sway and influence of their prototypes.

In spite of the continued dominance of rural conservatism, there were some political changes. They came insidiously, creeping in through the back door. They came through the interaction of the false largesse of Washington, and Southern poverty and insecurity. When dollars were offered, especially when their number exceeded those sent to Washington, Southern politicians tended expediently to ignore their States' rights tradition and were as ready as those of any other section to sell away to Federal authority area after area of state prerogative. Before the New Deal passed into history, Federal minions were dragging measuring tapes across every cotton and tobacco farm of the South. They had secured effective control of every state health department and employment service, to mention but a few of the areas sold out to Washington in years of the changing South.

Aided and abetted by Southern political leaders, along with their sister states, states of the South had slipped an irretrievably long way down the lucre-greased way from sovereign states to administrative units of an all-powerful national government. No longer were stirring calls for the defense of States' rights being heard—except when Federal authority threatened defiance of the "off limits" postings surrounding areas of state prerogative in interracial relations. Then only, with much of the appearance of special pleading, are the honored-in-the-breach principles of States' rights called to the defense.

Dangerous centralization of power in Washington and emasculation of constitutionally reserved powers of the states which permitted it were not changes special to the South, although there were effects special to the South.

But there was one great political change, although still largely potential in its effects which was *exclusive* to the South, although it was but part of a national movement. For three-quarters of a century, the white South had maintained all but exclusive political dominance of the region through its single party system. By restricting membership in the Democratic party to whites and ironing out all internecine differences in primaries, an unbeatable solid front could always be presented on election day. It was through circumstances rather than through any wide devotion to its principles that the Democratic party had come to be the South's single party bulwark of white supremacy. Keys to the success of the system had always been the restriction of party membership to white persons and the use of powerful political and social taboos against any party disloyalty, especially on the local level. In the years of change, both these keys were lost. Through a series of court orders, all racial restrictions on party membership were nullified. And, as the national Democratic party became increasingly anti-business, pro-labor, and pro-Negro, the taboo of party disloyalty lost most of its power. Indeed, in recent years, it was fast becoming a mark of distinction in the South to eschew the Democratic party.

For the moment, through sheer momentum, the political South continues to travel along in its old grooves, kept there by habit and the influence of party-loyal office holders, who treasure their seniority and dare not rock the boat. But the situation is too charged with incongruities to continue. There is an untenable absurdity in Southern Negroes affiliating with the party of white supremacy and voting in its primaries for candidates, all of whom are usually pledged above all else to the maintenance of racial segregation. There is equal political absurdity in the affiliation of those candidates with a national party equally determined to defeat the platform pledges of its Southern candidates and yet continuing to honor them with high positions as loyal party members. It is beyond possibility that such incongruities can continue for long. Those incongruities are certainly the seeds of drastic changes in the offing.

No discussion of the changing South can be adequate without noting its changing literature. For more than a century the use of words had been the South's only cultural feature, aside from the folk music of its Negroes. Although the changing South wrought little change in this exclusiveness, it did bring momentous changes elsewhere. The South had had successful writers in the era of the new South, but they had been repelled by the era. They, like so many of their fellow Southerners of the postwar South, were absorbed in the self-flattery of the glory that had been, enhanced by their imaginations.

Only Ellen Glasgow, from the remoteness of her detached individualism, utilized the rich material inherent in the South of that day. Other than Miss Glasgow's works, so little of cultural merit had come out of the South within the memory of man, that Henry L. Mencken, who counted himself a Southerner, gibed at the region unmercifully. It was the epitome of crudity, the "Bible Belt," the "Sahara of the Bozart."

No sooner had Mencken loosed his sharp tongue on the South's frailties than, as if in response to the hurt, dramatic changes began to appear in the desert. In the years that followed, to the amazement of the literary world, this desert became richly colored by a literary flowering unrivaled since that of New England, a hundred years before. Incidentally, it is interesting and significant that both those flowerings occurred as the sections were experiencing sweeping changes, moving them rapidly from an old, stable order into an utterly transformed society.

But the greatest change in Southern literature was in what Southern writers of the twentieth century felt compelled to write about. No longer, with the sole significant exception of *Gone With the Wind*, was it of glories past. It was now realism—bleak, stark realism. Through the widely popular works of such novelists and playwrights as William Faulkner, Erskine Caldwell, Tennessee Williams, Thomas Wolfe, and Paul Green, to mention but a few, the seamy side of Southern life was flamboyantly displayed before all the world.

Their immense success increased the South's difficulties in its relations with the world outside, for they had painted in the minds of those without first-hand knowledge of the region a picture of the South as one long Tobacco Road, peopled exclusively by ignorant, amoral sharecroppers, shiftless but philosophical Negroes, degenerate aristocrats, and crude, avaricious storekeepers—all twisted by frustration or congenital abnormality. There was no counterbalancing publicity for overwhelming millions of other Southern folk; professional men, merchants, farmers, artisans, mill operatives, and clerical workers. But for their accents, these differ little from their counterparts in Massachusetts, Illinois, or California. Although the tawdry pictures of Southern life depicted by Southern writers gave outsiders a grossly twisted concept of the South as a whole, the essential validity of the criticism underlying this literature contributed a needed stimulus to a rising social conscience in the South.

All these forces, and many more, were directing the changing South toward an ever-increasing similarity to the remainder of the country. But perhaps the most powerful forces of all were the educational and propaganda influences of mass communication and entertainment. Southerners saw the same movies, watched the same television shows, read the same magazines, and got their news through the same news agencies as did other Americans. Under their combined impact,

Southern views and Southerners' thinking were being inexorably, if insidiously, channeled into an increasingly uniform national mold.

Although most of the changes that were sweeping the South were little noted, enough of them were sufficiently obvious to exhilarate Southerners with a feeling that momentous events were occurring. They were saying that in the South "everything is on the move; cotton moving west, cattle moving east, factories moving south, Negroes moving north." However, few realized the full extent of changes in which they were involved. Fewer still realized the full implications of those changes, changes that spelled the early death of the South as an economic and sociological section apart from the nation.

A high degree of ruralism and agriculture, the Negro, poverty, and climate have for long kept the South a region apart. They were the essential ingredients of Southernism. Southernism was nothing more than the sum of their effects.

Changes of the twentieth century have altered and severely subtracted from every one of those elements—except, of course, the climate, and even it was being modified for millions through air conditioning. Ruralism had changed to urbanism. Agriculture had been both drastically altered and reduced to a minor element in the economy. Negroes had left by the millions and the conditions and attitudes of those who remained had been greatly transformed. The dire poverty that had made for Southernism had become only a relative poverty by comparison with other sections of a fabulously rich nation. For most, the poverty that warped remained only as a memory. By virtue of those subtractions from its components, Southernism had been steadily reduced to an approaching extinction. Or, perhaps it is putting it more accurately to say that Southernism was being inexorably moved to equation with Americanism.

If Southernism was dying, as it surely was, it was dying at the hands of Southerners. The most fascinating aspect of changes that were remaking the South in the national image is that all the primary changes were changes prayerfully sought or, more accurately, aggressively pursued by Southerners themselves. Southern states set a pattern for the country by establishing development boards, generously provided with public funds, to "sell" their states to industry. Every town of consequence had its Chamber of Commerce dedicated primarily to the same purpose. Southern states offered liberal tax exemptions to new industry. Some even went so far as to authorize political subdivisions to issue tax-exempt bonds to acquire plant sites and build plants for use by new industries. In no section was more restraint shown in enacting restrictive legislation in order that a "good industrial climate" might be offered whereas, to the same end, prolabor legislation always found the going tough.

The zeal Southerners displayed in fostering the growth of their cities was unmatched elsewhere. Atlanta, Baton Rouge, and Miami became classic demonstrations of metropolitan reorganization for the removal of legal impediments to growth. And everywhere, in small towns and cities alike, Southerners exhibited enormous pride in urban growth. Every little town hankered for industry and aspired to city status. Long-standing satisfaction with stagnation under the status quo seemed suddenly to have evaporated.

Fostering yet other changes, farm agents were busily weaning farmers from their old ways, from cotton and corn, and inculcating agricultural pursuits less demanding of a supply of cheap labor. They encouraged greater use of farm machinery. The trek of sharecroppers and farm laborers to the cities and the North was a measure of the farm agents' success.

Change swept the South in the twentieth century because Southerners themselves had warmly embraced change. They had ardently desired that increased prosperity which could come only through change and the greater ease of urban living. The "sensitive South" desired an end to its poor-relation status in the nation. However, most of the encouragers of change did not look beyond those immediate results of change. They had asked for industry and freedom from an outmoded agriculture and their prayers were answered. They had welcomed technology and a changed economy, but they had little reckoned inevitable consequences of the changes, accustomed as they were to thinking of their society as static. But change inexorably generates change, in endless chain. They had not realized that they would be unable to retain the past that Southerners inordinately treasured, that the dynamism of industry and technology and the impersonality of cities, alter the behavior, the manners, and manner of thinking as well as the economy.

Long ago, when the South first embraced change, it had unsuspectingly bartered away some treasured traditions of its past. At midcentury, it was being called upon for delivery and it was the delivery of bartered traditions that was proving painful, disruptive, and bewildering. It was that delivery in accordance with its barter that was tearing the South internally, to a degree unmatched in its long history of suppressed internal dissension. Some were satisfied with the barter and ready to deliver with all deliberate speed, seeing a better day in a future less fettered by the past. And there were those who, true to human nature, were reluctant, at this deferred payment date, to pay the price of things long enjoyed but who, at the same time, disliked the unease of conscience for their failure to deliver. They were the ones who realized that, for better or for worse, the bargain had been duly made and that they were already living in a changed world as a result and that there was little they could do about it. Also, there were those who maintained that they had not read the fine print and should therefore be relieved of its commitments. They were firmly convinced of the possibility of standing with one leg in the twentieth century and the other in the nineteenth; that they could keep their economy in the twentieth century and their society in an earlier century with an unbreachable wall between, all on the premise that society and economic life are separable entities, each operating in its own sphere. Finally, there were those few more consistent souls, enslaved to a past they adored, who claimed that the delivery was no obligation of theirs since they had never assented to the barter in the first place. Happy to eschew the stresses of a changing world, their only desire was to be left alone in the South, free to reject all change, past and future.

However great the measure of time which may be required to secure a composing of these dissident opinions sufficiently to effect a voluntary surrender of the fetters of the past, the South's commitments to change were already of too long standing, and too deeply enmeshed in its present, to permit any turning back. The measure of time necessary to resolve the South's diversities into a workable unison is uncertain. But there is no uncertainty in the conclusion, be it drawn with poignant regret or with longed for relief, that the irretrievable commitments of the changing South have equally irretrievably foreordained that, year by year, the South will be more American and less Southern.

Within the span of lives now in being, it will be but a geographical section of the nation and no longer a sociological entity within that nation.

A Postscript for the Day

21

IN MY TOWN there is a private school for Negroes, a survivor of numerous schools for freedmen established by the Methodist Episcopal Church in Reconstruction days. In the summer of 1956, under auspices of the home mission society of the church, a score of teen-age boys and girls, white and Negro, arrived at the school for a demonstration of interracial work, study, and living during the vacation period.

At the time of their arrival, rumors drifted around town that a large Klan group had just been organized in the county. No sooner had the presence of mixed groups at the school been discovered than rumors of the Klan were confirmed by a flaming cross on the school grounds and a threat, through an anonymous telephone call, that the school would be blown up unless the interracial session were discontinued.

As Mayor, I was immediately involved in the impending crisis. I held conferences with leaders of the group and with the young people themselves, advising them that, unfortunately, I thought they had overestimated the advance of racial tolerance in the deep South and

that there was, at least, a real possibility that the Klan might attempt
to carry out its threats and that, if so, instead of their session demonstrating successful interracial living in the deep South, it would have
demonstrated the opposite.

Meanwhile, as they were pondering my request that they avoid the
possibility of an ugly incident by moving their session to a more tolerant environment, I called the Governor's office and made a tentative
request for troops to protect the meeting, a meeting which was in no
way violating even South Carolina's strict segregation laws. When
sponsoring authorities decided to move the session to a border state,
excitement died down as suddenly as it had flared.

On the surface it seemed to have died down. But, a few nights
later, a cross was burned on my front lawn, apparently an expression
of disapproval of my determination to protect the group, had they
decided to stay on. The flaming cross was followed by anonymous
telephoned threats when my uncomplimentary opinions of the Klan
were reported in the press. Simultaneously, I received a letter signed
by some forty students at Columbia University, protesting my intolerance in handling the situation.

Here was a graphic demonstration of the great barrier of misunderstanding between sections on the racial problem in the South. It has
since become common knowledge that unless a Southerner vocally
subscribes to the rantings of racists, he is automatically branded in
the South as an "integrationist," whereas outside he will find his
moderation still classifies him as a bigoted "racist."

In the fall of 1957, came the fiasco at Little Rock. I had taken up
temporary residence in Boston to write a book on a subject unrelated
to this one. I was there when blaring headlines were reporting the
marches and countermarches of mobs and troops around Central
High School, as Governor Faubus and Federal authorities, each in
turn, plucked pages from the history of Reconstruction in the South.
The Boston press reported in minute detail everything that was happening there, as the old, familiar pattern of emotion-stirred action
was played out again in a modern setting, each move being made in
response to the emotional drive of opposing prejudices. The militantly intolerant were on one hand and their closely related kin, the

militantly tolerant, on the other. Between these extremes real tolerance seemed to vanish.

While Boston papers were playing up the Little Rock story for every nickel that was in it, almost to the exclusion of world events, and at the same time running columns of letters from irate readers, most of which were wholesale denunciations of the South and Southerners or displayed a complete lack of understanding of the problems presented by race question in the South, a series of dance hall and "rock and roll" riots occurred in Boston. Thousands were involved and dozens were injured. The papers in minor stories reported these disorders and "rock and roll" shows were banned by the city. But to this day, most Bostonians don't know that they were having serious racial disorders in their city, even as they were unmercifully castigating Southerners for their failure quietly and unemotionally to solve more difficult race problems. The Southern press tends to give exaggerated attention to its race problems, but the non-South press goes to extreme lengths to avoid all mention of race in connection with such incidents.

Again, here was an impressive illustration of the need for rational efforts to breach the wall of emotional misunderstanding which has risen between the South and the rest of the country, a wall which hampers the ultimate maturing of Southern society by feeding the fires of emotion, as Southerners struggle with enormous difficulties of adjustment.

That is how this book came to be—in the hope that it might play some part in helping the South solve its problems by giving both Southerners and outsiders a more rational picture of the South and its peculiarities and the historical bases of those peculiarities, that they may not appear so sacred to Southerners or so quixotic and silly to outsiders.

I have set down so far in this book, the conditions, events, and developments that have formed the background of Southern thinking, to show its inevitable evolvement through pride, yes, but more through circumstance. I have tried to be objective in that relation. If, in places, I have failed in that effort (it is always difficult, for example, for a Southerner to recount without emotional bias the injustices of

Reconstruction), my very failure, in a measure, should cast light on Southern thinking, for the account I have given is at least far more objective than the "history" that has been fed to most Southerners through the years, conditioning their thinking and creating to a large degree the problems that confront them today.

It remains now but to draw some conclusions from the account that has been presented and to discuss some features of the South's current problems in the light of historical backgrounds and realities of the present.

Both the facts of history as it actually happened and "history" with its added sectional tinting are of greater importance in understanding Southern thought than in other sections of the nation. While the people of other sections were being separated from their past by the intrusion of transforming developments, until recently, those of the relatively stagnating South continued through the generations to live intimately with their past. Under the impacts of recurring disasters, they were constantly turning back to the past for the solace it offered.

Another reason for the relatively greater importance of past events in Southern thinking lies in the personal continuity of the vast majority of Southerners with their history. Southern history, to a unique degree, is the story of fathers and forefathers of those living in the South today. In other sections, even in older ones, only a minority have a similar family continuity running back through their history, most of their present population being the issue of relatively late arrivals on the American scene.

The potency of the last century and a quarter in molding from the original pot of diversity in the South a remarkable uniformity of folkways is illustrative of the intimacy between the South and its history. Despite the cultural diversity of their origins and despite the fact that virtually all Southerners trace their loyalties back through allegiances to at least three and up to six flags, in contrast to the single flag in the new world history of most other Americans, Southerners have been molded into a sociological entity unmatched elsewhere. With the exception of what their history did to them, Southerners are much like Americans anywhere in the country. The failure to realize that that is true, failure to realize that their differences are mostly the products of history, a history that was far from being of their own making or their sole responsibility, is the greatest stumbling block standing in the way of outsiders' securing any real understanding of their compatriots to the south.

Now, at near mid-century, as the yet unsynchronized wheels of the history that made Southerners what they are attempt to mesh with those of the nation, there is rejection, clash, and a tearing asunder. Amid the fury evoked by disruptions of old patterns and the threat of greater disruptions to come, one hears that the South has arrived at a critical choosing of the ways.

Those who speak of an impending choice of ways speak without the perspective of history. There is no such choice. That choice was made years ago when the South embraced change, chose the American way, and sealed its choice by truly remarkable accomplishments and deep commitments. Now, the only choice remaining to the South is one of the means of resolving difficulties now flowing from its irrevocable commitments to the American way.

It is fatuous to think that there can be any revocation of those commitments to progress. Society, like all other living organisms, must grow or die. Nature tolerates no reverse process. It is essential that Southerners realize that, in post-World War II years, they were enthusiastically heralding the birth of what promised to be a magnificent, changed South of limitless promise and that, for better or for worse, that changed South, although still but a promising infant, is in being today. Realizing that, they should accept the fact that birth involves both pain and joy, relief and care, opportunity and responsibility. If Southerners can accept these truths and further accept the fact that just as man cannot be an island unto himself so, also, in the closely knit world society of today, no society can be an island unto itself, and if they can accept the fact that the dogmas of a stagnant past are inadequate to a dynamic present then, in one way or another, acceptable solutions to the South's formidable problems will be forthcoming.

In moving toward solutions to their problems (and everybody from the most fanatical integrationist to the most wild-eyed racist is looking for solutions), it is essential that Southerners accept a broader realism. Primarily, they must face the fact that there is not the remotest chance of undoing decisions of the Supreme Court on racial discrimination. Although the 1954 decision in the school segregation cases was widely anticipated in legal circles, since it was the only consistent culmination of a long line of decisions striking at racial discrimination in other fields, it was nevertheless shocking to most lawyers to realize that one minute "the Constitution" said one thing and that an hour later it said something quite the opposite. It was shocking that the legal sanctity of precedent had been given such short shrift and that provisions for the orderly amendment of the Constitution should have been ignored and by-passed, apparently without a qualm. Nevertheless, whether one dislikes the result in segregation cases or disapproves of the means by which it was made law of the land, it is now part and parcel of the Constitution which every lawyer and every public officeholder, from the president to local peace officers is sworn to uphold and defend. To proclaim otherwise is to proclaim anarchy. To proclaim otherwise necessitates a permission to anyone to obey only those decisions of the courts with which he agrees. That is anarchy.

Nullification and interposition are but a whit less patently absurd. The long debated Constitutional question of the sovereignty of states as against laws promulgated by the Federal government was the legal issue in the war of 1861; and the result of that war, whether we like it or not, fully and finally settled that issue in favor of Federal supremacy. Consequently, those who hold out hopes of nullifying the Court's decisions through nullification or interposition are engaging in nothing better than educated demagoguery.

Certainly the chance of securing from the Supreme Court itself a reversal, or even a modification of its school segregation rulings, is beyond possibility. All the appeals and all arguments that have been presented to the courts since the 1954 decision have only served to make it more firm and explicit. Only through fantastically wishful thinking can anyone imagine getting at least five men, of the firmness of character essential to one who has risen to the high estate of Supreme Court Justice, to reverse their views. Even if, through some miracle, five members of the Supreme Court were to be suddenly convinced that their affirmed and reaffirmed convictions in the school cases were erroneous, the enormous national and international political repercussions of a reversal would be ample deterrents.

I am convinced that few Southerners realize the extent of involvement of their domestic order in the national and world order. Many of them seem to have only a vague conception of the extent of the animosity against the South which has been engendered among people of other sections by the violence and economic pressure tactics employed to resist changes in its racial patterns. Reliable public opinion polls, taken just after the 1954 school segregation decision, indicated that barely half of white non-Southerners entirely approved of the decision. By 1958, less than ten percent remained opposed. And with each new act of violence in the South, pressure mounts for the adoption of prompt and powerful enforcement methods. Foreign newspapers the world over report every racial disturbance in the South and those reports are constantly handicapping the efforts of American diplomats in dealing with two-thirds of the people of the earth. Surely only the most unrealistic can imagine the national government voluntarily hampering its touch and go diplomatic struggle for survival in a dangerously restive world, by countenancing any retrogression in the non-discrimination rules its courts have laid down, simply to please a small minority of its people.

The most chimerical of all hopes through which Southerners have deceived themselves into the belief that their problems will somehow go away is the hope that Congress can be persuaded to undo the Court's decisions. The belief has been treasured and nurtured that, through loud enough and long enough protests, Congress can be induced to enact legislation restoring legality to the South's traditional caste system. Except that emotion has displaced reason (and most Southern thinking on the issue has been wishful thinking) one finds it difficult to believe that reasonably intelligent men can be persuaded that congressmen from outside the South will dare vote to support legislation which would violate the convictions of nine out of ten of their constituents. The action by Congress which appears far more likely, even all but certain if violence persists in the South, is abolition of the right of filibuster, so long a cherished bulwark against anti-

Southern legislation, and the enactment of a strong civil rights law sending the force of Federal enforcement into every Southern community.

Although slower in effect, inexorable economic forces are compelling the South to face its problems and take positive action. Unlike in 1860, the hand of the Federal government is now deep in our everyday lives. Everywhere we look, it is intimately involved; the social security system from which most people expect retirement income is Federal and the unemployment system is basically Federal. So are our public welfare and public health programs. Federal authority is the basis for order in our banking and home loan systems, our railways, airways, telephone, electric and gas systems, in our radio and television systems, and, to a substantial degree, in our law enforcement. Huge sums, with strings attached and susceptible to the attaching of additional strings, come to us from the national treasury for school aid, hospital construction, highway construction, airports and airline subsidies, for the improvement and maintenance of harbors, for sewage disposal systems, flood control, public power projects, irrigation and reclamation projects, and for watershed developments. There is Federal participation in most of the home loans of our urban dwellers; our farmers are now drawing about half their net incomes from the Federal treasury. And there are veteran's hospitals and military establishments, disproportionately concentrated in the South.

Finally, there are the hundreds of millions of dollars in Federal contracts annually let to Southern industries. Most of those involvements of the national government in our economy and our institutions are potential instruments of coercion should Congress elect so to employ them. Some are already being used. Non-discrimination clauses attached to grants to hospitals and airports and written into government contracts are examples. Unquestionably, others will be similarly employed.

Money speaks with great authority—sufficient authority, sometimes, to induce even ardent racists to waive principles in favor of principal. Witness the recent gift by the state of Mississippi of a site for a veteran's hospital, a gift approved by the state agency of Mississippi dedicated to the all-out protection of the Mississippi way from any encroachments upon it, despite the fact that the hospital will be unsegregated.

Beyond the powers of economic coercion inherent in government dollars are yet more ponderable economic considerations urgently demanding an end of tension on the Southern scene. No people have ever taken a greater pride in industrial progress than twentieth-century Southerners. Now it is beginning to dawn on those who have been dedicating themselves to that progress that the tension and uncertainty of future conditions are striking severe blows at further industrial progress. They are coming to realize that so long as parlous conditions created by the conflict between law and custom continue, few industrialists are going to elect to face the new and uncertain problems presented by that conflict, in place of the familiar problems of their old locations. Many new manufacturing establishments involve highly technical, largely automation processes, requiring the recruitment and importation of a high ratio of engineers and other skilled technicians, the preponderance of them young men with growing families. Recruiting such men for location in an area which is threatening to close its schools becomes patently impossible. The southward march of the most desirable types of industry to those states that are closing or threatening to abolish public school systems is being brought to a sudden and complete halt. Southerners must take their heads out of the sand and weigh that fact.

Nevertheless, bereft of the possibility of legal relief through the courts or Congress, a majority of the electorate in some Southern states are seriously pushing for the avoidance of even token integration, through the abolition of public school systems, despite the fact that no section of the country in the twentieth century has shown a greater devotion than the South to public education. That Southerners, despite that devotion, can now consider abolishing their schools as an alternative to integration emphatically illustrates the depth of their devotion to traditional social patterns.

One cannot avoid questioning whether those who advocate meeting integration problems by cutting off their noses to spite their faces are not quite devoid of historical perspective. Else they would understand that most of the South's past and present problems are largely attributable to an insufficiency of education. Are they ready to invite a new series of economic and social difficulties? Also, one wonders whether they have sufficiently considered that uncompromising determination to refuse to meet their problems in a positive way is only faintly reflected in the students themselves, the ones whose education it is proposed to sacrifice on the altar of the past. Will those children, in years to come, be grateful to their elders for requiring such a futile sacrifice? Finally, one wonders whether school abolitionists have given due consideration to the probability that, if school closings become widespread, the Federal government itself will step into the educational field and establish unsegregated schools for those to whom public education is being denied, and another state function will have passed from the states to the central government.

When school closing philosophy reaches up into the field of advanced education, wonder mounts. When Clemson College of South Carolina rejected a government grant for atomic research because the contract covering it contained the usual non-discrimination clause, one wonders whether authorities were motivated by fear of mass fear or whether they really felt that the remote possibility that a qualified Negro atomic scientist might apply for assignment to the project was so fraught with danger to the state's social system that it was preferable for South Carolinians to be denied training in the science of the future, unless they have money enough to leave the state and run the risk of seeking knowledge of the atom in the same laboratory with a Negro scientist in another part of the country.

Viewing this latter day abolition movement in that light, many a Southerner saw more tragedy than humor in the observation of Jonathan Daniels, editor of the Raleigh *News and Observer*, that, in 1860, the South seceded from the nation, but now it is seriously proposing seceding from civilization itself.

While much of the South's legally constituted leadership has been talking and following instead of thinking and leading, self-appointed leaders, among the worst elements, have been talking and acting in hope of creating and maintaining a state of fear that will prevent thought and indefinitely paralyze constructive action. Although few high-placed Southern leaders approve methods of the rabble, a considerable measure of responsibility for the disorders that have been occasioned by those elements in the South is, nevertheless, theirs. By harkening to the voices of the most vocal, who are all but invariably the most extreme, and mistaking those voices for the preponderant voice of their constituency, by seeking to please their constituency by feeding back to them the hate and defiance they hear; an atmosphere of tension, fear, and hate, conducive to violence, has been created in many areas. Sooner or later, Southern leaders must realize that, by failing to lead, they are permitting others to lead the South down a blind alley to dire consequences. Surely none but the perverted wants to face an indefinite future in a South, with a social pattern frozen in place by fears, a pattern that must be constantly fed with fear to forestall any relaxing of its hold. It is beyond belief that we will make that status quo, held in place by fear, the overriding Southern heritage we are to pass on to our children. It is beyond belief that Southern leadership, and even the dimwitted rabble rousers, will not soon recognize the awful cost and inevitable self-defeat inherent in absolute intransigence.

Most portentous of all the consequences of absolute intransigence and violent resistance is the harvest of ill will throughout the rest of the nation and all over the world. Unless something is done to check its growth, that enormous, composite voice from without will soon make the voice of protest in the South inaudible beyond the South itself. And that overwhelming voice will speak with commensurate authority, demanding coercive measures against the South. Such measures, once they are instituted, will preclude the long term, internally directed, and orderly transition which remains the South's greatest need and hope. If powerful coercive measures are to be invited by a continuing absolute intransigence, if a powerful civil rights bill is enacted and invoked, and crippling economic pressures are once brought to bear, in the process Southerners' cherished States' rights will have suffered derogations incomparably greater than in any period of the past.

In the process, it is likely that dreaded transitions, the resistance to which had invited coercive measures, would be precipitated and telescoped. No longer would the generous measure of time, which the South desperately needs for transition, remain available to it.

Those are but some of the costs of absolute intransigence. There are others. The economic and social cost in interruption of the South's industrial and commercial advance has been mentioned. There is the intangible but incalculable cost in race relations. It wasn't the decision of the Supreme Court in school segregation cases that blasted cordiality out of relations between races in the South. It was the things that happened afterward, and the millions of words of fear and hate that were written and spoken in the years that followed the decision, which wrung all cordiality from social ties between Southern whites and Negroes.

Nor was deterioration in race relations confined to the lower classes. Virginius Dabney, editor of the Richmond *Times-Dispatch*, cites an example from professional circles of that city. In 1955, well after the school decision, eighty-seven members, almost the two-thirds necessary for action, voted to admit Negroes to the Richmond Medical Society. Three years later, a new move to admit them got but three favorable votes. Wide cleavage between the races, created by the very nature of the policy of absolute intransigence, has served to deliver the leadership of both races over to the dictates of the extremes.

Across the chasm, spokesmen of the N.A.A.C.P. and White Citizen's Councils shout but never talk. Tactless and extreme Southern leadership, by giant steps, is delivering a full blown realization of what for generations has been the South's greatest fear—an organized and aggressive Negro electorate, holding a potential balance of power in the region. No more proof is necessary than a reference to sharply mounting figures on Negro registrations in the South in recent years. It is, perhaps, not too late to forestall the unhappy prospect of a formidable Negro political party based solely on racial interests. But the prospect remains remote of any appreciable number of white leaders emerging, ready to assume the political risks involved in a moderate approach to the region's problems which might gain the support of substantial numbers of Negroes and divide them along the lines of political principles.

If "over my dead body" intransigence carries such a high price tag, one may well wonder how it came to be dominant in half the South and widely influential all through the region. The 1954 school segregation decree, coming as it did before the South had adjusted itself to earlier decisions relating to discrimination in higher education, came as a shock to almost every Southerner. Suddenly confronted with its full implications, confronted with the prospect of altering social patterns of centuries, few Southerners, regardless of personal views of the decision, could longer cast a sanguine eye to the future. Loud protests from the more frightened and outraged overshadowed the quiet concern of those Southerners, perhaps more numerous, of moderate bent. Politicians with ears to the ground could hear little but sounds of violent protest. In an emotion-charged atmosphere most of them listened—and echoed before they thought, thereby committing themselves before thinking through to the consequences of their commitments. After that, the political survival of those so committed became dependent upon amplifying and multiplying the voices they had echoed. From the vantage points they occupied, as protagonists and expositors of the doctrine of "never" or "over my dead body," many were highly successful in building forces of the uncompromising. Rivals, observing their success, saw opportunity only in outhating the haters, and in ever more vigorously flaying the "Communist dominated" N.A.A.C.P., the "Communist infiltrated" Supreme Court, and Negroes, indiscriminately. Through that self-feeding process, an atmosphere was created such that all those who failed to subscribe to the moral rightness or even the wisdom of the doctrine of absolute intransigence were, *ipso facto*, categorized as traitors to the South—unless they kept their views strictly to themselves.

The atmosphere created by this latter day demagoguery of followship, in itself, gave encouragement to resistance through mass fears. In many places those fears have seized full control. Fear motivates unorganized resistance to change among poor and little educated whites, who fear economic competition of the rising Negro. Fear makes whispers of the voices of moderates. Fear drives the "red-necks" to don dunce caps and sheets to inculcate fear in those whom they deem insufficiently fearful. Fear of loss of face keeps anyone from proposing any change in traditional patterns, even those so silly as separate sanitary drinking fountains for blacks and whites (although whites, presumably the ones to be protected by such separate facilities, are if high born, probably scions of fathers or grandfathers who were suckled at the black breasts of Negro wet nurses and the blacks from whom they are being protected are perhaps doing more than they in the rearing and training of their children). But who is so free of fear that he will rise in a city council chamber or state legislature, risking being dubbed "integrationist" or "nigger-lover" by proposing an end to the absurdity? Fear grips ivory towers and keeps supplied the northward stream of the intellectually independent to less fettered realms beyond the restraints of fear. Finally, to complete the vicious circle, fear of defeat grips politicians who have embraced followship, compelling them to keep piling fuel on the fires of fear that they may continue their dominance through fear.

While in the paralyzing grip of that merciless entrapment, an unhappy, emotion-filled, tension-ridden South is being asked speedily to effect changes more drastic than any it has been confronted with in all its long past, excepting only those forced upon it at bayonet point almost a century ago.

Let no one underestimate the magnitude of that assignment. Even under optimum conditions, and nobody pretends that conditions in the South today meet that specification, it is a stupendous assignment to expect nearly fifty million diverse and individualistic folk, little inured to regimentation, suddenly to abandon, against their wills, deeply ingrained customs, traditions, and folkways, running back through more than a quarter-millennium of history, a history that has been uniquely cherished and retained. If the South is to make necessary changes and adjustments in fulfillment of the irrevocable commitments to change it has already made, millions of Southerners are going to have to change or modify many of the fettering predilections of their heritage. Also, if those adjustments are to be accomplished without resort to a second attempt at "Reconstruction" by force, with its inevitable harvest in blood, hatred, bitterness, and infamy, it is equally essential that many more millions outside the South must change many of their predilections and modify many of their attitudes toward the South and its unique problems.

So far as Southerners are concerned, a primary essential is wider acceptance of the inevitability of the changes they dread. For several years now, hundreds of high placed political leaders (most of whom know better and will privately admit it) and thousands of self-appointed resistance leaders have been energetically planting in the minds of the ignorant and gullible a conviction that the South can live indefinitely in a perpetual state of defiance of world opinion, sectional enmity, the power of the national press, power of the Federal government, the pressure of church leadership, the coercive power of national labor unions, the influence of the armed forces, and an unsympathetic rising generation in its midst—a multiple defiance which obviously cannot be long sustained.

But, until a sufficient number of devoted Southerners are willing to assume the risks involved in disabusing those who have been subjected to the heartless deception and demagoguery of the doctrine of perpetual defiance to overwhelming forces and influences, no real beginning can be made toward a tolerable solution to the South's problems. Until that can be accomplished, not through preachments from without but through reason from within, and until the potentially great voice of moderation within the South can be released from its whisper status, the present tension-ridden, incident-studded impasse will continue, with the ever present risk that, at any time, one of those incidents may bring down on the South the ultimate disaster of a second "Reconstruction" by force.

The South's ponderous current difficulties are complicated and multiplied by an overwhelmingly critical national press, which commonly displays a glaring lack of understanding of the South, a puerile lack of appreciation of the magnitude of the adjustments with which it is faced and, all too often, an intolerance almost as sweeping and indiscriminate as that commonly displayed by Southerners toward a Negro minority. Although lack of understanding and intolerance of the South, on the part of the outside press, tends to create a paralyzing defensive attitude in Southerners and an emotional atmosphere in the nation which deters a calm approach to the South's problems both from within and without, the basic error of people outside the South, reflected in attitudes of the press, lies in an apparent assumption that Southern whites are basically different from other Americans.

It would assist in creating an atmosphere of understanding if people everywhere, including Southerners themselves, could realize that Southerners, except for having a considerably higher proportion of Anglo-Saxon blood especially of the Celtic strain, differ from Americans elsewhere only to the extent that they have been uniquely molded by their history and environment and that the responsibility for that history and environment falls at least as heavily on the North as on the South.

Related to the preconception among outsiders that Southerners are fundamentally different from other Americans is the habitual tendency, throughout the country, to brand everything that happens in the South as Southern whereas, if the same thing had occurred in the North or West, it would not be branded as Northern or Western. Although examples of that tendency are constantly recurring, a particularly apt illustration grew out of the long Broadway run of *Tobacco Road*. The child marriage which was part of the plot of the play, set off, in the New York press, a full-scale tirade against a depraved and medieval South for countenancing child marriages, completely ignoring the fact that, for every Southern state permitting the marriage of girls under sixteen, there were two outside the South.

The field of relations between races in the South has long proved itself a productive field of fodder for braying demagogues. Discovery of that field was made well over a century ago and in intervening years, it has shown little signs of depletion. Although Southerners, with the issues nearer at hand, have been its most frequent visitants, they have by no means exercised a monopoly over it. They had no monopoly in the days of Abolitionists, nor in the days of Black Republicanism, and they have no monopoly on it today, despite the volume of their current braying. There is no doubting that the demagoguery which is currently thriving on the issue, in both the North and the South, is seriously hampering every reasonable and unemotional approach to the South's problems. And there is no less doubt that, even when reasonable solutions are found, their implementation will be constantly impeded so long as that demagoguery holds sway.

It is equally certain that there is no quick panacea for demagoguery. Since it lives by ignorance alone, its only cure in a free society, lies in the eradication of ignorance. That is a slow, slow process. From a practical standpoint, it means that the voice of the demagogue cannot be effectually quieted until an entirely new and far better educated generation takes its place in the electorate and the leaders of ignorance are forced into oblivion. That, through the dual influences of youth and education, a new and more liberal sociological climate, voluntarily embraced, is in the offing is obvious to all who take heed of younger voices. On every hand, there is unmistakable evidence of a directly proportional relationship between age and racial prejudice and an inverse relationship between education and prejudice.

The analysis of results of a recent survey of the sentiments of the Baptist clergy of Tennessee provides a revealing illustration of the influence of both youth and education in the integration issue. Almost eighty percent of those ministers holding degrees favored racial integration in the public schools, in marked contrast to the less than ten percent of those with only grammar school training, or less. Of the pastors under thirty years of age, more than sixty percent stood for integration as against less than twenty percent of those over fifty years old.

Allusion to the need of a generation for the South to adjust to impending changes is shocking to reformers who, ever and anon, are impatient to witness the millennium in their own time and are only rarely endowed with a balance of realism. However, in undertaking to change the deeply ingrained folkways of forty million people, their physical and social institutions, their customs and their laws, a bountiful supply of both patience and realism is essential.

I do not mean to imply that there is need for a generation of hiatus. All the while, through centripetal progress from the periphery, requisite adjustments can go forward. What I do mean is that it is unrealistic to expect a complete, voluntary adjustment to impending changes throughout the South, short of such a period for education and adjustment. And why, one may ask, should it require a generation for the South to change a few senseless laws and customs and be done with it? It is not so simple as that. In fact, few who haven't lived long in the South have any real conception of the difficulties involved. Some of those difficulties can be explained. Others defy explanation; they are only insidiously sensed.

The most convincing evidence of the truly formidable proportions of the South's adjustment problems is the practical unanimity of concern for the problems among Southerners of all strata, despite their diversity of origin and diversity of economic and social status. These problems are real and formidable to the old English of Virginia, Scots of the hill country, French Catholics of Louisiana, and the Yankees of Texas and Florida. Even to those whose consciences compel agreement with racial decisions of the courts, the problems are real and of first magnitude. They, too, recognize the imperiousness of the need for a generous measure of time.

Like their counterparts of the old South who opposed slavery but were forced to support it by the impatience of Abolitionists and fear of the only alternatives offered, there are millions of Southerners whose consciences oppose segregation, but who are so fearful of the consequences of precipitate abolition of long established ways, that they are being forced by the intransigent and impatient integrationists into the camp of the intransigent segregationists.

In the resistance of many men of unquestioned integrity and ability, there is further proof of the enormity of the South's problems and also of the fact that there is considerable merit in the South's contentions that, as a minority section, it is being unjustly and roughly manhandled by a powerful majority, through the derogation of its traditional Constitutional rights and immunities. A cause cannot be without merit and yet receive the whole-hearted support of men who have long since been graduated from politician to statesman—men such as James F. Byrnes, Walter George, Richard B. Russell, John L. McClellan, and Harry F. Byrd. They are neither lightweights nor demagogues. When men such as they, with intimate knowledge of the problems, add their voices to the protests, it should be sufficient, in itself, to give pause to militant reformers of lesser ability and lesser familiarity with the problem.

Consider some aspects of the South's problem in more detail. One of the imponderables that must be faced by everyone in meeting the challenges of change is the Southerner's unique nearness to his history, which has already been pointed out. The effect of the South's retention of its past upon today's problems can be seen in its current reactions to the school integration problem. A definite relationship is apparent between the resistance being encountered and the extent and horrors of the Reconstruction era in the area involved in the integration process.

Another imponderable is the relatively low educational level of the bulk of the South's mid-century electorate, it being the product of prevailing ruralism and poverty, which, in turn, were the product of the destruction of the war and the re-destruction of postwar years. Ignorance, of course, harbors error and fear, the building blocks of demagoguery. But in meeting the school integration crisis, the paucity of schooling of the average Southerner of middle age or older is of itself an especially fecund source of bitterness and resentment. It would be difficult to exaggerate the depth of resentment of those men, when they look back on the miserable little school to which they trudged long distances for a few years, when farm work permitted, and compare what was offered them with the grand modern school to which Negro children are daily being transported in relative luxury. When the Negro registers protest in the face of opportunities the like of which were denied to older whites by the poverty which they feel that the Yankee produced, the white's unreasoning resentment is boundless.

Although usually unrecognized as such, economic influences play a major role in the South's racial patterns. Except temporarily in war times, through all its history, the South has suffered from a labor surplus, a constant threat to job security. Even before they became directly competing freedmen, the lower living standards of Negroes have made the race a terrifying competitive threat to poor whites and to the little security they enjoyed. That economic threat was a major factor in the creation of the caste system, as poorer whites sought to wall Negroes off from their jobs by legal and social restrictions. Although most of these whites do not recognize this fear of economic competition as the basis of their blind hatred of the Negro, it is among lower economic groups of whites that racial prejudice is most rampant.

However, fear of cut-rate competition from the Negro is but part of the economic aspect of the South's racial difficulties. Another part, comparable in influence, is the Southern manifestation of ordinary American economic snobbery. I am constantly amazed that, in all that is said and written about the South's racial problem, this aspect of it is almost invariably ignored, despite the fact that it is a powerful factor which will probably complicate the problem even beyond another generation. In a typical Black Belt community, where white and Negro school children are about equal in numbers, if one were to divide all the school children into two groups according to the income available for their support, the results of that economic segregation would be very nearly identical with that obtained by simply drawing the color line.

The fact that racial segregation in the public schools substantially accomplishes economic segregation is one of the reasons why there are so few private schools in the South. It lessens the incentive of the more affluent to remove their children from influence of the less privileged by sending them to private schools. But, most of all, the economic differential between the races serves to confuse with racial attributes those qualities attributable simply to the environment of poverty, thereby greatly magnifying the popular conception of an innate Negro inferiority. Disease, filth, few clothes, and the brutalizing influences of large families crowded into one or two rooms—these qualities, when they are frequently observed as attributes of Negroes, are, understandably enough, easily confused with innate Negro attributes rather than being simply the indicia of poverty, regardless of race.

The average Southerner's conviction of the identity of those attributes with black skins has been based upon a lifetime of observation and association, and no amount of words can disabuse him. The only way he can be convinced that filth, disease, slovenliness, low moral standards, and uncouth ways are not necessarily Negro racial traits is by raising the economic standards of the race to a level that will permit eradication of the evil results of abject poverty, and that will require time—a generous allotment of time. Until then, any general integration of white and Negro children, especially in rural areas where economic disparity between the races is greatest and where generally the Negro has made the least progress toward acceptable standards of living would, of course, border on the tragic, not only for the white children but for Negroes as well.

Of course, the most patent difficulty in effecting racial integration in the South is the very size of the Negro minority. About twenty percent of the population of the whole section is Negro, with variations between the states, running from well below ten percent in Kentucky and Oklahoma to more than forty percent in Mississippi. Between districts and counties, Negro concentration shows much greater variation, running from negligible percentages in some mountain counties to well over eighty percent in many counties in the Black Belt. Both sociological studies and experience have indicated that integration can be effected, usually without great difficulty, in those areas with Negro concentrations of less than twenty percent. It is those areas where Negroes exceed twenty percent of the population which will need time to make their adjustments; time, too, for a better educated and more liberal citizenry to rise to power, time to raise the economic and social standards of Negroes, and time for continuing Negro migrations to reduce the problem by reducing Negro ratios.

In, for example, areas like Clarendon County, South Carolina School District No. 1, situs of one of the original school segregation cases, a rural area where there are something like eight Negro school children for each white, and most of them from Negro homes where economic and social standards have more characteristics of homes of the newly freed slaves immediately after the war than of what we think of as average American homes, successful racial integration of the schools is out of the question for the foreseeable future. If, by coercive measures, integration were to be forced upon such a community, it would soon become obvious that the whites, not the Negroes, would have become the injured minority, with the practical result that "integrated" schools would be exclusively Negro schools.

The net result would be no gain for Negroes at the price of incalculable injury to the whites. It is the regions where such conditions prevail which call for the fullest measure of patience and understanding, while long-term programs, to alleviate the basic conditions which make integration in those areas impossible in this generation, are inaugurated and carried forward, in the interest of developing a more receptive environment for another day in the indefinite future.

Some readers will feel that the opinion of those who are convinced of the impracticality of racial integration in the public schools where the Negro population exceeds twenty percent is belied by the present existence of integration in some metropolitan centers of the North and Midwest where Negro percentages approach that figure. Actually, for many reasons, the successful integration of even much higher ratios of Negroes in those areas would not make them case histories demonstrating the possibility of obtaining equally successful results in the relatively rural South.

Integration in those non-Southern areas was not inaugurated under the burden of long established customs to the contrary, nor under any comparable climate of prejudice. Also it was inaugurated when Negro ratios were far smaller, before relatively large numbers began to influence fears. Also, there is no comparable economic disparity between the whites and Negroes in those metropolitan centers. Moreover, generally speaking, the Negroes being integrated into Northern schools are the cream of the race. Negro migrants from the South are usually the more energetic and ambitious. As a group, they have had twenty percent more education than those left in the South.

Moreover, and this is the most significant difference of all, Northern metropolitan integration is more technical than actual, a situation usually impossible in the South. Residential segregation in Northern cities is far more concentrated and rigid than appears anywhere in the South. Most Northern cities have but a single large ghetto for their Negro population, in marked contrast to Southern cities which usually have several, frequently ill-defined Negro districts. In practically all Southern rural areas, Negroes live here, there, and everywhere. Consequently, the vast majority of Negro children living in cities in the North, and virtually all Negroes in the North live in cities, attend "integrated" schools that are exclusively Negro schools, simply by reason of propinquity of residence. Also, the concentration of Negroes into a single district in these Northern cities tends greatly to reduce the extent of periphery areas where racial difficulties are usually encountered.

Finally, it is essential that Southerners rationally face the most terrifying, most irrational fears connected with the racial integration issue—the fear of racial amalgamation, of "mongrelizing." Although the fear of intermarriage, or "mongrelizing," is, without doubt, the most compelling force behind the die-hard resistance of militant segregationists, it is actually the least realistic in point of fact and justification and the most overworked of all the fears of integration.

I recall a mulatto worker for integration shocking his white listeners by an affirmative response to the question of whether or not he *believed* in racial amalgamation. But then he added: "How can I not believe in it? Look at my skin. It is a fact, and how can anyone not believe in a fact? Now, if you ask me if I am in *favor* of racial amalgamation, I can give you a different answer—a definite 'no.' "

The fact that more than three-fourths of all Negroes in the South carry a noticeable infusion of white genes in their body cells is tangible evidence of amalgamation in the past under rigid segregation rules represented first by slavery and then by the caste system. For my part, I cannot follow the logic of opposing any change in a system which has already proved itself productive of an alarming degree of racial amalgamation, by basing the opposition to change on fear of amalgamation. An advocate of racial assimilation might more logically urge retention of the caste system as an encourager of racial amalgamation.

When the impassioned fearful ones keep asking the question, "Would you want your sister or daughter to marry a Negro?" I am ever amazed that they fail to recognize the implied insult in the question. Do they suppose that suddenly all the sisters and daughters of white men will be deprived of their right or inclination to say "no" if they have any contact with a Negro man?

So far, I have discussed principal difficulties confronting the South in adjusting to the changes to which it is committed. I have mentioned principal areas of misunderstanding between the sections and some of the fond delusions of both Southerners and non-Southerners which are impeding the South's orderly adjustment to change. However, there are many others which I have not covered, some of which are too important to be ignored.

I have given weight to the damaging effects of Southern demagoguery feeding on racial issues, but I have mentioned only in passing its Northern counterpart which, although less damaging, is certainly a serious deterrent to any orderly solution of issues.

When members of Congress from Northern and Midwestern states, where there are large concentrations of Negro voters, insist on invading a field of regulation reserved to states under the Constitution by supporting Federal anti-lynching bills, Southerners, with considerable justification, assume that their interest is more in the Negro votes in their districts than in the protection of some Southern Negro from being the victim of a now nonexistent crime.

When Governor Averell Harriman hampered New York's police services by removing from Negroes drivers' licenses the useful description of "Negro," insultingly implying that Negroes are ashamed of being identified as such, Southerners, thereafter, saw little more than vote seeking demagoguery in Harriman's immoderate criticism of the ways of the South.

Certainly the press, of urban centers of the North having large Negro populations, is not contributing to the intersectional understanding essential for an orderly solution of the South's racial problems when it subscribes, as it commonly does, to the hypocritical policy of censoring the news of local happenings to conceal all racial aspects, while playing up stories of similar incidents when they occur in the South. If those news agencies were interested in helping with the solution of the South's problems, which have suddenly become national problems, they should certainly inform their readers of the difficulties incidental to integration in their own bailiwicks. If for no other reason than to arouse their own public to the need for finding solutions to racial problems, they should fully report, rather than suppress, the facts showing, for example, the large problem presented by the Negroes' tendency to violence, North and South. But that is one of the segregationists' most powerful arguments and so the facts supporting it are generally taboo.

The whole problem is complicated by being made to appear more simple than it actually is when New Yorkers, for example, are not informed that from their Negro fourteen percent in 1957 came over half of all the city's criminals; when Chicagoans are not made aware of the fact that more than half of the arrests in their city for homicide, rape, and robbery were from their fifteen percent Negro population; and when the people of San Francisco are not made aware that more than half their robberies were committed by Negroes, although they represent but seven percent of the city's population. Perhaps if non-Southerners were given such facts, they would realize that the process of integration, where Negro ratios are far greater, is not so simple as they are prone to believe and a more patient and understanding attitude toward the South, which is fully aware of such facts, might result.

It would help, too, if non-Southerners more fully realized the truth of the observation that, whereas the South formalized segregation but never completely practiced it, the North formalized social integration but never completely practiced it. To a great extent it is the problem of de-formalizing segregation that is so difficult for the South. That is something non-Southerners find difficult to understand. An example, even from the opposite side of the world, may help in understanding the difficulties of de-formalizing anything traditional, even a silly folkway or superstition, one as senseless, for example, as separate sanitary drinking fountains for the races, a vestigial custom which originated in the days of the open bucket of ice water and a common dipper. Among the Hindus, white cows are sacred creatures and are permitted to roam at will, unmolested. We, and I suspect many Hindus also, think that custom completely unreasonable—even silly. Nevertheless, I am quite certain that the Indian government would be even sillier if it suddenly issued an edict requiring that henceforth all white cows must be removed from the villages or slaughtered.

There is yet one more common misconception of the South which is sufficiently prevalent among non-Southerners to call for attention. Everywhere outside the South, I sense a feeling that the South is hopelessly provincial, a place that scarcely knows what is going on in the world beyond its narrow confines.

In response, for defensive comfort, I think of the record of the centuries. I think of Carolina traders and their imperial dreams, dreams in advance of high placed ministers back in the halls of empire. I think of a whole group of Southerners so little fettered by sectional interests that they hazarded their all to stand for liberty against the mother country for whom they had little grievance but her treatment of New England colonies. I think of Jefferson in France and Jefferson acquiring Louisiana. I think of Monroe announcing his doctrine to forestall the threats of empire builders of less breadth of vision. I think of much later days when Southern leaders fought a noble, but losing, battle for acceptance of the world concepts of their fellow Southerner, who literally gave his life to establish a League of Nations. I think of the support they later gave Tennessean Cordell Hull in sealing the "Good Neighbor Policy" with reciprocal trade treaties. Then I think of the crucial part Southern leadership played in the establishment of a United Nations which yet remains the greatest single hope of the world. I think of these things, and I know the South is not inherently provincial.

It is essential that non-Southerners give due thought to all those things—and one thing more, and it is the prime essential. Those who claim the heritage of the North must think long and fairly of the measure of responsibility inherent in and inextricably involved in that heritage for the predicament of the South today, a responsibility that runs the gamut from New England fortunes built on the slave trade, through those which had their origins in protective tariffs that impoverished the South, through the ruin of a war that was not of the South's choosing, and a postwar compounding of its ruin by a combination of corruption and stupidity. And, finally, from the lessons of that record, they must realize that undue coercion has never proved the right answer in dealing with the South and only stupidity can suggest its employment again.

Those are the manifest and minimum obligations of non-Southerners. Upon Southerners, themselves, far more is incumbent. They must awaken not only to all those things which already have been pointed out but many more.

When Southerners ring the changes on States' rights, in defense of their caste system from outside interference, they should realize how hollow is the sound of that defense in light of their own record of readiness to surrender other aspects of States' rights, when dollars flowing south in return for those rights were the inducement. They must give more thought to the fundamental economic truism that the prosperity of any society is strictly limited by prevailing standards at its base. In keeping with that truism, the South will never enjoy economic standards comparable with other sections so long as it maintains a large substratum of poverty. It must awaken to the ultimate futility of all attempts to retain its caste system by economic pressures in a mobile, interdependent economic system; that the weapon of economic coercion is a two-edged sword—a game that can be played by both sides, with equal risks to the players.

Southerners must somehow learn to restrain those ignorant and frustrated individuals who are wont to exchange their wool hats for dunce caps and bed sheets for, whenever they ride, they serve only to advance the cause of militant integrationists by increasing the incentive for employment of irresistible coercive measures against the South, and reducing the time which would otherwise be available to the South to effect an orderly transition. In fact, the Klan, with its kindred terrorist groups, is proving to be the veritable right arm of the N.A.A.C.P. Klansmen must somehow be made to see, both because it is right and because it is expedient that, although violence may win a skirmish, it can never win a struggle.

Since tension took hold of the South, after the 1954 school segregation decision, most of the lines of communication between whites and Negroes in the South have been severed. Now, as Southern Negroes go about in their smiling black masks, Southerners continue to think that they know what the Negro thinks. With no basis for their beliefs but the usual smiling black faces and the usual sounds of high gaiety emanating from their groups, most Southern whites continue to believe of the Negro what was once true of him—that he has no real desire for change, that he is satisfied with things as they are, that the only discontent is among a handful who have been stirred up by outside agitators, or lured into revolt by N.A.A.C.P. money.

That is perhaps the greatest delusion abroad in the South today.

Southern whites should stop fooling themselves and learn the facts from the studies and surveys that are available, revealing Negro sentiment as it actually exists. If they do, they will learn that now the Southern Negro is overwhelmingly in favor of change and that there is no longer the remotest chance that he will abandon his fight. He is reaching for the ballot in formidable numbers, developing his own leadership, and standing up for his rights as never before. It is essential that the white South realize that, hereafter, the Negro, himself, will be an assertive political and sociological force on the Southern scene.

Another commonly held error relates to the decision of the Supreme Court which started all the trouble. Most Southerners are firmly convinced that the Court, in effect, ordered the South to integrate its public schools. It did nothing of the sort. Its holding was a negative one, not positive. What it actually held was that discrimination in public school education cannot be based solely on race. From the practical standpoint, it decreed an adjustment, rather than the revolution which many Southerners assume to be its implications. That fact, plus a reasonable application of placement laws of the type enacted by Alabama and upheld by the Supreme Court, can serve to give all the time reasonably necessary to make requisite adjustments in compliance with the law of the land if, and only if, Southern leadership will proceed to face the problem and move, in good faith, toward accomplishing those minimal adjustments required by the law as it now stands. Attitudes of defiance or heels firmly planted against moving an inch can serve only to stimulate coercive countermeasures and thereby shorten the time available to make adjustments which are inevitable.

Although many Southerners have been giving thought to all these issues, many others, under the sway of a leadership more given to emotion than thought, have been too distracted by the heat of the struggle to think long thoughts. And, unhappily, too many who have been thinking long and realistically upon the South's problems have been cowered by social and economic pressures into keeping their thoughts to themselves. In places, those pressures have become so powerful that there is grave concern that Southerners may be sacrificing, on the altar of their traditional racial patterns, an infinitely greater privilege—that fundamental of American liberty and democracy, freedom of speech.

And, from the practical standpoint, the South now stands more in need of the talents and long thoughts of all of its people, of all shades of opinion, than it has in generations.

If Southern leadership can be brought to turn from an inevitably futile emotional approach to the region's problems, if they can bring themselves to commend cool consideration on the part of distracted ones, if they can assume the obligations of their role and abandon followship, if they can move their ears from the ground, realizing that in that ungainly position, they can move neither forward nor backward, if they can harken to the quiet voices of reason amid the tumult of the ranters . . .

If they can heed the wishes of those millions of Southerners who love the South too well to wish for it an indefinite future of strife and tension and those tens of millions everywhere who see the world implications of what they do, or what they fail to do, and the very fate of the nation in a parlous world resting in their hands . . .

If they can be inspired by those quiet voices of reason and those prayerful wishes of millions gallantly to face problems to which the South is heir, with a full realization that they cannot be solved by looking backward, boldly to accept their challenge with the limitless opportunities they offer, opportunities that can be met so as to secure the admiration and respect of the world . . .

If they can do these things—and, with an abiding faith born of devotion, I am persuaded that some way or another they can and will . . .

Then a Southern sun will continue to shine upon and Southern rains will continue to refresh and rejuvenate a happier land where, from the harvest of the seeds of time, the forces of pride and circumstance will have winnowed the good from the evil, where that which was noble in its past will be retained and the best in its heritage secured for the future, even as the opportunities and privileges of a changed world are embraced and kneaded into a truly triumphant South.

Index

Abolitionism, foci of, 52
Abolition societies, rise of, 57
Abolitionists, disillusionment of, 172; militant, 64; Southern opinion of, 68
Adams, John, and Declaration of Independence, 40
Adams, Samuel, stature of, 153; and view of Constitution, 47
Agrarianism, Southern, 216
Agrarian revolt, Southern, 216–19
Agriculture, Southern, contrast with Northern, 114; diversification in, 239, 255; progress in, 254; statistics on economy of, 86–88; wartime changes in, 125
Alabama, radical control of broken, 177; radical government in, 163
Alabama-Mississippi region, cotton boom in, 70
Alamance, battle of, 34
Alliance, the. *See* Farmers' Alliance
Aluminum Company of America, bauxite monopoly of, 237
Amalgamation, racial, fear of, 77, 297
American Anti-Slavery Society, 67
American Colonization Society, and Liberia, 62
American Temperence Society, and anti-slavery issue, 67
Ames, Adelbert, 179
Amnesty Act, extension of, 178
Anderson, Major Robert, 120
Antietam, battle of, 123
Anti-slavery, rise of, 64; Jefferson on, 45
Appeal, on slave revolt, 65
Appomattox, Confederate surrender at, 132
"Appomattox, spirit of," Reid on, 151–52
Aristocracy, in early colonies, 18, 25; islands of, 72
Aristocrats, Southern, allied with Jacksonian Democrats, 204
Arkansas, joins Confederacy, 121; radical control of broken, 177; radical government in, 166; railroad scandals in, 155; and reinstatement to Union, 143
Articles of Confederation, inadequacies of the, 44
Ashby, H. S. P. ("Stump"), as demagogue, 220
Ashley, J. M., character of, 154
Ashley River, first Carolina settlement on, 18
Atlanta, Ga., devastation of, 129, 137
Atlantic Coast Line, Northern control of, 233
Atlanta *Constitution,* on "new South," 206
Atomic Energy Commission, Southern plants of, 247, 249

Back countrymen, Carolina, and Cornwallis, 42; discord with coastal settlements, 27–28, 33
Bacon, Nathaniel, 32
Bacon's Rebellion, 32
Bank of the United States, and Panic of 1819, 57
Barbados, influence of in early Charleston, 18–19
Bauxite, Northern monopoly of, 237
Beauregard, Gen. Pierre G. T. de, 118
Beecher, Henry Ward, disillusionment of, 172
Bilbo, Theodore, as demagogue, 221
Biloxi, Miss., French settle, 20
Birmingham, Ala., founding of, 209–10; as iron center, 232
"Birmingham Differential," the, 233
Birth rates, Southern, 261, 264
Black Belt, the, 89–90
Black Codes, and civil rights, 146; Radicals' reaction to, 147; Southern states adopt, 145
Blaine, James G., character of, 155
Blair, John, and Constitutional Convention, 44
Bland, Richard, on rights of government, 38, 40; and slavery issue, 41
Blease, Cole L., as demagogue, 221
"Bloody shirt," use of, 167, 173–75, 177
Boll weevil, destruction of the, 238, 243
Bond servants, role of in New World, 15; trek west, 17, 23
Booth, John Wilkes, 144
Boston Tea Party, 38–39
"Bourbons," alliance of with Northern money interests, 203–04
Boutwell, George S., character of, 154; and Credit Mobilier, 170
Brierfield, Jefferson Davis' home at, 112
British East India Company, and Boston Tea Party, 38–39
Broilers, as leading farm crop, 254
Brooks, Rep. Preston, whips Sen. Sumner, 78
Brown, John, emancipation seal of, 80; raid of, 80; as symbolic figure, 81
Brown, Gov. Joseph E., 130
Bull Run, Battle of, 122
Bullock, Rufus, corruption of, 166; sends for Federal troops, 177
Business, Northern, alliance of with Southern Bourbons, 203–04
Butler, Sen. Andrew, 78
Butler, Benjamin "Beast," character of, 154; and hatred for South, 138; as Louisiana's military governor, 161

Byrd, Sen. Harry E., 267, 292
Byrnes, James F., 292

Caldwell, Erskine, and Southern literature, 270
Calhoun, John C., philosophy of government of, 58; and President Jackson, 59–60; and tariff issue, 58–59
Calhoun, Patrick, as symbol, 209
Cameron, Simon, character of, 155; as Secretary of War, 169
Carolina, expands trade, 19, 22; first settlement in, 18; French settle in, 13; fundamental constitution of, 18; slave economy of, 19; and Spanish Florida, 20
Carolina Regulator movement. See Regulators, Carolina
Carpetbaggers, and constitutional conventions, 158
Casas, Bartolemé de las, 10
Caste system, Southern, beginnings of, 224; extension of, 226; outlawed, 248, 251; B. T. Washington on, 228
Chandler, Zack, character of, 155
Change, eras of in South, 261–69; South's commitment to, 273–74
Cheasapeake Bay, London Company settles in, 13–14
Charleston, aristocracy in, 19, 25; desolation in, 201; falls to British, 41; rise of trade in, 19
Charleston News and Courier, on "new South," 206
Chattanooga, Tenn., founding of city of, 209
Child marriages, 290
Cities, Southern, growth of, 272
Civil rights law, 149; problems surrounding Negro, 302
Civil Rights Act of 1866, provisions of, 148
Clarendon County, South Carolina, integration in, 295
Clay, Sen. C. C., on poverty of South, 114
Clay, Henry, and Compromise of 1850, 75
Clemson College, 284
Clinton, Sir Henry, miscalculates Americans, 41–42
Cobb, Howell, 122
Cobb brothers, the, 130
"Code Noir," in New Orleans, 22
Colfax, Schuyler, character of, 155; and Credit Mobilier, 170
Colonial economy, Southern, 204, 232, 253
Colonies, lost, 13
Columbia, S. C., devastation of, 129
Communication, means of, in early Virginia, 17; in South, 95, 102, 139
Compromise of 1850, 75
Confederacy, the, economic losses of, 128; and Georgia, 130; inevitability of defeat of, 131–32; and North Carolina, 130; organization of, 120; reasons for fall of, 131–32; Southern reverence for, 135–36, 199–200
Congress, corruption in, 147–48; and Pres. Johnson, 160; Lincoln's growing breach with, 143, 144; and South, 160–68; vengeance of radical, 156
Conkling, Roscoe, character of, 155
Conscription laws, abuses of, 130–31; Southern reaction to, 130
Conservatism, Southern, 29, 96
Constitutional Convention, the, 44–48; conflicting interests in, 45; and creation of "the South," 45–48
Constitutional conventions, in seceded states, 157–60
Constitutional Union Party, the, 83
Constitutions, Reconstruction, 159–60
Constitution, U. S., compromises in, 45
Convict lease system, abuses of, 219
Cooke, Jay, 138; and Simon Cameron, 169; power of, 156
Cooper, Thomas, on opposition to tariff, 58
Cooper River, first settlement at, 18
Cornwallis, Lord, and Greene, 43; miscalculates Americans, 42; surrenders, 43
Coromantees, the, as slaves, 24
Cotton, Ashley River crop, 18; as basis of Southern economy, 57, 70; as "King" of South, 52, 55–56; no longer main crop, 239; prices of decline, 71, 215
"Cotton diplomacy," failure of, 123
Cotton gin, invention of, 53–54
Cotton Snob, 113
Cotton tax, 129; abuses of the, 151; as instrument of vengeance, 167
Credit Mobilier, scandal of the, 170–71
Crime rates, Southern, 106–08, 264–66
Culture, in old South, 104–05; in new South, 269–70

Dabney, Virginius, on race relations, 286
Dale, Gov. Thomas, on race prejudice, 15
D'Alyllon, colony of, 13
Daniels, Jonathan, on Southern secession, 284
David, the, 126
Davis, James H. ("Cyclone"), as demagogue, 220
Davis, Jefferson, as Confederate President, 120; early popularity of, 122
Davis, "Jeff" (of Arkansas), as demagogue, 220
Dawson, Francis W., on new South, 206
Death rates, Southern, 261, 263–64
Declaration of Independence, Jefferson on, 40; and slavery issue, 45
Demagoguery, Northern, 290, 298
Demagogues, Southern, decline in, 224; and election frauds, 222; influence of, 221, 290; and race relations, 223; and violence record, 221–22
Democratic Party, attempt of to oust Louisiana Radicals, 181; discrimination against, 170; 1860 convention of, 83; post-war strength of in South, 148; Southern, 219–20, 268–69; strange alliances within, 204, 269
Democrats, Jacksonian, alliance of with Southern aristocrats, 204
Depew, Chauncey, on opportunities in South, 204–05
De Soto, Fernando, 6; expedition of, 10, 12

Discovery, the, 13, 18
Disfranchisement, Negro, 224–25
District of Columbia, Negro suffrage in, 157
"Dixie," 136
Drayton, William Henry, 40
Dred Scott Decision, results of, 78
Duke University, efforts of to survive, 202
Durham, N. C., as tobacco center, 207

Eboes, the, as slaves, 25
Economy, Southern, advances in, 261–63; and agriculture, 49–50
Edmonds, Richard H., on new South, 206
Education, Southern, 102–04; advances in, 239; changes in, 262–63; higher, 240, 263; and Reconstruction, 196; and the war, 201–02
Election board, South Carolina, Supreme Court reverses action of, 184; Florida, 184; Louisiana, 184
Election frauds, in South, 222
Ellenton riots, the, 183
Elizabeth I, Queen of England, and New World settlements, 13
Emancipation, Negro, movement for, 63–68
Emancipation Proclamation, justification for the, 144
England, abandons slavery, 65; after French & Indian War, 36; rise of social conscience in, 21

Fair Employment Practises, 248
Farmers' Alliance, and Democratic Party, 217–18; and Populism, 219; spreads through South, 216–17
Farming, cash crop, in post-war South, 215–16; modern, diversified, 239, 254
Farm tendency, system of, 256
Faubus, Gov. Orvil, 276
Faulkner, William, and Southern literature, 270
Filibuster, right of, 281–82
"Fire-eaters," the, 87, 121
Fisk, Jim, 138; power of, 156
Florida, boom in, 244; and Carolina, 13; and election of Hayes, 175; French settlements in, 13; radical control of broken, 175, 182; radical government in, 166; Spanish grip on, weakened, 35
Force Bill, and Nullification Crisis, 60; provisions of, 61, 219
Forests, Southern, descreation of, 211; modern culture of, 256–57
Forrest, Gen. Bedford, as Grand Wizard, Ku Klux Klan, 180
Fort Hill, Calhoun's home at, 112
Fourteenth Amendment, the, 185; evocation of by corporations, 168; as part of radical plan, 149, 167
France, loses American empire, 36; settlements of in New World, 13; settles on Mississippi, 22
Franklin, Benjamin, and Constitutional Convention, 44; and Declaration of Independence, 40; stature of, 153

Freedmen's Bureau, abuses in, 150; insufficiency of, 146
French and Indian War, results of the, 35–36
Frontier, South as, 71–72, 101–04
Fugitive Slave Laws, 78

Gaboons, the, as slaves, 25
Gadsden, Christopher, 40
Galveston, Tex., commission form of government in, 217
Garner, John, 267
Garrison, William Lloyd, as bigot, 138; and insurrection of slaves, 66
Gates, Horatio, defeat of, 42
Gates, John, oil interests of, 236
Geography, and the formation of the South, 26
George, Sen. Walter, 267, 292
George III, King of England, and taxation of colonies, 36
Georgia, and Confederacy, 130; and Indian lands dispute, 57; radical control of broken, 177; railroad swindles in, 166; settlement of, 21; slave economy of, 45–46; and slavery issue, 66
Germans, immigrate to South, 25
Gerry, Elbridge, and Constitutional Convention, 44
Glasgow, Ellen, and Southern literature, 269
Glen, Gov. James, on backwoods living, 28
Gone With the Wind (Mitchell), 270
Goodspeed, the, 13
Gorgas, Josiah, and Southern industrialization, 125–26
Gorgas, William C., 125
Government, municipal, Southern innovations in, 217
Government, theories of at Constitutional Convention, 46–48
Grady, Henry, and "new South," 206, 212
Grange movement, in South, 216
Grant, Pres. Ulysses S., and "Beast Butler," 161; and Gen. Lee, 132; presidency of, 161ff; and radicals, 155–56, 182–84
Great Awakening, results of the, 28
Great Depression, in South, 245
Greeley, Horace, 138; disillusionment of, 172
Green, Paul, and Southern literature, 270
Greene, Nathaniel, and Cornwallis, 43; military tactics of, 43
Greene, Mrs. Nathaniel, and Whitney, 53–54
Gregg, William, and Southern industrialization, 205
Grenville, George, taxation efforts of, 36–38
Gulf Company, the, 236
Gulf states, cotton culture in, 70

Habeas corpus, writ of, suspension of, 130
Hamilton, Alexander, and Constitutional Convention, 44; and U. S. Constitution, 46–48

Hammond, Sen. James H., on role of cotton, 82
Hampton, Wade, and Negro vote, 158; as symbol of good government, 182
Harriman, Gov. Averell, as demagogue, 298
Hartford Convention, and sectionalism, 56
Hayes, Pres. Rutherford B., election of, 160–62; removes Federal troops from South Carolina, 184
Helper, Hinton, antislavery tactics of, 79
Henry, Patrick, and Stamp Act, 37; and U. S. Constitution, 47
Herty, Charles H., and Southern paper industry, 247
Higginson, Thomas, 80
History, South's reverence for, 278, 293
Homicide, Southern rate of, 222
Hookworm, control of, 229
Hospitality, Southern, 98–99
House of Burgesses, Virginia, beginnings of, 14; protests Stamp Act, 37
Howe, Samuel, 80
Hughes, Price, 23
Huguenots, immigration of to South, 25
Hull, Cordell, "Good Neighbor" policy of, 300
Hunter, David, wartime devastation of, 127

Illiteracy, Negro, and Reconstruction, 196; Southern rates of, 103, 230
Illustrated London News, on North-South chasm, 49
Immigration, to Southern colonies, 25–26
Impending Crisis of the South, The, (Helper), 79
Indians, Carolina's trade with, 22–23; confined in Gulf region, 8–9; and the early South, 7–11; heritage left by, 9–10
Industry, Southern, 124; in new South, 205–06, 209–10, 232–36, 283; post World War II, 249, 252; in wartime South, 125–26
Ingersoll, Sen. on issues of campaign of 1876, 174
Inquiry into the Rights of the British Colonies, An (Bland), 37
Integration, racial, deformalizing, 299; relation of size of Negro minority to, 295; Southern unpreparedness for, 283, 291–96
Iron industry, in South, 232–34

Jackson, Pres. Andrew, feud of with Calhoun, 59–60; and Nullification crisis, 60; paves way for Florida annexation, 70
Jackson, Miss., devastation of, 129
Jamestown, Va., settlement of, 14–18
Jefferson, Thomas, and Declaration of Independence, 40; liberality of, 44; and Louisiana Territory, 56; and slavery issue, 45, 61; stature of, 153; and view of Constitution, 47
"Jim Crow" laws, enactment of, 225–26
Johnson, Pres. Andrew, battle of for principles, 160; continues Lincoln's reconstruction program, 145; impeachment of, 160; Radicals' opinion of, 160; relations of with Radical Congress, 160; stature

of, 153; and understanding of South, 142
Johnson, Sen. Hiram, upholds caste system, 226
Johnston, Albert Sydney, "plantation" of, 111
Johnston, Gen. Joseph E., surrender of to Sherman, 137

Kansas-Nebraska Bill, the, 75
Kellogg, W. P., and Louisiana radicals, 182
Kelly, William D. "Pig Iron," character of, 154
Kentucky, as Confederate ally, 121
King, Rufus, and Constitutional Convention, 44
Knapp, Seaman A., demonstration farm movement of, 238
Ku Klux Klan, in Alabama, 178; in Arkansas, 178; in North Carolina, 177; objectives of, 180; in South Carolina, 180; in Texas, 178

Labor, changing categories of in South, 253–54
Lafayette, Gen., and Cornwallis, 43
Laurens, Henry, 25, 40
Law, Southern disrespect for the, 106
Lee, Richard Henry, proposes Declaration of Independence, 40
Lee, Gen. Robert E., and Confederate morale, 122–23, 132; stature of, 153
Le Moyne brothers, and French colonies, 20, 22
Liberality, Southern, 44
Liberator, the, on slave revolts, 66, on Southern aristocrats, 77
Liberia, and American Colonization Society, 62; establishment of, 62
Lien merchant, and share cropping, 214
Lien System, evils of the, 215–16
Lincoln, Pres. Abraham, assassination of, 144; and attack on Ft. Sumter, 120; Congress' breach with, 143; and election of 1860, 83; issues Emancipation Proclamation, 144; and reinstatement of Southern states, 143; stature of, 153; and understanding of South, 142
Literature, Southern, changes in, 269–70
Little Rock, integration controversy in, 276–77
Locke, John, drafts Fundamental Constitution, 18
London, Bishop of, on Negro slaves, 16
London Company, and settlement of Jamestown, 14
Long, Huey, as demagogue, 267
Louisiana, corruption in government of, 181–82; and election of Hayes, 175, 181; radical control of broken, 175, 181; radical elections in, 163; reinstatement of into Union, 143; under military government, 161; under radicals, 162–63
Louisiana (Territory), Jefferson acquires, 56
Louisville Courier-Journal, on new South, 206
Louisville & Nashville Railroad, and Birmingham, 210; Morgan gains control of, 233; and Southern iron industry, 232

Lynching, gradual disappearance of, 265; and Populists, 219; in South, 106, 265; Southern record of, 265

Mackey, Charles, on North-South chasm, 49

Madison, James, as Father of Constitution, 44; plans of for freeing slaves, 61; and slavery issue, 41; stature of, 153; and U. S. Constitution, 47

Malaria, as Southern scourge, 24, 229

Mandingos, the, as slaves, 25

Manufacturers' Record, on new South, 206

Marion, Francis, 43

Marshall, Chief Justice John, solidifies central government, 47

Martial law, in South, 182–84

Mason, George, and Constitutional Convention, 44; and slavery issue, 41; stature of, 153

Matthews, Maurice, 23

McClellan, John L., 292

Mencken, H. L., on Southern culture, 269

Merrimac, the, 126

Mexico, Spain subdues, 12

Mexican War, the, 74–75

Migration, from farms, 243, 260; from South, 247–48, 260–62; to South, 260, 261

Military organizations, Southern respect for, 127

Mississippi, radical control of broken, 178–79; radical government in, 165–66

Mississippi River, geological formation of, 5–6

Mississippi Valley, North's invasion of, 122

Missionary work, in Southern back country, 28

Missouri, as Confederate ally, 121; slavery issue in, 57

Missouri Compromise, and sectionalism, 63

Mobile, Ala., French settle, 20

"Mongrelizing," fear of, 297

Monitor, the, 126

Monroe, Pres. James, on freeing slaves, 62

Morgan, Gen. Daniel, defeats Tarleton, 43

Morgan, J. P., and Southern industry, 232–33; and Southern railroads, 233–34

Morton, Oliver, character of, 155

Moses, Franklin, and South Carolina radical government, 164

NAACP, 286

Nagoes, the, as slaves, 24

Nairne, Thomas, 23

Nation, the, on Southern whites, 176

National banking system, restoration of, 185

National public works program, as instrument of vengeance, 167

Negro, the, and changing South, 260–62, 302; at constitutional conventions, 159; disfranchisement of, 224–25; emergence of as political and social force, 268–70, 302; growing influence of in Southern politics, 161–63, 266; influence of in South, 266; in Jamestown, 16; in Louisiana radical government, 161; mi-

gration of to North, 227, 243, 260–62; in Mississippi radical government, 165–66; in the North, 248, 261; of North and South compared, 261–62; "poor whites" hatred of, 93–94, 223; and Populism, 216–18; problem of intensified, 190; problem of as common denominator in South, 135; reaction of radicals to, 171–74; as scapegoat, 220; shifting of population of, 248, 261–62; social progress of, 266; in South Carolina radical government, 164, 165; Southern reaction to, 89–90; vital statistics of, 86, 228, 260–62, 263–64; wrongs suffered by, 191–92

Negro minority, size of as determining factor in success of integration, 295

Negrophobists, caste system of, 224–25

Negro Seamen Acts, 65, 106

New Deal, concentration of on South, 245–46, 267–68

New England, economy of, 300; loses textile industry, 234–35; slavery in, 52; and slavery issue, 61

New Orleans, settlement of, 20, 22; sugar economy of, 72

New York *Tribune*, on plantations, 77; on post-war South, 201

North, economy of the, 46, 56; and exploitation of Southern sources of wealth, 87–88, 209–11; industry of gains control in South, 208; Negroes in the, 227, 243, 248, 261; and profit from Southern plantation economy, 88; Southern distrust of, 188; and War of 1812, 56

North Carolina, and Confederacy, 120, 130; joins Confederacy, 121; lack of democracy in, 112; radical control of broken, 177; radical government in, 167

Northern Methodist Church, as seat of bigotry towards South, 138

Nullification Convention, South Carolina, and tariff issue, 58–60

Oak Ridge, Tenn., atomic installation at, 247

Occupation forces, demoralizing influence of, 151

Oglethorpe, James, and settlement of Georgia, 21

Ohio Resolution, and Negro emancipation, 64

Ohio River Valley, abolitionism sentiment in, 52

Oil, discovery of in Texas, 236; Northern interests dominate, 237–38

Old Providence, Puritans settle, 52

Olmsted, Frederick Law, on Southern homes, 111

Orientals, caste system for, 172

Othello (Shakespeare), on British race prejudice, 15

Page, Walter Hines, 134; as constructive critic, 198; on "Forgotten Man," 231; and Southern education, 202, 231; and Southern public health movement, 229

Panic of 1819, the, and sectionalism, 56–57

Paper industry, Southern, 247

Pardo, expedition of, 12
Paris, Treaty of, 36
Parker, Niles G., and South Carolina radical government, 163
Parker, Theodore, 80
Parliament, British, slave debates in, 57, 65
Patterson, "Honest" John, and South Carolina radical government, 163, 164
Pawpaws, the, as slaves, 24
Pee Dee River, Welsh settle, 25
Pellagra, control of, 229
Pendleton, Edmund, and slavery issue, 41
Pensacola, Spanish settle, 20
Petigru, James L., moral bravery of, 105
Phillips, Wendell, as bigot, 138
Pickens, Andrew, 43
Pike, Albert S., disillusionment of, 172
Pinckney, Charles, at Constitutional Convention, 44
Pinckney, Charles Cotesworth, at Constitutional Convention, 44
Pitt, William, and repeal of Stamp Act, 37
"Pittsburgh Plus," system of, 233
Plant System, the, 233
Planter-aristocrat, the, 92–93, 104; and sense of obligation to public service, 88, 98
Plantations, beginnings of in Jamestown, 17; number of in old South, 86–87; economy of, 88–89
Pocahontas, 15
Poinsett, Joel, 105
Politics, Southern, conservatism of, 96, 267; growing influence of Negro in, 266; incongruities in, 269
Polk, Pres. James K., and War with Mexico, 75
Polk, Leonidas L., 219
Poll tax, abandonment of, 266; effects of, 266
"Poor whites," and fear of Negroes, 93–94; and Reconstruction, 192, 197–98
Populism, defeat of, 219; and Farmers' Alliance, 218
Poverty, in South, 114
Press, the, and race problems, 276, 289–90; subservience of, 298
Private academies, in South, 103
Proclamation Line of 1763, 27; and Grenville, 36
Prostrate State, The (Pike), 173
Protective tariff, the, as instrument of vengeance, 216
Public health programs, Southern, 229, 263
Public offices, sale of, 166, 171
Public schools, Southern. See schools, Southern
Public school systems, move to abolish, 283
Puritanism, Southern, 97–98

Race issue, and Reconstruction, 172–74; 190
Race relations, post World War II, 248, 286; in South, 90–92
Racial patterns, Southern, economic influences in, 293–94

Racial problem, Southern, barriers to understanding in, 275–76
Radicals, and Fourteenth Amendment, 143; reaction of to Black Codes, 147; refuse Congressional admission to Southern states, 143; and seceded Southern states, 161–68; and Southern Negroes, 159
Railroads, Southern, control of, 208; discriminatory rates of, 233
Raleigh, Sir Walter, and New World settlement, 13
Raleigh News and Observer, 284
Randolph, Edmund, and Constitutional Convention, 44
Randolph, John, and slavery issue, 41
Randolph, Thomas, on slave freedom, 62
Reciprocal trade treaties, Hull's, 300
Reconstruction, devastation wrought by in South, 187–88
Reconstruction Acts of 1867, provisions of, 156
Red Shirts, activities of in South Carolina, 183
Reed, Walter, work of in malaria, 229
Reformers, disillusionment of the, 172
Regulators, 42–43; in North Carolina, 33; in South Carolina, 33–34
Reid, Whitelaw, on post-war South, 201; on spirit of Appomattox, 151–52
Religion, revival of, 62; social aspects of in South, 97
Republican party, embraces Abolitionism, 82
Revolution, economic aspects of, 140–42
Revolution, second American, 140
Rhett, Barnwell, 81, 122
Rice, introduced into Carolina, 19; and slavery, 24, 54
Richmond, devastation of, 129
Richmond Medical Society, 286
Richmond Terminal Company, 209
Richmond Times-Dispatch, 286
Richmond and West Point Terminal Company, 233
Roanoke, founding of, 209
Robertson, Thomas J., 163
Rockefeller, John D., and Southern public health movement, 229
Rolfe, John, 15
Royal African Company, 21
Ruffin, Edmund, 81, 122
Ruralism, Southern, 29, 85–86, 95–96, 267
Russell, Richard B., 292
Rutledge, John, 40; and Constitutional Convention, 44; and Regulators, 33–34

St. Augustine, establishment of, 13
Santee River, settlement near, 25
Savannah, British capture, 41
Savannah River Plant, 249
Scalawags, and constitutional conventions, 158
Schools, Southern, private, 103; public, 102, 129, 230, 240, 262–63
Scotch, the, immigration of, 25
Scotch-Irish, immigration of the, 25–26
Scott, Robert K., and South Carolina radical government, 163

Seaboard Air Line, Morgan organizes, 233
Seceded states, constitutional conventions in, 157–60
Secession, as immediate cause of war, 118; ordinance of, 84
Second American Revolution, the, 140
Sectionalism, as moral issue, 56; and Panic of 1819, 56–57; and protective tariff, 56; in Scotland, 199; varying forms of, 199; and War of 1812, 56
Segregation, economic, 294; racial, 297; residential, 296
Segregation laws, enactment of, 225–26; judicial destruction of, 301
Senegalese, the, as slaves, 24
Seven Years' War, the, 36
Shakespeare, on British race prejudice, 15
Sharecropping, rise of, 150; system of, 213–16
Sheridan, Gen. Philip, and hatred of South, 138; as Louisiana's military governor, 161; returns to Louisiana, 181; wartime devastation of, 127
Sherman, William T., on Southern desolation, 137; on Southern forage, 125; and surrender pact with Johnston, 137
"Slave Code," beginnings of, 16
Slavery, apparent Southern solidarity regarding, 116; beginnings of, 15–17; in Carolina, 19; and Declaration of Independence, 41; England abandons, 65; as moral issue, 172; in New England, 52; "positive good" doctrine of, 75–76; reaches saturation point, 54; as Southern obsession, 73; in U. S. Constitution, 45–48
Slaveholders, Negro, 113
Slaves, market for increases, 23; qualities of Negro races as, 24–25; trading of in 1734, 24
Smith, Cerrit, 80
Soil mining, as by-product of sharecropping, 215; in South, 114
South, the, and Abolitionism, 68; adjustment problem of, 272–74; agricultural economy of, 30, 50–51, 86–87; changes in, 125, 186, 272–74; changing economy of, 244, 251; changes in education in, 251; changing literature of, 269–70; conservatism of, 29, 96; and Constitutional Convention, 45–48; controls national government, 63; crippling effects of war in, 132, 139; dedication of to past, 197, 200; and distrust of North, 188; economic cost of war to, 128–32; economic factors in, 86–88, 261; efforts to industrialize, 125–26, 205–06; and enshrinement of past, 278; external unity of, 115–16; frontier conditions in, 71–72, 101–04; geological formation of, 3–6; homes of, 17, 110–11; Johnson's understanding of, 142; lack of provincialism in, 300; liberalism in, 44; Lincoln's plan for reinstatement of, 143; Lincoln's understanding of, 142; "lost colonies" of, 13; low educational level of, 221, 293; manufacturing prowess of revealed, 134; mechanical innovations of in wartime, 126; mineral production in, 237–38; mineral wealth of, 236; military organizations in, 98; military tradition of, 127; myth of the old, 109–14, 116–17; as a political unit, 266–69; poverty of, 114, 133–34, 196; racial constituency of, 261; racial prejudice in, 89–90; realism in, 45, 270; religious revival in, 62; and return of frontier, 124, 133; rise of anti-slavery in, 45; "slave economy" of, 86–87; solidarity of, 95; stagnation in, 194; standard of living in, 253; subsistence living in, 124; urbanization of, 207–08, 259–60; and War of 1812, 56; "wealth myth" of, 114; World War I boom in, 243; and World War II, 247–48
South, the new, educational advancement in, 230–31; era of, 229–41; illiteracy rates in, 230–32; iron industry developed in, 232–34; and Negro, 240, 260–62; progress in, 205–08, 228–41, 262ff
South Carolina, aids New England, 39; and battle for textile industry, 234–35; corruption in radical government of, 163–65; economy of, 19, 24; and election of Hayes, 175, 182–84; lack of democracy in, 54; Nullification Convention in, 58–60; radical control of broken, 182–84; radical rule in, 163–65; secedes from Union, 84, 119; and slavery issue, 41; two governments in, 184; and Virginia, 20
Southerner, characteristics of the, 194–95; duties of the, 196; in national government, 40–41, 63, 194, 195–96, 241
Southernism, decline of, 271–74
Southern press, and Pres. Davis, 122
Southern Railway, Northern control of, 233
Spain, colonization efforts of in North and South America, 13, 19–20
Spindletop, Texas, discovery of oil at, 263
Squatter sovereignty, doctrine of, 76
Stamp Act, defiance of the, 37–38
Stamp Act Congress, the, 37
Standard Oil Company, the, 236
Stanton, E. M., character of, 155
States' rights, loss of, 268; South's devotion to, 130, 285; time conflicts, 130
States' sovereignty, Southern campaign for, 75, 119
Staunton, Va., city manager government in, 217
Stearns, George, 80
Stephens, Thaddeus, 139; ruthlessness of, 153
Stowe, Harriet Beecher, disillusionment of, 174; Uncle Tom's Cabin, 76
"Stretch out" system, 246
Subsistence living, in wartime South, 124
"Sub-Treasury Plan," the, 218
Suffrage, Negro, in District of Columbia, 157; in North, 172, 266; in seceded states, 158
Sulphur, 237
Sumner, Charles, as bigot, 138; character of, 154; disillusionment of, 172; whipped by Brooks, 78
Sumter, Thomas, 43
Sumter, S. C., city manager government in, 217

Supreme Court, during Grant administration, 160; outlaws racial discrimination in education, 250, 302; on segregation, 225, 280
Susan Constant, the, 13
Swiss, immigration of the, 25
Synthetic fibre production, rise in, 254

Taney, Chief Justice Roger B., and Dred Scott decision, 78
Tariff of 1828 (Tariff of Abominations), Southern reaction to, 58–59
Tariff, protective, and sectionalism, 57; and South Carolina Nullification Convention, 59
Tarleton, Banastre, and Cornwallis, 42
Tea, British tax on, 38
Tennessee, joins Confederacy, 121; postwar government of, 143, 156; radical control of broken, 177; radical government of, 167
Tennessee Coal, Iron, and Railroad Company, as industrial giant, 232
Tennessee Valley Authority, the, 245
Texas, early settlers in, 72; as Indian territory, 20; radical control of broken, 177; radical government in, 167
Texas Company, the, 236
Texas-Mexico affair, Southern part in the, 74–75
Textiles, synthetic, 254
Textile mills, Southern erection of, 206; success of, 233–35
Thirteenth Amendment, seceded states ratify, 145
Tillman, "Pitchfork" Ben, 218, 220
Timber, Southern, development of, 257; exploitation of, 211
Tobacco, exported from Jamestown, 14; as major Southern industry, 52, 207
Tobacco Road (Caldwell), 270, 290
Tompkins, Daniel A., on new South, 206
Tonti, and New Orleans, 22
Toombs, Robert, 122, 130
Tories, and War of Independence, 35–40
Townshend duties, American reaction to the, 38
Trade, in early Charleston, 19; influence of on colonization, 22–23
Treasury agents, abuses by, 151
Tryon, Gov. William, and Regulator movement, 33
Turner, Nat, and slave revolts, 66
Typhoid fever, control of, 263

Uncle Tom's Cabin (Stowe), influence of, 76
Underground Railway, 79
Union League, demoralizing influence of the, 150–51
Union Pacific, and Credit Mobilier, 170–71
Union Sulphur Company, 237
Urbanization, Southern, 207–08, 259–60

Vardaman, James K., and race issue, 220
Venereal disease, campaign on, 263

Violence, role of in South, 106–08, 264
Virginia, aristocracy in, 25; beginnings of legislative body in, 14; charter, 14; Negro slavery in, 23; joins Confederacy, 121; 100 years after settlement, 16; protests Stamp Act, 39; radical control of broken, 177; radical government in, 167; slavery debates in, 66–67; slavery declines in, 45, 54; slavery increases in, 16–17, 24; and South Carolina, 20
Virginia, U. of, war losses of, 128
Virginia Dynasty, the, 63, 112

Wade, Ben, character of, 154
War, material destruction of the, 128; mechanical innovations in art of, 126
War of 1812, the, and sectionalism, 56–57
War Hawks, the, 58
War of Independence, the, 41–43
Warmouth, Henry Clay, and Louisiana government, 161–63
Washington, Booker T., on caste system, 228
Washington, George, and Constitutional Convention, 44–48; defeats Cornwallis, 43; and slavery issue, 41; stature of, 153; and U. S. Constitution, 47
Watson, Tom, as demagogue, 220
Watterson, Henry, on new South, 206
Welch, Thomas, 23
Welsh, immigration of the, 25
Weld, Theodore Dwight, and antislavery, 67
West Indies, plantation society in, 24
West Point, corruption in appointments to, 171
White Citizens' Councils, 286
White League, formation of, 181
Whitney, Eli, and cotton gin, 53–54
Whydals, the, as slaves, 24
Williams, Tennessee, and Southern literature, 270
Williamsburg, settlement of, 17
Wilson, Henry, and Credit Mobilier, 171; and Pres. Grant, 155
Wilson, James, and Constitutional Convention, 44
Wilson, Woodrow, as Southern president, 241
Winston, N. C., as tobacco center, 207
Wisconsin Primary, origin in South, 217
Wolfe, Thomas, and Southern literature, 270
Womanhood, Southern reverence for, 99–100
World War I, and South, 241–43
World War II, and South, 247–48
Wythe, George, and Constitutional Convention, 44; and slavery issue, 41

Yancey, William L., 81, 122
Yankee, Southern hatred of, 134–35, 187–88
Yellow jack, control of, 263
Yorktown, Cornwallis' surrender at, 43